URBANIZATION IN INDIA

URBANIZATION IN INDIA
Spatial Dimensions

V L S PRAKASA RAO

CONCEPT PUBLISHING COMPANY PVT. LTD.
NEW DELHI-110059

ISBN-13 : 978-81-8069-966-5(P.B)

First Published 1983
Reprinted 2013

Vadhiparti Lova Surya Prakasa Rao (*b.* 1917)

Published and Printed by :

Concept Publishing Company Pvt. Ltd.
A/15-16, Commercial Block, Mohan Garden
New Delhi-110059 (India)
T: 25351460, 25351794, *F*: 091-11-25357109
E: publishing@conceptpub.com, W: www.conceptpub.com
Editorial Office: H-13, Bali Nagar, New Delhi-110 015, India.

Foreword

THERE can be no argument about the importance of the theme of this book: it concerns the spatial dimensions of India's towns and cities—without of course excluding the social, economic and political, indeed it deals with spatial or areal manifestations of these. The sheer numbers of urban dwellers are impressive: 62 million in 1951 (17.6% of the total population after a large upsurge following the disruption and mass transfers of population following Partition); 78 million in 1961 (18.3% of a larger population yet a modest proportional growth that disappointed many concerned observers anxious that urban-industrial growth should alleviate poverty among economically vulnerable rural groups); 107 million in 1971 (20.2% and with an annual growth of 4 per cent in urban population compared with just over 2 per cent for India as a whole); and 156 million in 1981 (23.7%).* While many indigenous commentators and a few foreign ones hope for rapid urban growth for the reason just noted, no one pretends that even the existing rate of urban growth is unattended by serious problems, while the less well-informed foreign visitor or television-viewer is apt to be so blinded by horror at the street-dwellers of Calcutta and Bombay (or even of Madras or Bangalore) as to regard faster urban growth with ill-concealed horror. Prakasa Rao and his team of researchers face all these problems, make them explicit and quantify them where data permit. Their inter-disciplinary perspective is wide: alerted by the social anthropologists, for instance, their broader, spatial surveys make us aware of the functions performed by the urban slum, for instance, as well as its drawbacks, even its disgraces.

*Excludes Assam and Jammu and Kashmir.

While they are abreast of modern theoretical and applied ideas about towns and cities in both developed and developing countries, their choice of initial slogan quoting from Wolfgang Stolper is significant of their vocation as urban geographers: '. . . truth must come before originality'. In this volume they are synthesizing about the Indian city as a whole after many years, individually and in collaboration, spent in very detailed survey and analysis in particular cities like Bangalore, Vijayawada and Vishakapatnam. All students of India's urban scene, at home and abroad, owe them a heavy debt of gratitude.

In discussing practical problems, planning problems, their concern is towards better physical or perhaps better physical-cum-social planning, more decentralized, more regional, more sensitive to local issues, local means of livelihood, local social structure, than has perhaps been the accepted ethic or paradigm in town and country planning, at least since Sir Patrick Geddes worked in India over 60 years ago. They write hopefully of the future role of positive planning of this complexion, seeing genuine concern for decentralization in the Sixth Plan as compared with lip-service in earlier ones. On my last visit to India in November to February last, my first since the Emergency, I sensed that planning at the national level had moved away from the heady ideas of the Second Plan period—though now as then with a radical left in dissent—and was groping towards some way of influencing the course of national progress in the interests of the less privileged that was compatible with domination of the fast-moving parts of the economy by capitalist undertakings. (This presumably need not exclude nationalized undertakings prevailing in certain of the commanding heights of the economy).

If this feeling, for it was hardly a judgment after a ten weeks' visit, was perchance correct or even partially so, where do the positive views and aspirations of Prakasa Rao lead in relation to the great fund of hard empirical data that he presents? If one takes as a limiting case the view Russel Ackoff once expressed that 'planning is finding out what is going to happen and then taking the credit', then the patient down-to-urban-earth surveys and analyses of our author, and his regional perspective, are equally valid and useful, perhaps even more so. Suppose that we accept that the future health of

India's society, economy and presumably polity too are in fact to depend, as he believes, in the evolution of what he calls a rural-urban continuum (in contrast with a strongly hierarchical urban structure, relatively little integrated with rural society, that is only very partially in 1982 related to the period of colonial domination). Suppose further that the role of the professional planners is to be relatively less important in future, and that the transformation of the poor and unworthy parts of India's scene, both rural and urban, is to depend on a very kind of ecological enlightenment very widely diffused through capital and labour, landowner and landless labourer, peasant and merchant. In such event, while this will not be the book to attempt the widest diffusion of facts, trends and ideas—if only for linguistic reasons—it may still point a pathway in the linking of urban and regional scholarship to both Gandhiji's ideas of rural uplift and Patrick Geddes's advocacy of what he called 'conservative surgery' compound by compound and mohalla by mohalla in India's towns and cities.

June 1982
MILTON KEYNES

ANDREW LEARMONTH
The Open University

Preface

"... truth must come before originality"
—*Wolfang F. Stolper*

THIS book presents the results of empirical analysis of urbanization in India with some theoretical underpinnings and policy implications. The point of view is that of a geographer, although there are implications for the other social scientists and urban and regional planners.

To bring out the significance of spatial dimensions, the urbanization process and patterns are analysed at the national, state, sub-regional, city-regional and intra-city levels. To gain better insights, the city/town is taken as the unit of analysis. At the city-regional level, the village is taken as the unit of analysis, and at the intra-city level, the units of analysis are households, establishments, wards and ecological units.

After the introductory section I, the book is structured and organised in two sections: inter-city (Urban India) and intra-city (Indian City). These two sections set the stage for the concluding section which discusses some urban development policy issues.

The focus of Chapter 1 is on the complexities underlying the urbanization process, patterns and correlates. This is followed by an analysis of the structural and behavioural aspects of the urban system and the city system (Chapter 2). While the functional gaps in the urban system are brought out in Chapter 2, the spatial imbalances based on the analysis of the urban and regional interrelationships are brought out in Chapter 3. Recognising the increasing emphasis on the welfare connotation of urbanization, the problems associated with the dispersal of urban infrastructure are analysed in Chapter 4. While the analysis at the inter-city level is based on the urban and regional hierarchic framework, the analysis at the intra-city level is based on the ecological zonal framework, with the distance from the city-core/centre, taken as the major determinant of the city structure. Analysing the processes and patterns underlying the city-sprawl and the emerging density gradient profiles, the multi-dimensional and transitional city-structure, combining both 'pre-industrial' and 'post-industrial elements' is brought out using our empirical study of Bangalore (Chapter 5). Associated with the 'pre-industrial' and 'post-industrial' elements, are the rich, the middle-class and the poor strata of the urban society. Noting the significant share of the poor in the city-ward migration, and their imprint on the city-structure, the distribution of city slums and the socio-economic status of the slum dweller are analysed in Chapter 6. With the increasing emphasis on the quality of the urban environment, the impact of slums on the urban environment, and the role of the city in creating climatically altered, sometimes inhospitable, environments are analysed in Chapter 7. The concluding chapter draws attention to some of the important urban development policy areas.

V L S Prakasa Rao

Acknowledgements

I SHOULD like to express my gratitude to the Indian Council of Social Science Research, New Delhi, for awarding the Council's Senior Fellowship for a period of three years (1979-82) to work on a theme of my choice, and to the Indian Institute of Management, Bangalore, and specifically to Prof. N S Ramaswamy, the Director of the Institute, for granting affiliation to work in the Institute during the tenure of my fellowship.

I should like to acknowledge my indebtedness to Dr V K Tewari (Chs. 1, 2, 5 and 6), Dr H Ramachandran (Chs. 1, 2, and 3), Dr Neera Ramachandran (Ch. 4), and Mr. G S Sastry Chs. 1 and 2) for their valuable and substantive contributions to different chapters. Dr Tewari and Mr. Sastry took the additional responsibility for data processing and computer analysis. The contributions of the teams of workers to Chapter 6 and 7 are acknowledged in the relevant sections of the study. I have drawn extensively from the doctoral dissertations of Dr C Parvati and Dr Ranjana Talwar. I am equally indebted to these two scholars. Dr V K Bawa's critical and helpful comments on the policy chapter are gratefully acknowledged. For the cartographic excellence of the maps in the book, the credit goes to Mr B G Kulkarni. I should also like to express my gratitude to Professor A T A Learmonth for writing the Foreword to this book and his critical comments and editorial changes, and to Dr Afzal Mohammad for his assistance in the final scrutiny of the text and the maps. I wish to express my appreciation to Smt. Grace Pushpamanjari for secretarial assistance and typing the text, and to the Administrative and Accounts Sections of the Institute for administering the Fellowship.

BANGALORE
3 April 1982

V L S PRAKASA RAO

Contents

List of Figures

List of Tables

Eopolis to Dynopolis

The first is 'eopolis' the rise of the village community with permanent habitation. The second is 'polis', and association of villages with a common site. This is essentially a town for defence. The third stage is metropolis or mother city. The fourth is megalopolis: the beginning of the social decline of the human community. The fifth stage is 'tyrannopolis, an urban pattern which is parăsitic' and the sixth and the final stage is 'nekropolis' with ghost towns, the manifestation of war, famine and disease. In contrast to this horrible city of the future, we have the 'invisible city', the product of revolution in communications and electronic transmissions. Even the remote village can have the urban component of life, and yet avoid the city, we do not want to live in. There is yet another stage: the 'dynopolis' not only for the man but also for his cars, aeroplanes, helicopters, and may be rockets.

—LEWIS MUMFORD AND DOXIADIS

INTRODUCTION

It is difficult to organize statistical data on urbanization without defining what is 'urban'. It is equally difficult to define 'urban' owing to its multi-dimensional structure: demographic, social, economic, physical, geographical and political/administrative. The fact that urbanization is frequently equated with "the quality of life" and "the quality of environment", further complicates any exercise in measurement. According to the definition of the 1961 census (and also in 1971), a human settlement is defined as "urban" if it had (i) a minimum population of 5,000; (ii) 75 per cent of the male working population engaged in non-agricultural activities; (iii) a density of at least 1000 per sq. mile and (iv) distinct urban characteristics (e.g. industrial areas, areas of tourist importance, etc.). A settlement which is a municipality, corporation, cantonment or notified area is also classified as a town. Anomalies arise in the population size band of villages: 5,000 to 10,000 and above, and towns: less than 5,000 to 20,000, in the whole settlement spectrum (Fig. 0.1 and Table 0.1). This is the rurban band of the spectrum (Bhaskara Rao 1977). In this band, it is the functional structure which is more important than population size. It could be hypothesized here that some of the accessible large villages (5,000-10,000 size class) are more urban than some of the equally accessible small towns (less than 10,000, which are more rural. There were 290 class VI towns (less than 5,000) in 1971. There were 7,974 villages in the population size class 5,000-10,000, and 1358 villages in the 10,000 and above size class (1971). While the census definition of a town is standardized, and is a welcome measure, its rigidity leads to both declassification and reclassification of villages and towns. Here the unresolved problem relates to the precision in the criteria, particularly 75 per cent in non-agricultural population and 1000 population density per square mile. If the administrative criterion is applied, then statistically defined towns need not be administratively urban. Inter-state variations in the recognition of the administrative status of a town, and in the patterns of urban-rural profiles (e.g. Kerala) further complicate the problem of definition. Here, any national aggregate urban analysis conceals the structural realities underlying urban definition with its emphasis on demographic criteria.

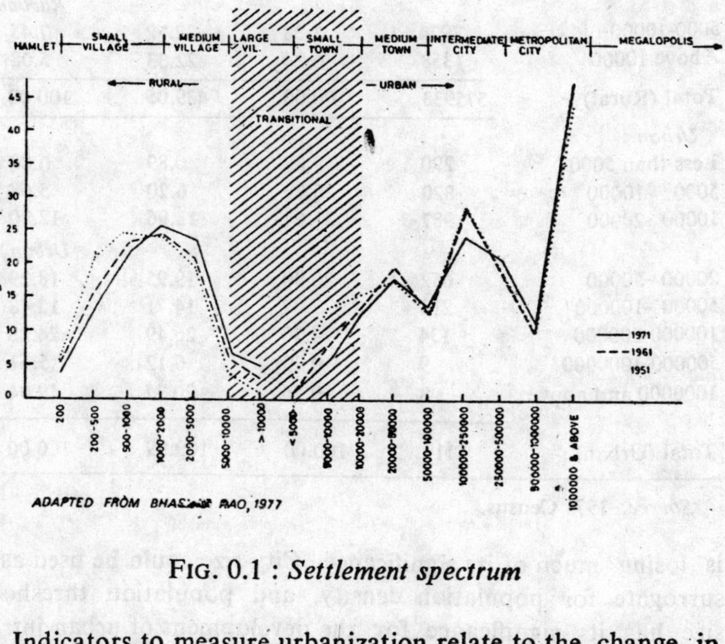

FIG. 0.1 : *Settlement spectrum*

Indicators to measure urbanization relate to the change in the characteristics of people, place/area, technology and functions. The mixing up of the descriptive and normative aspects of urbanization only adds to the problem of measurement. Urbanization could be treated as a dependent variable (economic-social-political), and also as an independent variable (population size-density-intensity). With the changing structure and patterns of urbanization and structural inter-relationships, and owing to policy intervention, this compartmentalization

TABLE 0.1 : **Settlement spectrum (1971)**

Population size class	No. of settlements	% to total no. of settlements	Population (in million)	% to total population
Rural				*Rural*
Less than 200	150072	26.06	15.25	3.47
200 -500	168561	29.27	56.63	12.89
500 -1000	132990	23.09	94.41	21.50
1000-2000	81973	14.23	113. 6	25.78
2000-5000	36005	6.25	104.55	23.82
				Rurban
5000-10000	7974	1.38	32.72	7.45
Above 10000	1358	0.24	22.33	5.08
Total (Rural)	575933	100.00	439.05	100.00
Urban				
Less than 5000	290	9.30	0.89	0.82
5000 -10000	820	26.29	6.20	5.68
10000 -20000	987	31.64	13.96	12.80
				Urban
20000 -50000	652	20.90	19.95	18.29
50000 -100000	219	7.02	14.71	13.48
100000-500000	134	4.30	26.49	24.28
500000-1000000	9	0.29	6.12	5.61
1000000 and above	8	0.26	20.77	19.04
Total (Urban)	3119	100.00	109.09	100.00

Source: 1971 Census.

is losing much of its significance. City-size could be used as a surrogate for population density, and population threshold size has its significance for the development of urban infra-structure. But city-size often obscures the underlying inter-relationships between the different structural elements. In this context, city-size becomes an "intervening variable" (Richardson 1973). Compared to city-size and the associated demographic criteria, land-use, functional structure and the level of urban infra-structure are more sensitive measures of urbanization (Rao 1964, Mitra 1965, Alam and Khan 1972, Desai 1969). If weightage is to be given to an urban area and its land-use and functional structure, there is the problem of the deviation between the legal city, the built-up or urbanized area, and the functional area. This poses problems in the delimitation of an urban area, and in working out urban densities and population projections. In spite of the awareness of these problems, no steps are taken in disaggregating the urban areas. Delimitation becomes more difficult with increasing sub-urbanization, concentration of non-agricultural population and urban land-uses in the city fringe, and periodical expansion of city limits, incorporating the adjoining villages. The break between the urban area and the functionally inter-related adjoining the villages which are in the different stages of urban transformation is not always clear-cut. Data constraints will be more in the case of the analysis of city-regional and inter-city linkages. Reconciliation and fitting the different categories, statistical with physical and socio-economic will be a continuing problem. Some of the problems in making the urban-rural land-use and settlement structure base more refined and up-to-date should be resolved by the technological revolution in landscape inventorying that is now taking place (e.g. aerial photographs, satellite (LANDSAT and RADAR), and computer graphic).

To bring out the size, shape, contiguity, concentrated and dispersed patterns in space, inter-settlement distance, and regional setting, cartographic techniques are the best. The map provides the base for distance measurements and hence, the scale of the map becomes a critical factor for map generalization and analysis. There is as yet no indication of the error for a given map scale for a given theme, though the methodological problem has been considered (Reid and Learmonth, 1966). Regional variations in structure of the transitional and contact zones and urban-regional inter-relationships are best brought out by chorochromatic (or 'place-time') mapping techniques. Here, the map is used as a 'sieve' to extract and highlight the critical regional elements. A map showing the location of large cities with rapid growth, both in numbers and urban area, overlaid on natural land units, watershed zones and areas of structural instability and flood hazard, provides a more appropriate regional base for zoning, than a series of maps showing these regional elements separately. Here, the scale of the base map becomes critical in map generalization. If maps are used liberally, without taking into account the underlying errors, they become more dangerous than statistics. It needs no emphasis that for map generalization, there is a need judiciously to integrate maps on the field and the topographic scales with maps on the chorographic scales.

Urban versus Rural

In 1971, a total urban population of 109 millions (20 per cent of the total population) lived in 3,119 urban settlements, while 439 millions (80%) lived in 5,75,933 rural settlements. While 49 per cent of the total urban population lived in cities with >1,00,000, 12.5 per cent of total rural population lived in large villages with >5000. As many as 64 per cent of the total rural population lived in villages with a population of less than 2000. Rural settlements with population size ranging from 5000—10,000 and above, and small towns with a population size ranging from less than 5000 to 20,000 could be classified as rurban settlements: semi-rural and semi-urban. Just over 76 millions (14 per cent) live in these 11,429 rurban settlements (Table 0.2).

TABLE 0.2 : **Rural-Rurban-Urban settlements**

Population size class	No. of settlements	% to total no. of settlements	Population (in millions)	% to total population
Rural				
<200-5,000	566,601	97.85	384.00	70.06
Rurban				
5,000-20,000	11,429	1.98	76.10	13.88
Urban				
20,000-10,00,000+	1,022	0.17	88.04	16.06
Total	579,052	100.00	548.14	100.00

Source: 1971 Census.

Urban and Rural dualism is sharp in demographic and economic characteristics.

Birth and death rates are both lower in urban than in rural areas. The birth rate in urban areas was 29.7 per 1,000 population and 38.9 per 1000 population in rural areas. The death rate was 10.2 per 1000 in urban areas and 17.3 per 1,000 in rural areas (1970). Consequently, the natural increase was lower in urban (19.5) than in rural areas (21.6). Yet the urban growth rate during 1961-71 was 3.8 per cent per annum while the rural growth rate was 2.2 per cent.

Urban males (61.3 per cent) and urban females (42.1 per cent) were more literate than rural males (33.8 per cent) and rural females (13.2 per cent). The sex ratio was lower in urban (858) than in rural (949) population. Rural areas had a higher percentage of children (43 per cent) and aged persons 6 per cent than urban areas (39 per cent and 5 per cent). In contrast, the urban areas had a higher percentage of population in the working age group (56 per cent) than rural areas (51 per cent) (1971).

Table 0.3 brings out the urban-rural differences in the industrial categories of workers. As many as 85 per cent of rural workers were in agriculture in 1971. The rural component in the urban sector persisted with 13 per cent of urban workers. The workers in household industry (5 per cent) also reflect the persistence of the rural dimension in urban life. This is mainly because many of the urban centres are overgrown villages, and there are rural areas in many of the city-corporation areas. Of the urban workers, the service sector had the largest share (25 per cent) followed by factory industry (23 per cent). Of the total workers employed in rural areas, only 5 per cent were in the service sector, and 2% in factory industry. The contrast is sharper in the commercial sector with 30 per cent in urban and 3 per cent in rural. The urban-rural differences narrow down in the household, mining and quarrying and construction activities.

Rural incomes are lower than urban incomes. The average household income (1975-76) in rural areas was Rs. 3,897 and Rs. 7,074 in urban areas (NCAER, 1980). Both the NCAER study and National Sample Survey data show that income distribution in urban areas is slightly more unequal than the rural distribution, and that inequality has declined in both urban and rural areas between 1963-64 and 1973-74 (Mills, 1980).

TABLE 0.3 : **Industrial categories of workers, 1971**

(in thousands)

	Urban		Rural		Total	
	Number	%	Number	%	Number	%
Agriculture	4,089	12.78	1,25,874	84.78	129,963	72.02
Mining and Quarrying	321	1.00	602	0.41	923	0.51
Manufacturing: Household Industry	1,589	4.95	4763	3.21	6,352	3.52
Factory Industry	7,314	22.85	3402	2.29	10,716	5.94
Commercial: Trade and Commerce	6,415	20.04	3623	2.44	10,038	5.56
Transport storage and communication	3,191	9.95	1210	0.82	4,401	2.44
Construction	1,119	3.57	1096	0.74	2,215	1.23
Other services	7,960	24.88	7895	5.32	15,855	8.79
Total	31,998	100.00	1,48,465	100.00	1,80,463	100.00

Source: Pocket Book of Population Statistics, 1972, *Table* 7.

The percentage of population below the poverty line (Rs. 65 per capita per month in rural and 75 per capita per month in urban: 1977-78 prices) was 51 in rural areas and 38 in urban areas. Yet the percentage of population suffering from protein or calorie deficiency or both, was 28.8 in rural areas and 32.6 per cent in urban areas. This is calculated on the basis of 2,400 calories per person in rural areas and 2,100 per person in urban areas (Sixth Five Year Plan 1981).

Within the overall characteristic of sharp breaks in urban-rural profiles, an urban interface between urban and rural is emerging, particularly in the metropolitan regions and in the developed regions with agro-industrial and commercial base. This is mainly due to improvements in transport and communications to metropolitan centres, and urban-industrialization and commercialization of the rural areas, and consequent improvement in the incomes of the people. Is there then an urban-rural continuum emerging? On this issue, see Chapter 3.

URBAN INDIA

1

URBANIZATION PROCESS, PATTERNS AND CORRELATES

THE DIVISION of the human habitat into 'urban' and 'rural' is based on a distinction of certain attributes of population of the habitat. Although, the two constructs are associated with dichotomies of 'modern' and 'traditional', and 'industrial' and 'agricultural', apparently one finds urban attributes in rural population and areas, and rural attributes in urban population and areas. Urbanization, then, involves the transformation of rural attributes to urban ones. That rural precedes urban is therefore implied.

The urbanization process relates to concentration of people engaged in non-agricultural occupations and concentration of non-agricultural land-uses in a specialized area, a 'place', as a consequence of population, occupational and land-use shifts. Urbanization thus involves:

(a) concentration of people at population densities higher than those associated with agricultural populations with only very rare exceptions on either side;
(b) population shift (migration) from rural to urban areas;
(c) occupational shift from agricultural to non-agricultural; and
(d) land-use shift from agricultural to non-agricultural.

These shifts, associated with economic development are not always coterminus, contiguous or sequential, and are accompanied or should be accompanied by rise in incomes, and a consequent improvement in standard of living, change in 'life style' and changes in the institutional framework. Thus, there is a chain of shifts.

While population shift implies a physical shift of population from rural to urban, occupational and land-use shifts can take place *in situ* i.e. without change in residence. This leads to sub-urbanization (near the city): staying in the village, and commuting to the city for work. The 'place' is not just physical habitat but is also the human habitat—the settlement. The human settlement scale ranges from farmstead to megalopolis. The human settlement scale is dynamic, and has both horizontal and vertical links. While the horizontal links are intra-settlement (micro) and inter-settlement—regional (meso) and national (macro), the vertical links are hierarchical. Both types of links function within a resource-base and also within a transport and communication network. People, goods and services and information constitute circulating flows through the settlement system. The urban settlement may be treated as a point location at regional and national levels, though at the 'site' level, it has an areal extent. The point locations of urban settlements may usefully be analysed geometrically from some view points such as inter-urban spatial relations; but also to the points may be attributed for purposes of analysis certain differentiating characteristics such as the degree of concentration of non-agricultural production and exchange. Inherent in the process of concentration is functional specialization. Equating the urbanization process with concentration, the process involves not only an increase in concentration at a point but also multiplication of points of concentration—the urban settlements. The concentration points are primarily of consumption, processing and service functions, with different levels of economic, social and technological attributes, which are inter-related and are time-culture specific, as hypothesized in Table 1.1. Population size, growth and function may all be arranged in rank order separately or according to some composite index of degree of urbanization. While such a ranked array may be interpreted as hierarchical or as a continuum (on the hierarchy/continuum issue, see also Chapter 2), it is clear that the degree of concentration, specialization or diversification tends to differ; and that the extent of

TABLE 1.1 : **Human settlement spectrum : attributes of urbanization***

Time-Culture Scale

Human Settlement Spectrum	Social	Economic (Occupational)	Technological (Transport)	Linkage
Farmstead hamlet village	Folk society, social groups place bound	Primary with small traders, artisans and service workers	Pedestrian, Bullockcart	Isolated-limited contacts
Town city City region	Preindustrial ecological groups, place-work-folk isomorphism	Secondary workers (trade, transport) construction) whole sale traders	Roadways railways, airways	Regional links through movement of people, goods and services-information
Metropolis conurbation	Late industrial class groups, increasing spatial mobility	Tertiary services, industrialist entrepreneurs, Financiers	Television, computer, satellite	National and international links
Megalopolis hyper-urban	Post-industrial interest groups unbound	Quarternary services, business executives, Research scientists	Satellite, skylab, space shuttle	Increased international links Through space
Dynapolis ecumenapolis	?	?	?	?

*Adapted and expanded from Friedmann (1966). There is no implication or suggestion of sequence of events in this hypothesization. The impact of time is always uneven. While some events leap-frog, others get telescoped. Each successive period carries with it the relicts of the earlier periods.

inter-relationships between the attributes of urbanization can often be viewed as dependent on the hierarchic level of the urban centre.

The relationships between urban settlements take the form of reciprocal linkages with their respective hinterlands, though not in all regions (e.g. mining regions), and in all types (project towns). In the context of the development process, urban centres depending on their size, type and functional scale, often spread innovations from urban to rural areas. Innovations may also flow from rural areas to urban, and from periphery to core (Slater, quoted by Friedmann and Wolf 1976). In this process of diffusion, different urban development patterns may develop: development poles may develop with often gradual, sometimes sharp distance decay; or arterial/corridor patterns; or dispersed patterns. Diffusion of urban development could also lead to an urban-rural development continuum. An urban-rural continuum could be in family size and type, land-use, occupational structure and urban amenities and the way of life.

Urbanization as a process of concentration is characteristic of both developed and developing countries. The difference between the two lies in the structure of urban-industrial relationships, city size and spatial distribution, and urban-rural relationships. It is necessary to identify here different scales in the process of urbanization—metropolitan cities usually with much industry of particular types; market towns with the commercial sector as the key urban sector, rooted to the regional resource base; and small towns with the service sector as the key sector to serve the adjoining countryside. One can envisage associated subprocesses such as metropolitanization-growth of cities with advanced technological and quaternary base; urban-commercialization—growth of market towns of medium size with an agricultural production and servicing base, with appropriate technology; and rural urbanization-growth of small towns with a service base again with appropriate technology.

Metropolitanization refers to the growth of metropolitan centres rooted in industrial and tertiary economic base. A metropolis is a distinct form of settlement, characteristically with sprawling of its built-up area, and includes its inter-dependent nearby villages, and even towns. The metropolitan region is the most intense commuting field, and has a certain minimum critical size. The metropolis is best epitomized in its tertiary core. The metropolitan centres are a class by themselves, characterized by large scale consumption and a large quantum of flows of people, goods, services and information. The high degree of nodality of a metropolis is best reflected in the high order communication network and the very radial network of national and regional transport routes.

Different from metropolitanization is industrial-urbanization, consequent upon national economic policies. Recognizing steel as one of the core sectors of the Indian economy, industrial cities like Bhilai, Rourkela and Durgapur have been developed, which contributed greatly to the national economy but could not diffuse development in their immediate vicinities. These cities are rooted to localized resources of national importance, and have all the characteristics of implanted centres which developed 'enclave' economies.

Distinct from metropolitanization and industrial-urbanization, is urban-commercialization associated with regional clusters of market towns of medium or intermediate size of cities. Increased commercialization of agriculture due to the Green Revolution has given a new impetus and special status to many market-towns in the collection and distribution of surplus produce. This has induced the development of market infra-structures from village level (cleaning, grading-storage); to selling depots and processing units in central villages and agri-towns; to commercial grading and modern warehousing, crop insurance and communication facilities in the market cities. Market function is getting reoriented and realigned to higher order urban functions particularly through retail and wholesale trade. Market-towns with agro-based industries, market infra-structure and other central place functions serve the countryside, while the farmers with increased incomes develop productive links with market-towns and change their life styles for the better. In the economic sector, production, processing and distribution get better integrated. A milk production factory in a market city, located at the apex of a prosperous and a highly populated delta with its paddy-sugarcane economy has its maximum impact on its 'milk-shed' area and is most integrative, involving thousands of farmers who have improved their quality of life even within a short period of two to three years. The potential for backward linkages exists through a well developed packing industry if properly planned (Waheeduddin Khan, 1975). If the steel city of Bhilai located in the backward Chota Nagpur plateau reflects enclave economy, the market city of Vijayawada located at the apex of prosperous Krishna delta on the east coast plain of India reflects an integrated urban-rural economy (Prakasa Rao and Ramachandran, 1975).

The third sub-process is urbanization of the countryside through the growth of small towns and large central villages to serve their rural-hinterlands. In economic structure, these settlements are more rural than urban. Most of the rural settlements are not linked to the urban system through the transport network, and where they are so linked, they tend to be eclipsed by nearby larger centres owing to sub-standard urban services and amenities. While in the developed countries the different sub-processes of urbanization tend to get integrated with the metropolitan system, in India, as in other developing countries, the sub-processes operate independently or function with a disproportionate mix, resulting in a disjointed pattern. Thus the process underlies the pattern, for example, if clustering or agglomeration due to economies of scale is the process, then

TABLE 1.2 : **Urban process and patterns**

Process	Pattern	Attributes
Centralisation—Polarisation	Primate	Key attribute: manufacturing industry and tertiary sector: trade, transport and services.
Decentralisation or Decentralised concentration—Commercialization	'Puncti form'	Key attribute: Commerce, agro-based industries, and tertiary sector: transport and services
Urbanization of the countryside	Dispersed pattern	Key attribute: lower order urban services and amenities

cluster is the emergent pattern. A primate pattern is consequent upon concentration/agglomeration, while a decentralised concentration leads to 'punctiform' pattern. Associated with the process and associated pattern are distinct attributes (Table 1.2). It is difficult to compartmentalize the different sub-processes, patterns and attributes due to changing development patterns and due to planning and policy interventions. There is telescoping or overlapping of functions, both vertically in the level of specialization, and horizontally, i.e. spatially.

Urban Patterns

Global

At the world scale, there is an overall relationship between the level of urbanization and the level of economic development. The world pattern of distribution of the levels of urbanization, measured by the percentage of urban to total population and the pattern of distribution of wealth, measured by the GNP per capita, have a positive correlation (Table 1.3). At

TABLE 1.3 : **Percentage of urban population to total population and GNP per capita**

	GNP per capita (1964)	Percentage of urban population to total population (1970-1971)
USA	2000+	75
Canada	,,	75
UK	1000-2000	79
German Federal Rupublic	,,	82
Australia	,,	88
Netherlands	,,	72
Japan	,,	83
USSR	500-1000	62
China Republic	200-500	64
Ghana	100-200	34
Ceylon (Sri Lanka)	,,	17
Nigeria	<100	21
India	,,	19

Source : Urbanization—Sector Working Paper, *World Bank*, 1972.

the world level the generalization is that the higher the level of urbanization the higher the per capita income level. This positive correlation is attributed to such factors as rapid industrialization, increase in productivity, higher literacy, higher living standards, and greater socio-economic interaction among people. Here it is important to distinguish the effects of high rates of urban population growth. That rapid urban population growth fosters rapid increase in a nation's wealth or productivity, cannot be inferred from the positive correlation between higher proportion of national population in urban areas and high levels of per capita GNP (Andrei Rogers, 1978). Of course, the urban impact on development will also depend on the city-size structure and city hierarchy. World urban patterns emerge in the patterns of urban primacy also. High degrees of primacy are asscciated with lower income countries e.g. Thailand, Latin American countries and Uganda, to mention a few. However, high primacy is also associated with higher incomes and higher rates of urbanization, e.g. France and Denmark. As a generalization, at the world level, high urban primacy is associated most frequently with countries with a small areal extent and dense population, low per capita income, export-oriented and agricultural economies, a colonial history and rapid rates of population growth (Linsky 1965). Yet as exceptions like France and Denmark show, the relationship between primacy and development is still not clear. It is too simple to equate primacy with parasitism (Richardson 1973). Primacy in its classical form is best expressed in 'the law of the Primate city' of Jefferson (1939) which states: 'All over the world it is the law of the capitals that the largest city shall be supereminent, and not necessarily in size but in national influence'. The primate city model and Friedmann's (1966) core-periphery model have some characteristics in common.

All over the world, the urban patterns are changing: in the levels of urbanization, in the pattern of spatial distribution, and in urban-rural relationships. In the United Kingdom, the urban pattern has reached the maturely developed megalopolitan stage, an urban climax, where the regional urban core and its fringe, and the city-regions are integrated and interlocked. It is reckoned that 90 per cent of Britain's population live within one hour's journey from central city services. This measures the degree of megalopolitan scale and urban continuum (Smailes 1971). In USA, the once dominant Boston-Washington megalopolis has given place to other megalopolises like the one in the Pacific North-West and the one south of the Great Lakes. The emerging trends in technology and communications network are drawing the metropolitan peripheries into daily commuting urban systems, and the metropolitan cores and peripheries are being drawn into the 'urban field' with its structural profile of 'metropolitan core-regions and inter-metropolitan peripheries' (Friedmann and Miller 1965). The emerging new urban systems in USA are defying the traditional bases of urbanization, and are tending to be "multi-nodal-multi-connected social systems, sharing national growth and offering a variety of 'life styles' in a variety of environments" (Berry 1977). The basic pattern that underlies this changing spatial urban pattern is set by the revolution in communication technology and the structure of transport network resulting in 'corridors', of urbanization* with a network of nodes of different urban scale. Though this corridor form of urban landscape is a deviation from Christaller-Lösch landscape, it has its roots in the "traffic principle" and the city-rich sectors. In the Netherlands, there is a trend toward the development of a second urban 'conglomeration' and two more zones of urban concentration, next to Randstad (ring-city), which is threatening to become a megalopolis, but is being interrupted by planning intervention in the form of green belts and buffer zones. Dispersal of urban conglomerations outwards, along corridors, is being promoted; resulting in "concentrated decentralization". Within the European framework, plans are being prepared for further expansion of Randstad but preserving its "open structure".** In Germany, the Ruhr

*Corridors are linear urban systems with both time and spatial dimensions and represent a sharp distortion of Christaller-Lösch landscape. An urban corridor like megalopolis implies a strongly interacting linear urban development linked by a highly developed transport and communication axis. In this linear urban system, the population size is of the order of 10 million to 250 million (Papaioannou 1969; Whebell 1969).

**Physical Planning in Netherlands, Second Report, The Hague, 1966.

cities have developed as regional urban system through metropolitan transport and communication network system. The Ruhr urban system is a unique case where the Rhineside cities are crumbling in their economic base with the regional shift of the mining economy from the Rhineside to the Lippe. Here the regional urban pattern is being geared to a motorized community and circular metropolitan commuting. The urban system of the Ruhr is identified as having reached the stage of 'industrial urban neurosis'. Associated with these patterns of urbanization are life styles changing with increasing mobility, and a craving for an uncontaminated environment to reside, and commute to the polluted core for work.

Urban Patterns

Asia

In contrast to the trend toward megalopolitan and urban climax in the developed West, urbanization patterns in Asia are primate patterns, and urban-rural dichotomy is sharp. The primate pattern is partly the result of colonial legacy and partly due to sectorally oriented national development policies. Unlike the primate and high income countries, the primate patterns of low income Asiatic countries display a spatial pattern where the primate metropolises stand out as 'enclaves' of development poles with sharp distance decay in the levels of development. The primate cities of India, particularly the national cities like Calcutta and Bombay carry 'the imprints of colonialism'. These are categorized as "satellite primate cities" which function as 'enclaves' with extra regional links at least in considering their evolution over the last century or so in the colonial period, and perhaps the early decades since independence. The city's socio-economic and demographic structures reflect essentially a core-periphery exploitive relationships (Moonis Raza *et al.* 1979). The failure of the primate cities to diffuse development is attributed to the overall low level of development and the very structure of the wider economic system (McGee, 1971). The process underlying the primate patterns is associated with low income, poor nutrition, low levels of food consumption and low levels of education, characteristics, typical of not only Asian but all developing countries

(Berry 1973). Here the crucial factor is the overall and continuing rapid growth of rural population and city population. The process underlying the unconformity between the urban and rural population growth, and the imbalanced economic development and social transformation have been labelled as "pseudo-urbanization (McGee 1971)," "false-urbanization" (Kantseboskaya 1976) and "dysfunctional urbanization" (Moonis Raza *et al.* 1979).

In between the Western and the Asian patterns of urbanization, Japan illustrates a case of blending of megalopolitanism of the Western type with the typical village rooted rural way of life, built around kinship and ethnic ties with local neighbourhoods (Berry 1973). India is a typical case of dual and transitional patterns with a highly polarized and spatially imbalanced urban system, sharp urban-rural and core-periphery dichotomy and sharp regional variations in urbanization patterns. Some of the urban-regional patterns of the West, like urban-industrial corridors, regional urban clusters, inter-metropolitan linkages and daily urban systems with increasing distance range and with greater mobility are emerging in India but with a different structure and low level of intensity. The million cities are developing into a national metropolitan system with greater international links, and developing some of the traits of post-industrial structure. The two large agglomerations, Calcutta and Bombay, crossing 7 million and 5 million mark respectively join the group of the world's largest agglomerations in population size (Table 1.4).

In the world setting, the level of urbanization in India with its 19.9 per cent of total population (1971) is low. But in terms of sheer size: absolute numbers of urban population i.e. urban scale, India with 109 million, stands next to USSR with 136 million, and USA with 149 million (1971). What further adds to the scale, is the net increase which was of the order of 24 million during the decade 1961-71. This increase is equivalent to the total populations of many countries in Europe. Thus the urban scale and its increase claim a high rank for urban India in the urban world.

TABLE 1.4 : City and population size

City	Million (Year 1975)
Tokyo	18.1
New York	17.0
Shanghai	11.4
Mexico	10.9
London	10.7
Sao Palo	10.2
Los Angeles	9.8
Buenos Aires	9.5
Paris	9.2
Peking	8.5
Calcutta	8.4
Rio de Janeiro	8.2
Bombay	7.5

Source : Development Forum. Dec. 1975, Habitat Conference, *Human Settlements*, Vancouver, 1976.

Urban India as a national aggregate

The annual growth rate of urban population during 1901-71 was 4.6 per cent. In absolute numbers, urban population increased by 84 million. This 70 year-period was characterized by slow growth or decline in the proportion of urban to total population in the early decades (1901-21) partly due to natural disasters, and partly due to the very slow pace of industrial and economic development; then rapid growth during 1941-51 due to political disasters and the consequent refugee migration to cities. The plan periods 1951-71 were characterized by fluctuating growth (Table 1.5). With such varied pattern of growth, long term analysis of trends in urban growth loses much of its meaning.

The substantial increase in urban population during 1951-71 (46.65 million), and a modest increase in the proportion of urban to total population (2.57 per cent) had taken place against the background of an occupational structure where the proportion engaged in the primary sector showed an increase,

TABLE 1.5 : **Urban population growth in India**

Year	Urban Population (in millions)	Growth rate	Percentage of urban to total population	
1901	25.85	—	10.85	Natural disasters
1911	25.94	0.34	10.29	
1921	28.09	8.28	11.18	
1931	33.46	19.12	12.00	
1941	44.15	31.95	13.96	Political disasters
1951	62.44	41.42	17.30	
1961	78.93	26.40	17.98	The era of Planned development through the Five Year Plans
1971	109.09	38.21	19.87	

and that in the secondary sector showed decrease contrary to expectation. The tertiary sector showed a slight recovery (Table 1.6). Thus the degree of urban-industrialization and planned development through the Five Year Plans could not bring about a significant shift in occupational structure, comparable with the developed countries. In India, the problem relates to both urban growth (3.8 per annum) and rural growth (2.2 per annum) during 1961-71.

TABLE 1.6 : **Occupational structure—All India**

Year	Primary	Secondary	Tertiary
1951	72.1	10.6	17.3
1961	72.3	10.6	17.1
1971	72.5	9.5	18.0

Even within the urban sector, there is a distinct traditional/rural component of occupational structure which is not insignificant, though it showed a decline during the decade 1961-71. This brings out the still persisting, and unabsorbed rural element in the urban sector, mostly in the periphery of the large urban settlements and in the medium and small towns, with a strong agricultural base. It appears that the urban-commercial sector responded more to urbanization than did the industrial sector in terms of working population. The nebulous service sector which in the census classification includes both professional and domestic services, showed a decline during 1961-71 (Table 1.7).

TABLE 1.7 : **Urban occupational structure in India**

Census Industrial categories	Number employed (in '000)		Percent to total workers	
	1961	1971	1961	1971
Primary Traditional/Rural:				
Cultivators	1730	1632	6.5	5.1
Agricultural Labourers	910	1919	3.5	6.0
Household Industry	2090	1589	7.9	4.9
Total	4730	5140	17.9	16.0
Mining, Quarrying, Livestock, Fishing	660	859	2.5	2.7
Total	5390	5999	20.4	18.7
Manufacturing				
Processing, Servicing and Repairs	5540	7314	21.0	22.8
Commercial				
Trade and Commerce	4320	6415	16.3	20.1
Transport, Storage and Communication	2130	3191	8.1	10.0
Total	6450	9606	24.4	30.1
Other Services	8090	7960	30.6	24.9
Construction	960	1119	3.6	3.5
All Total	26430	31998	100.0	100.0

The degree of imbalance in terms of high population concentration in cities, and multiplication of cities, and the near-static proportions in Class II and III towns, accompanied by a decline in small towns, are emphasized by many researchers on Indian urbanization (Table 1.8). The large cities of today were not born large but have steadily grown over years. There were only 25 Class I cities (>1,00,000 population) in 1901. Of

TABLE 1.8 : **Urbanization trends—Distribution of towns and urban population of India by size classes 1901–1971**

Size Class	Number of Towns								% of total urban population in each size class							
	1901	1911	1921	1931	1941	1951	1961	1971	1901	1911	1921	1931	1941	1951	1961	1971
Cities 1,00,000+	25	24	29	34	48	77	105	148	25.81	27.15	28.89	29.99	36.83	43.38	50.23	55.83
Medium towns 50,000—1,00,000	42	39	45	54	78	96	130	183	10.79	9.90	10.22	11.16	11.80	10.40	11.09	11.32
Small towns 20,000—50,000	136	143	154	195	248	336	459	582	16.03	16.84	16.42	17.80	16.63	15.95	17.51	16.32
Urban villages 10,000—20,000	395	367	374	446	514	631	745	873	20.87	19.64	18.21	18.25	16.12	13.99	12.99	11.31
5000—10,000	756	727	753	816	939	1156	763	678	20.23	19.54	18.85	17.24	15.19	13.08	7.25	4.71

TABLE 1.8—*contd.*

	Number of Towns								% of total urban population in each size class							
	1901	1911	1921	1931	1941	1951	1961	1971	1901	1911	1921	1931	1941	1951	1961	1971
5000 less	494	535	616	555	437	596	219	172	6.27	6.93	7.41	5.56	3.43	3.20	0.93	0.51
Total	1848	1835	1971	2100	2264	2892	2421	2636*	100.00	100.00	100.00	100.00	100.00	100.00	100.00	100.00
									(25.85	25.94	28.09	33.46	44.15	62.44	78.93	109.09)
																(Millions)

Source: Census of India.
*Urban agglomeration is taken as a unit.

the additional 123 Class I cities (between 1901 and 1971) 42 were Class II (50,000—1,00,000), 47 were Class III (20,000—50,000), 21 Class IV (10,000—20,000), 6 Class V and VI (10,000), and 7 were villages in 1901. Of the 183 Class II cities in 1971, 2 were Class II, 67 were Class III, 70 Class IV, 23 Class V, 4 Class VI and 17 were villages in 1901. Of the 582 Class III towns in 1971, 18 were Class III, 216 were Class IV, 150 Class V, 20 Class VI and 178 were villages in 1901. Thus towns in one size class in one census period get upgraded to the next higher size class in the next census period. This upgrading accounts for the negative growth rate in certain size-classes. Of course a few towns got downgraded. These facts get concealed in aggregate tabulation (Table 1.8).

The following two tables for Karnataka towns bring out the differences in the two types of tabulations: one without taking upgrading into account (Table 1.9) and the other, wherein the growth of each town under various classes in 1961 is aggregated irrespective of its reclassified status of 1971 (Table 1.10). Only, the towns defined as urban for the first

TABLE 1.9 : **Urban population growth rates by size-classes: Karnataka**

Class	Size Range	%Growth 1951-61	%Growth 1961-71
I	100,000+	34.25	67.87
II	50,000–99,999	70.38	—11.38
III	20,000–49,999	42.33	39.39
IV	10,000–19,999	35.69	34.19
V	5,000–9,999	–52.26	–24.25

TABLE 1.10 : **Urban population growth rates by size-classes: Karnataka**

Class	%Growth 1961-71
I	35.56
II	75.88
III	22.16
IV	14.53
V	18.84

time in 1971, are omitted. The Table clearly brings out that the medium towns have grown at a faster rate than the large cities (for urban-size growth-type relationships on an individual city/town basis, refer pp. 64-66).

Even after allowing for these statistical traps, urban India is highly imbalanced. The imbalance is best typified in the concentration of urban population in large cities with 52 per cent to total urban population concentrated in 5 per cent of the total number of urban centres. Associated with this concentration of population is the concentration of metropolitan functions, particularly in the million cities, leading to functional gaps between metropolitan and non-metropolitan cities. The problem is one not only of functional gaps but also spatial gaps. While the increase in the number of Class I cities from 25 in 1901, and 77 in 1951 to 148 in 1971, and the metropolitan cities (more than 5,00,000) from 3 in 1901 and 9 in 1951 to 19 in 1971, reduced the spatial gap in metropolitan functions whatever be their scale, the location pattern of cities is such there are still wide spatial gaps. The problem gets compounded with the sharp inter-state and inter-regional variations in urban patterns relating to both size-class and spatial distribution. These variations are analysed in the following sections.

Inter-State variations Tables (1.11 and 1.12)

The different states are ranked on the basis of growth, number of towns per 10,000 square miles and percentage of population in cities, medium towns and small towns during the decades 1951-1961 and 1961-1971, into three categories: High, Medium and Low. High growth and high rank in cities indicate metropolitanization; in medium towns indicate urban commercialization; and in small towns, indicate rural urbanization.

According to the 1961 classification and ranking, Maharashtra and Gujarat were the metropolitan States (conforming to the national aggregate urban pattern), and Madhya Pradesh, Orissa and Assam were the States with rural urbanization. Bihar, Madhya Pradesh and Kerala were the states characterized by commercialization. It is necessary to note that in Madhya Pradesh the growth and percentage of population in both cities and medium towns were high. In Gujarat and

TABLE 1.11 : **Urbanization patterns—1961**

Growth rate of population in cities (1951-61)	Percentage of population in cities to total urban population		
	High	Medium	Low
High	MH(M)* GJ(M)	—	PH(H)* OR(L) AS(L)
Medium	TN(H)	RJ(L) BH(M)	MP(L)
Low	WB(H) UP(H)	AP(L) KN(M)	KE(H)

Growth rate of population in medium towns (1951-61)	Percentage of population in medium towns to total urban population		
	High	Medium	Low
High	BH(M) MP(L) KE(H)	AP(M)	KN(M)
Medium	PH(H) AS(L)	OR(L)	WB(H)
Low	—	GJ(H) TN(H)	MH(L) UP(M) RJ(L)

Growth rate of population in small towns (1951-61)	Percentage of population in small towns to total urban population		
	High	Medium	Low
High	MP(L) OR(L) AS(L)	BH(M)	WB(H) PH(H)
Medium	KN(H)	TN(H) KE(H)	—
Low	RJ(L)	AP(L)	MH(M) UP(M) GJ(M)

*For explanation,—See Notes, p. 33.

TABLE 1.12 : **Urbanization patterns—1971**

Growth rate of population in cities (1961-71)	Percentage of population in cities to total urban population		
	High	Medium	Low
High	—	KE(H) BH(M)	MP(L) OR(L)
Medium	AP(L) GJ(M)	KN(M)	RJ(L)
Low	MH(M) UP(H) WB(H)	TN(H)	AS(L) PH(H)

Growth rate of population in medium towns (1961-71)	Percentage of population in medium towns to total urban population		
	High	Medium	Low
High	BH(H) KE(L) OR(L)	TN(H)	KN(M)
Medium	—	RJ(L)	MP(L) MH(M) UP(H)
Low	AS(L) PH(H)	AP(M) GJ(H)	WB(H)

Growth rate of population in small towns (1961-71)	Percentage of population in small towns to total urban population		
	High	Medium	Low
High	AS(L) RJ(L)	GJ(M)	UP(M) WB(H)
Medium	MP(L) KN(H) OR(L)	PH(H)	—
Low	—	BH(M) TN(H)	AP(L) KE(H) MH(M)

Maharashtra though the growth of population in cities was high but the growth in both medium and small towns was low and coupled with low and medium proportions of population in these towns. Based on this, one could formulate a hypothesis that in Gujarat and Maharashtra, metropolitanization is inhibiting the growth of both small towns and medium towns. It needs no mention that Maharashtra is a State where the "urban shadow" of metropolitanization is maximal, and medium and small towns are more scattered than cities. Thus Maharashtra is also characterized by a high degree of urban concentration. High degree of metropolitanization and high city concentration only reveal that urbanization is imbalanced, both in space and structure. There was no State where the urban structure was balanced between the three types. In West Bengal, though the share of urban population in small towns was low, the growth rate was high, while the share of city population was high, its growth rate was low. In one of the least urbanized states (Orissa), the small towns had a higher share, and they were also growing faster, along with the fast growth of the cities. If the density of cities per 10,000 square miles is taken into account, West Bengal ranks first, and Kerala ranks second. Kerala was less imbalanced in the density pattern of the different town/city size-classes. In contrast to

Notes :

1. AP—Andhra Pradesh
   AS—Assam
   BH—Bihar
   GJ—Gujarat
   KE—Kerala
   KN—Karnataka
   MH—Maharashtra
   MP—Madhya Pradesh
   OR—Orissa
   PH—Punjab (Punjab & Haryana)
   RJ—Rajasthan
   TN—Tamil Nadu
   UP—Uttar Pradesh
   WB—West Bengal
2. Cities—Class I and II towns, medium towns
   Class III towns and small towns
   Class IV and V towns, as defined in Census of India.
3. High-ranks : 1 to 5
   Medium-ranks : 6 to 7
   Low-ranks : 10 to 14
4. H, M and L in brackets along with State names indicate the State position as High, Medium and Low according to the number of towns per 10,000 square miles.

this, there was not even one city per 10,000 square miles in Assam, Madhya Pradesh, Orissa and Rajasthan. Thus, there are city-rich and city-poor states. In Madhya Pradesh, Orissa, Assam, Bihar, West Bengal and Punjab, the pattern was one of urbanization of the countryside, may be at a sub-standard level. High growth of small towns could be taken as an evidence for this tendency.

The patterns of change during 1961-71 indicated that the metropolitan states of Maharashtra and Gujarat did not show high growth of cities during 1961-71 though the share of population in cities remained high. While Gujarat is in the high-medium cell, Maharashtra is in the high/low cell, thereby indicating that the rate of metropolitanization is slowing down. The pattern of urbanization (commercialization) in Bihar and Kerala did not change during 1961-71 while the pattern of urbanization did change in the case of Orissa from rural urbanization. The emergence of Rajasthan in the first cell, along with Assam during 1971, suggests that the urbanization pattern in Rajasthan and Assam is one of rural urbanization. At the national aggregate level, metropolitanization is certainly increasing as evident from the increase in the number of cities, proportion of city population and city growth rate.

Inter-regional variations

Sharp contrasts in natural and economic landscapes lead to sharp inter-regional and intra-regional differences in urban patterns. It must be mentioned here that variations in the industrial resources base and regional accessibility to transport and power lead to sharper regional urban variations than variations in the agricultural resources base (Berry and Prakasa Rao, 1968). Broadly, four regional urban patterns emerge :

1. Metropolitan regional pattern with its national and inter-national links and shadow effect on its periphery.
2. Urban-industrial pattern associated with industrial development mainly rooted in the region's agricultural and industrial resources, and well developed power and transport network.

3. Agro-based urban pattern associated with irrigation agriculture.
4. Least urbanized pattern associated with hill-forest areas.

Metropolitan regional pattern

The degree of imbalance that is created in the urban and regional system by a metropolis of first order becomes evident if the dominance of the metropolis in its region/state is examined. Development trends in metropolitan Bombay for example, confirm to core-periphery dichotomy. If the twin city project takes full shape, the Bombay metropolis should have 12 million by 1991. Strictly speaking, the Bombay metropolis should be treated as a part of the emerging megalopolis with Bombay and Ahmedabad as the primary nodes, and Poona, Surat and Vadodara as the secondary nodes. This adds up to an urban population mass of about 10 million even by 1971. The level of economic concentration in Greater Bombay becomes evident from the following facts.

With 12 per cent of the total population and 59 per cent of factory workers of the State, Greater Bombay dominates in electricity consumption (69 %), disbursement of bank credit (85 %) and in the concentration of joint stock companies (85 %) 1971-72. The metropolitan regions of Bombay and Poona together captured 97 per cent of the State's net increase in factory workers during the 15-year period ending 1971. In year 1977, Greater Bombay had 89,730 industrial units (registered and unregistered) employing 1.5 million workers. More than 68 per cent of the units were concentrated in the Bombay city area. Majority of the key-industries belonged to the innovative and capital-intensive type—electronic, engineering and chemicals in contrast to the stagnating, and even declining cotton textiles and agro-processing industries located in the low production peripheral regions (Aurangabad and Nagpur). Thus even the industrial sector is characterized by modern and traditional dichotomy. In the economically lagging rural areas, isolated pockets of prosperous areas like the sugarcane belt with its sugar town of Kolhapur stand out amidst wide areas of dry farming and consequently unstable agricultural economy. When there is some resource potential, as in the forest and mineral rich areas (Nagpur and Chandrapur) and fishery areas (Konkan), their level of utilization is low. The rural landscape of the peripheral areas as in the upper valleys of the Tapti, Godavari and Krishna, is characterised by distinct zonation between valley plains with concentration of agriculture and the adjoining uplands and inaccessible watersheds with grass lands, shepherds, nomads and tribals (the Sahyadris and the Satpuras). Thus the limited natural resource endowment and intra-regional inaccessibility and the dominance of Bombay all have truncated the urban system. While the cities developed links among themselves, the town clusters are yet to function as diffusing nodes. The urban growth is weak and discontinuous, and the majority of the coastal and interior towns with an unstable agricultural base and declining household industry base, could not develop regional relationships. The demographic balance and man-land ratio are upset due to heavy migration to Bombay and other larger cities. The interstitial areas remain as depressed areas in spite of their proximity to the metropolis. Thus while Bombay metropolis is tending to become a megalopolis with inter-city, national and international links, the rural areas and the small and medium towns are lagging, excepting in a few and isolated pockets, and remain structurally unrelated to the metropolis. In the Bombay metropolitan region (South Konkan) the trading function of some of the Konkan ports was squeezed out and weekly markets collapsed. But migration, high dependency ratios, high sex ratios and stagnating and declining towns are attributed to the shadow effect of the metropolis which has contributed to the weakening of the socio-economic structure of this part of the metropolitan region. There is some change now, with the development of industries and improvement of accessibility and a specific development policy of Bombay Metropolitan Development Authority to promote industries in the periphery of the metropolis. Yet the core-periphery socio-economic gap persists (Johri 1980, Brahme 1977, Deshpande 1976, Sita 1972).

Urban-industrial pattern

The pattern of urbanization in the agro-industrial Coimbatore district is a deviant from the national pattern of urbanization of metropolitanization at the expense of small and medium towns and rural areas. In Tamil Nadu, Coimbatore district ranks third in the level of economic development, with the metropolitan district of Madras and the plantation district of Nilgiris ranking first and second respectively. The major thrust for urbanization came from industrialization rooted in the region's resource base, mainly cotton, the proverbial 'colonial crop', and hydel power development during 1931-61 which was instrumental in industrial dispersal. The 13-year period from 1961-1974 was characterized by growth in both urban-industrial and commercial agricultural sectors. On the agricultural front, the district is characterized by highly diversified cropping, and all the 26 crops grown enter markets. Jowar, groundnut, sugarcane, turmeric, tobacco and of course cotton, are important in terms of production and marketable surpluses. The pattern of localization of the commercial crops is such that the respective commodity markets are located in towns of different population sizes located in the zones of respective crop concentrations. The zone of production concentration of cotton, groundnut and cholam lies along and on either side of the Coimbatore-Erode axial belt. This is the zone of maximum concentration of industrial and market centres. The population size class of urban centres varies from small towns to class Icities. The population size of market villages varies from just above 2600 to 24,000. Coimbatore and Tiruppur the cotton cities, Pollachi, the groundnut city, and Erode, the turmeric city, have well developed market complexes, well served by the telecommunication link system, and are well linked with Madras, Cochin, Bangalore and Bombay. The Coimbatore-Erode axial belt is the zone of concentration of weekly markets also. All the urban and market centres have a high degree of connectivity, measured by shortest path, and are well connected by the transport net. Even the villages are well connected to urban centres with no village located more than 20 km from an urban centre.

Coimbatore, which held a dominant position in the region till 1961, has shared its importance with Tiruppur located at a distance of 80 km. Erode located at a distance of 130 km. and Pollachi at a distance of 40 km. Coimbatore, Tiruppur and Pollachi recorded a decline in the rate of population growth, while Erode city and the medium size market towns like Udumulpet, Gopi and Bhavani recorded an increasing rate (1961-71). Of the 33 urban centres in the Coimbatore-Erode axial belt, Coimbatore, Tiruppur and Erode are industrial beehives supported by well developed market complexes. Both industrial scale and industrial climate in the region promoted a powerful and dynamic industrial entrepreneurship. Some of the cotton farmers have become innovative and enterprising industrialists and ploughed back their farm profits into industry. The Coimbatore farmers' responsiveness to agricultural and industrial development and package programmes is well known. The cotton textile industry at Coimbatore has become the springboard for the development of textile machinery manufacture, spare parts, electric motors and pumpsets. Apart from these industries, there are more than 3500 registered small scale units which manufacture a wide range of products—agricultural machinery, machine tools, transport equipment, chemicals and chemical products and steel structurals to mention a few examples. Tiruppur has developed as a hosiery complex with over 1200 small hosiery factories operating in the small scale sector. There are over 400 small batik enterprises in and around Erode employing thousands of women and men for printing and dyeing cloth especially sarees, and 100 leather tanning and leather industries. There are also thousands of handlooms. About 500 small ancillary units take up job works for medium and large scale industries. Small industries undertake job and ancillary work for the public sector undertakings at Bangalore and Madras.* Thus the region's urban-industrial cities function as a part of the country's industrial and market network and contribute their share in the development of national economic space. In contrast, at the intra-regional level, the disparity between the axial belt and the northern (irrigated agriculture) and southern regions (dry farming and livestock farming) is sharp. There are also sharp functional and spatial gaps in urban and market infra-structure. This is attributed to the absence of regional

*Industrial Focus on Coimbatore, special supplement. *The Indian Express*, November 1980.

planning in spite of designating the Coimbatore region as a planning region (Parvathi 1977).

Agro-based urban pattern

At the macro-regional scale, the Gangetic plains, the agricultural heartland of India with its high rural population densities and well developed transport and power network is highly urbanized and metropolitanized. Between two of the four metropolitan apexes, Delhi and Calcutta, are urban-industrial islands like Kanpur-Lucknow, Agra and Varanasi located in an area of high rural population density, agriculturally rich. Unlike the agriculturally poor inter-metropolitan troughs between Delhi and Bombay and Madras, the inter-metropolitan trough between Delhi and Calcutta is mainly agriculturally rich, and is also a city-rich region. (Fig. 1.1)

In contrast to the Gangetic plains, the core areas of the Mahanadi, Godavari, Krishna and Cauvery deltas have a different urban pattern, and are less urbanized mainly because of regional inaccessibility to transport. These deltaic areas, have medium and small towns, mostly based on trade, transport, household industry and services. Many of these towns are slow-growing or stagnant or even declining. Owing to regional inaccessibility to transport, there are not adequate incentives to develop growth-promoting industries in spite of agricultural prosperity and high rural population densities. It is after the impact of the green revolution that some of the delta towns of the Godavari and Krishna started playing an important role in the marketing of agricultural surpluses, and responding to the development of market infra-structures. It was found that the pattern of agricultural development in the Godavari and Krishna deltas influenced the growth rates of the accessible medium and small towns in the deltas (West Godavari). Agricultural development is reflected in the rate of mobilization of agricultural surpluses in the highly productive and rapidly commercializing agriculture (Pothanna, 1979). In such a dynamic setting, urban centres also became dynamic through multiplication of agricultural input and servicing facilities, growth of agro-processing units, and increase in the number of retail trade shops to cater to the increased demands in the city and the city hinterland. These prosperous delta

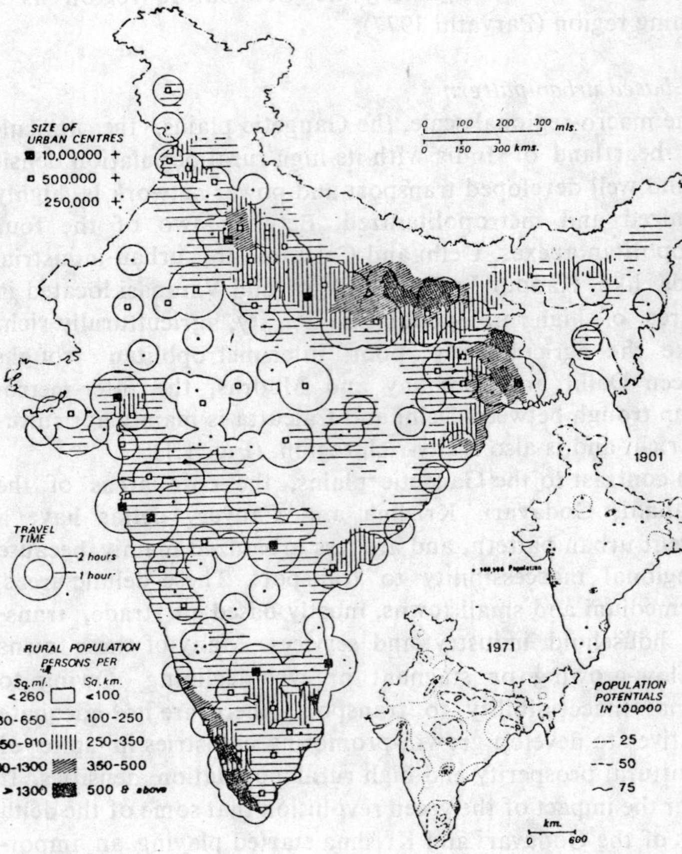

FIG. 1.1 : *Urban India—1971*

areas depend on the cities located at the delta apexes for city benefits even on a sub-standard scale. Even these cities do not have a strong industrial base and they are mostly commercial and service cities. Consequently a majority of them either showed a declining growth rate or only a slight increase during 1961-1971. In other words, these cities are not growing by high migration, as there is no inducement to migrate, real or even perceived. Where there is some industrial development in the city periphery, the growth rate tends to be high—Vijayawada Rajamundry, Tiruchirapalli and Cuttack. In the absence of an industrial economic base, the intensity of urban patterns does not sharply differ between one agricultural tract and another, for example between Krishna-Godavari delta, Tungabhadra valley and Warangal-Nizamabad (Andhra Pradesh).

Punjab is yet another example of an agriculturally highly productive and prosperous state which is characterized by small and medium-sized cities and towns to the exclusion of large cities dominating the others. The largest city, Amritsar has just under half-a-million in population size (1971). The population of the next ranking cities varies from 3,00,000 to 4,00,000. Thus there is no large population size gap and consequent functional gap between one city and another. These cities along with medium and small size towns, provide the needed economic infra-structure for agriculture and agro-processing, and social infra-structure for the rural folk. These examples bring out clearly that a rich agricultural base with commercializing agriculture does not by itself lead to more intensive urban patterns (Berry and Prakasa Rao 1968).

Least urbanized pattern

The least urbanized areas are the inaccessible and hill-forest areas, and here, even at this low urban level, there are intra-regional differences. The hill-forest areas of the Godavari valley (Andhra Pradesh) are relatively more urbanized, and some of the areas have even a higher level of urbanization than the irrigated agricultural areas, the core of the Godavari delta. The higher degree of urbanization in these areas is due to mineral and industrial resource base, and relatively better accessibility to transport and power. Nilgiri district (Tamil Nadu) with its plantation economy and tourist industry is more urbanized compared to other hill forest districts. Population density, if that is any index at all, varies from 100 to 300 per square mile in the more developed urbanized forest areas. In the less developed, less accessible and least urbanized forest areas, population density is below 100 per square mile.

Malnad, the hill-forest region of Karnataka, like other hill-forest regions, is characterized by low population density (less than 200 per square mile) and low level of urbanization with 13 per cent of the region's population living in 35 towns, and with an average annual growth rate of 1.5 per cent (1961-71). The distribution of size classes of towns indicates that Malnad is a region of small towns, 6 belonging to size class 10,000-20,000, and large villages, 22 belonging to size classes of 5000-10,000 and below 5000. The largest Malnad town has population of about 42,000 (Chikmagalur), followed by Sirsi, Sagar and Dandeli with populations ranging from 25,000 to less than 29,000. Chikmagalur is a trading and a district headquarters town with a diversified functional base, while Dandeli is an industrial town with industries rooted to local resources. Sirsi and Sagar are trading and transport towns. Mercara, the coffee estate town is a small town with less than 20,000 population and a declining growth rate. Most of the other towns are agricultural, household industry and trading towns.

Even at this overall low level of urbanization, the sharp intra-regional variations are related to the density of forest cover, accessibility to transport and type of regional economy which is locally getting transformed owing to improvements in transport and power, and the State's specific region-oriented development policies. The change is from subsistence forest and agricultural economy to more specialized forest-based and industrial and plantation economy, and commercialized agriculture with horticulture as an important sector. Within the overall changing pattern of Malnad economy, three zones stand out distinctly, the northern as the paddy-ragi zone dominated by forestry; the central as the paddy-spice zone, and the southern as the coffee, spices and paddy zone. This resource structure with its export orientation has set the functional base for the majority of towns as collection and distribution centres with extra regional links: 24 out of 35 towns developed extra-regional linkages, and 18 towns are located on highways.

One of the major problems of urban Malnad is the low or sub-standard level of urban infra-structure, and consequently, the southern Malnad is drawn into the metropolitan field of Bangalore and the urban field of Mysore. The central Malnad depends on Shimoga while the northern Malnad depends on Dharwar and Belgaum for higher order urban infra-structure. Chikmagalur, the largest Malnad town, has a functional score of 0.44 the maximum, followed by 0.35 for Sagar and 0.34 each for Sirsi and Mercara. The functional scores for the majority of Malnad towns are low with less than 0.1. How low the score is for the largest Malnad town (0.44) becomes evident by reference to Bangalore with a score of 14.1 followed by Hubli-Dharwar 3.8 and Mysore 3.2.

Urban correlates

Migration

Migration constitutes the very foundation of the process of urbanization, and is recognized as the chief mechanism by which urban centres continue to grow. One view is that urbanization stops when migration to urban centres stops. Yet urban centres grow partly by natural growth (excess of births over deaths) and partly by inter-town movement. Such a migrationless situation could be identified as urban continuum in terms of redistribution of population which is a consequence of the very process of development. It is being recognized now that this type of interpretation is rather simplistic, and even demographic explanation of migration in terms of age-sex-education-occupation syndrome does not bring out the diversity and complexity underlying migration, particularly in the developing countries.

A young male adult who is educated is identified as a typical migrant. Sex composition gets more balanced with the migrant moving with his family. Migration of educated females to cities in search of employment is an indication of social change. There is no suggestion of sequence here, and all the characteristics of migration can coexist in a developing country. Continuing migration over a long period from polyglot source areas into a resource potential areas like plantation area, transforms the migrant groups into "miniature plural societies", as in Coorg and Nilgiris in the Western Ghat region of South India (Steen Folke 1968).

The migration scheme (Bhaskara Rao *et al.* 1980. Figure 1.2 and accompanying Table) has four migration zones: two migration-source-areas, and two migration-receiving-areas; two less developed and two more developed. The four zones are: (1) distressed areas with small villages with no infra-structure and limited natural resource endowment, and hence less developed; (2) areas with resource potential and with some development but with limited infra-structure and with larger

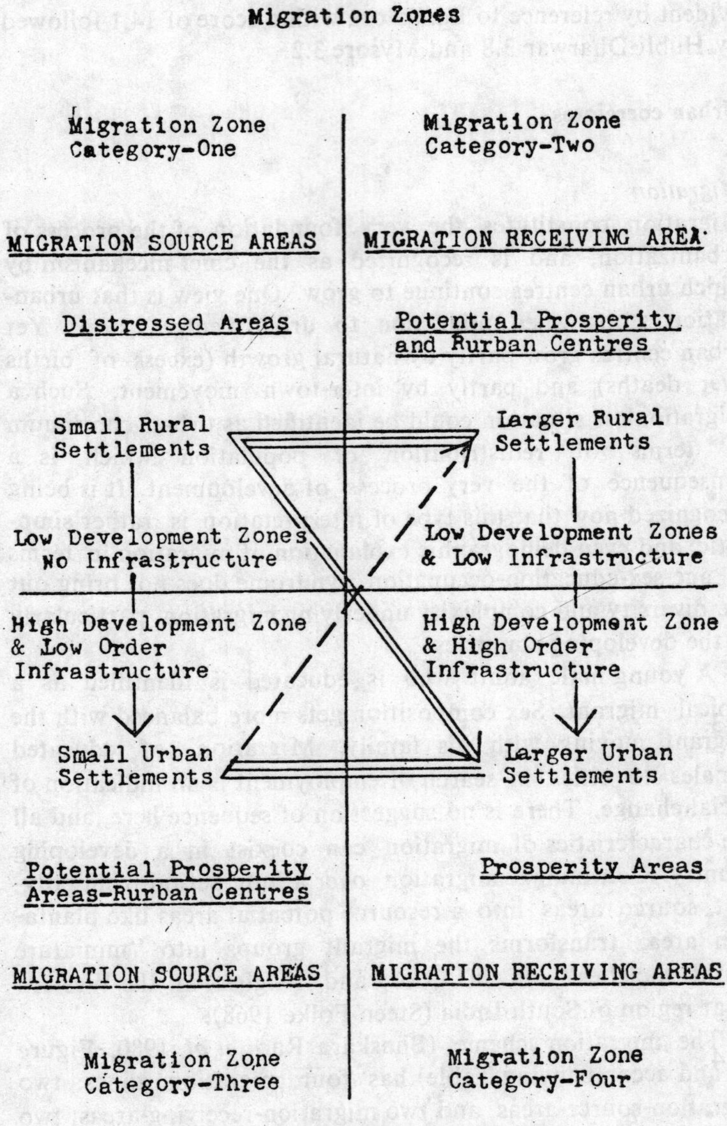

FIG. 1.2 : *Migration flow models*

The Migration Zones and their characteristics

Settlement Type and Nature	Migrants Characteristics
1. *Migration Zone Four: Metropolis and other larger cities*	
* Industry/Tertiary * State or Regional Administration and large institutional headquarters * Higher order urban infra-structure—education, health, transport, communication, etc. * Prosperity areas and highly developed	* Educated * Skilled * Long-distance or medium distance Intra-state migration is high * Short-distance migration is less * Urban-Urban migration is high * Step migration (more pronounced) * Investors and entrepreneurs * Self-employment in small and medium size activities
2. *Migration Zone Three: Medium-size towns and rurban centres*	
* Market and Service * Trade and Commerce * Zonal and local administration centres * Medium order urban Infra-structure * Less potential areas and less developed	* Less educated and more illiterate * More semi-skilled and artisans * Short and medium distance migration (Intra-district and Inter-district) * Low or no income group * Rural to Urban Migration is high * Urban to Rural migration is just appeared * More of direct migration—less step migration. * Entrepreneurship; small scale activities * Out migration
3. *Migration Zone Two: Larger rural centres and small towns*	
* Service Centres * Settlements in agricultural prosperous areas * Low industrial development * Potential areas of commercialisation * Low infra-structural facilities	* Rural to Rural migration is high * Urban to rural migration is marginal * Artisans and less skilled * Casual Labour * Low literacy rate * Low or no income group * Migration is still a *social* field

Rural-Rural migration sex ratio indicates "*marriage migration*" (more predominant in third zone though it is in other zones).

Settlement Type and Nature	Migrants Characteristics
4. *Migration Zone One: Smaller rural settlements/hamlets*	
* Migration Source Area * Primary production areas (agriculture, mining, forestry, etc.) * Marginal or no infra-structure * Distressed areas	* Out migration * Declining Trend * High illiteracy * Low earning and low income

villages; (3) more developed, but with low order infra-structure and small towns. Both large villages of zone two and small towns of zone three have the potential to become 'rurban' centres under integrated planning; (4) highly developed and resource rich areas with cities and higher order infra-structure. This is the zone of maximum pull from all the other three zones; and the distance factor has little or no significance in migration. This is the zone of metropolitanization where the immigrant cities have a strong industrial base or diversified occupational base with a developed tertiary sector. Zones two and three are the potential areas for reverse migration, if infra-structure and resource endowment are developed. Here the key sectors are commercial sector and resource-based industry. These zones act as migration filters if urban infra-structure is well developed. The real problem zone is the first zone which consists of small villages and hamlets, which are not viable economically. These settlements are stagnant or declining, and are the main sources of outmigration. The resource base consists of mining, forestry and subsistence agriculture, and infra-structure is at near zero level. Any development thrust in this zone, through highly capital-intensive industrial centres only pulls migrants from other areas and increases the socio-economic distance between the residents and the migrants. The industrial nuclei, dominated by migrants, stand as enclaves of prosperity amidst poverty, contributing more to national development than regional or local development.

It must be mentioned here that this clear cut zonation gets blurred as the different zones are drawn into the spiral of development through planning and policy intervention. Here, not only the metropolises and the urban-industrial nuclei but also the mineral based industries, plantation areas in labour-deficit hill forest areas, irrigation projects and land reclamation schemes act as magnets for migration. Migration in these contexts has some balancing function. In a situation where the city's employment capacity is outpaced by the unemployed migrant labour, migration has an imbalancing function, either increasing the level of urban unemployment or under-employment.

Migration streams in India are sectoral—to rural from

rural and urban, and to urban, from rural and urban; and territorial—short distance (intra-district), medium distance (inter-district) and long-distance (inter-state). It is the urban pull that operates over long and medium distances. In contrast, the short distance migration—rural to rural is identified as essentially marriage migration, and the "marriage field" unlike the "employment field" is limited only to adjacent areas. Economic migration of females is low, just over 3 per cent (1971). Here the streams are not clear cut. Migration from one urban to another urban area is on the increase. The percentage increase of reverse migration from urban to rural areas (1961-1971) is a characteristic of migration in India. This urban to rural migration stream is explained by both pull of the rural areas due to varied rural based development programmes, and "push back" from large cities (Bose 1970).

During the decade 1951-61, the net rural to urban migration accounted for 40.6 per cent of the decade's urban growth. Thus migration played a major role in urban growth. During 1951-61 decade, 11.62 million persons moved from rural to urban areas, and reverse movement during the decade was of the order of only 3 million persons, both males and females. In contrast during the 1961-71 decade, while the rural to urban migration was 10.98 million persons, reverse migration (urban to rural) was in much larger numbers (5.33 million persons) (Premi 1981). Distinct from the urban and rural migration streams is the rural to rural stream which was the largest in both the decades.

Rural to rural seasonal migration of agricultural labour over both short distance and medium distance is important. In the case of flue cured virginia tobacco labour migration as in coastal Andhra, the migration stream tends to be job (skill) specific, and consists of adult males, females, boys and girls, and travel over distances varying from 150 to 250 km. during tobacco season—October to April. The size of the migrant streams in one season would be of the order of 4000 and above (M.S.A. Rao 1978). The seasonal migrant labour associated with sugarcane harvesting from November-mid May is yet another example. The scale of impact of sugarcane factories can be measured by the fact that one single factory in a Gujarat district could generate migration of 25,000 workers.

The source region for the majority of the migrants, belonging mostly to low castes, is the dry agricultural area of low productivity, located in the rain shadow of Maharashtra, which is the (cheap) labour reservoir (Bremen 1978).

There is another migrant stream belonging to low income but highly skilled, who both out-migrate and in-migrate. These are the artisan classes who due to lack of demand for their products and skills are forced to leave their traditional profession and become agricultural labourers and join the seasonal migrant group (Manmohan Singh 1979). These are not drawn into any specific development plans at micro regional level, and they often get lost in the ocean of 'weaker sections'.

In contrast to these seasonal migrants, the rural to urban migrant streams are becoming highly desperate and polarised: one large stream consisting of the illiterate poor in search of livelihood, and another, consisting of the rich educated and the elitist, in search of better opportunities. Proximity to a city or a highway acts as a pull factor. The poor are pushed out of the village, while the rich are pulled into the city. One stream consists of the younger generation whose parents belong to upper and middle income groups, majority belonging to land owning and business classes, and hence rooted to villages, but with city links. One result of these links is the realization of the need for education and the associated skills. This leads to a tendency to spend on education, a prelude to greater migration (Connel, *et al.* 1976) That propensity to migrate increases with increased education was also confirmed by Greenwood's regression study of internal labour mobility in India (Greenwood 1971).

Migrants to Class I cities based on their place of last residence, accounted for 38 per cent of the total population of these cities (1971). The million cities have 42 per cent of their population as migrants; half a million cities have 31 per cent, while the percentage increases to 39 for cities with less than half-a-million. If a city's annual growth rate of 4 per cent and above is regarded as a clear indication of growth by migration, there were as many as 73 cities out of 144 cities (1951-1971). The city's migration stream is dominated by young adults. Long distance industrial pull, youthfulness of the migrants, and long distance service pull are found to be significant factors explaining the city-ward migration (Premi, 1978).

*The migrant to Bangalore**

In Bangalore, the migrant household heads were 62 per cent of the migrants to the city, 58 per cent were from Karnataka—medium distance migrants; and 21 per cent from Tamilnadu, 8 per cent from Kerala and 8 per cent from Andhra Pradesh—long distance migrants. The migrants from the rest of India and from outside India were 4 per cent and 1 per cent respectively. Thus in terms of migration pull, Bangalore with 95 per cent of migrants from South Indian States is a migration magnet for the macro-region of South India. The proportion of migrants who came direct to the city was 76 per cent and that of step migrants was 24 per cent. As distance from the city increases, step migration becomes more significant, relative to direct migration, though step migration is always less than direct migration. The single and the most significant direct migration stream to Bangalore was urban-urban accounting for 40 per cent of total migration. The rural-urban migration stream accounted for 36 per cent. Of the total migrants, 46 per cent came to the city alone, 33 per cent with wife and children, 20 per cent with other close relatives and 1 per cent with friends and others. The reasons for migration were—in search of employment (29%), after securing employment (25%), on transfer (12%), as dependants, (13%), for education (6%), due to marriage (3%), and due to family differences (3%). There was a change in the reasons for migration over time. Reasons: "came in search of employment" and "came with parents" had declined in importance. 'Transfer' as a cause of migration had increased in importance.

Migrants differ from residents in demographic characteristics and social structure. By marital status, the percentage of unmarried migrants was higher (7) than that of residents (4). In education, at the graduate level and above, migrants

*Source: Household survey 1974-1975. A Migrant is defined as one who was not born in Bangalore city, but was residing in the city at the time of the survey (Prakasa Rao & Tewari, 1979).

had higher educational attainment than residents. Considering the general literacy level, about 77 per cent of male migrants and 55 per cent of female migrants were literates. Thus the overall education level of the migrant was higher than that of the resident. Urban migrants were comparatively more educated than rural migrants. Apart from the better education level of the migrants than that of the residents, the migrants' awareness and adaptability were higher, as evident from their response to development and planning programmes like e.g. family planning programmes.

In terms of social composition, the migrant households were more heterogeneous than resident households, represented by Hindu, Muslim, Christian, Jain, Sikh and Zoroastrian religions, and different castes: brahmins with maximum proportion of migrant households, followed by agricultural castes, artisan and servicing castes, and scheduled castes, the least among migrants. The proportions of fragmented and nuclear households were more among migrants. Group migration can be explained in terms of castes and places of origin. Migrants of the same caste or from the same village stay and live together and maintain regular contact with places of their origin. Bangalore is a polyglot city with as many as 16 languages. Of the different language groups, Malayalam, Konkani, Tulu and Gujarati speaking groups were mostly migrants.

Bangalore city is a city of middle class households with 59 per cent having a monthly household income of Rs. 300 to Rs. 999. The mean monthly income of the migrant households (Rs. 685) was more than that of the resident households (Rs. 612). The per household expenditure in the household with migrants as heads (Rs. 615) was more than that of the resident households (Rs. 559). More households with migrant households heads (24%) spent Rs. 750 and above than the resident household heads (19%). The number of migrant households spending more than Rs. 1,000 was about 14 per cent, while only 10 per cent of the resident households spent more than Rs. 1,000. A larger proportion of the migrant households belonged to the higher income group than the resident households. The per capita income of the migrant household heads was higher (Rs. 151) than that of the resident household heads (Rs. 103). Also, 21 per cent of the migrant household heads had a per capita income of more than Rs. 200, against 10 per cent of the resident household heads. While 19 per cent of the migrant households were earning more than Rs. 1,000 per month, only 15 per cent of the resident household heads belonged to this income class. Thus the migrant is better placed in terms of income, than the resident.

A majority of the migrants (71%) maintained links with their place of birth or place of origin. The links were both ways—migrants visiting places, and friends and relations visiting the migrants in the city. Distance from the native place, duration of stay, the cultural background of the migrant, and property links, determined the frequency of visits and the strength of links. Social compulsions like weddings, provided common occasions for the migrants' visits. These accounted for just above 60 per cent of the trips. About 21 per cent had property at their place of birth. In frequency of visits, next to social visits are visits for illness (48%), and for festivals (47%). For the same reasons, migrants were also visited by friends and relations from the places of origin. All the three distance ranges were involved in movements. The longer the distance the less the frequency. The most common frequency (36%) of visit was 'occasionally'; 24 per cent visited yearly and 18 per cent half-yearly; 7 per cent visited monthly and one per cent weekly. These links acted as information channels to diffuse the city's image—its 'bright lights', new development programmes, job prospects and concessions to 'target groups'.

From the above analysis it becomes clear that macro. analysis of migration based on census data needs to be supplemented by micro analysis of the migrants. Among migrants, there are different types—permanent migrants, seasonal migrants and return migrants. Using the term liberally, even commuters are classified as migrants—daily migrants. These variations pose problems in definition.* To understand the complex process of migration in relation to the process of urbanization, the widening of data base is being advocated. The decision making process of the movement and

*For census definitions refer 'Birth Place Migration in India', S.K. Merhotra, Census of India 1971. Special Monograph No. 1, Ministry of Home Affairs, New Delhi 1974.

psychological factors, migration histories and impact of migration on source areas are emphasised in addition to the conventional details relating to socio-economic characteristics and place of birth and last residence (Escap 1979).

Urban-industrial correlates

Out of a total of about 320 million urban working force (1971) in India, only about 7.3 million (22.8%) were employed in the manufacturing sector. In 1961, the percentage of the work force in manufacturing was 21. Thus the percentage increase between 1961 and 1971 was very small: 1.8.

As the city-size increases, the range in the population engaged in different sectors among cities of similar size decreases and proportion of workers engaged in manufacturing increases (Table 1.13). The process of spatial and sectoral concentration continues till a very large city size of the conurbation or megalopolitan scale, coupled with decentralization policies, repel industrial concentration from large cities. But

TABLE 1.13: **Proportion of workers in manufacturing, trade, commerce and services by size class of cities (1971)**

Industrial classification of occupation category	Maximum, Minimum and Average proportion of workers in cities of population size			
	1,00,000 to 2,50,000	2,50,000 to 5,00,000	5,00,000 to 10,00,000	10,00,000 and above
Manufacturing				
Max.	61.2	56.2	35.8	44.7
Min.	5.5	9.7	13.2	20.2
Av.	22.7	25.8	23.8	33.8
Trade and Commerce				
Max.	33.8	29.4	25.6	22.5
Min.	8.3	12.1	13.3	15.5
Av.	20.1	18.5	19.8	21.4
Services				
Max.	60.7	44.6	43.2	37.8
Min.	9.2	9.7	6.7	20.3
Av.	27.9	25.1	21.4	25.7

then, instead of industrialization of medium towns or small cities, the periphery of the large city gets industrialized.

Of all the size classes of towns, cities have the maximum number of agglomerations: 87 out of 148 cities. These are located at the city periphery. While the population of the cities of the million size group grew by 35 per cent during 1961-71, the agglomerations grew by 51 per cent. The population of the agglomerations of the half-a-million size group grew much faster (82%). To mention a few specific cases, identifying agglomerations with the city periphery, the periphery of Madras grew by 13 per cent while the main city grew by 43 per cent; Ahmedabad periphery by 97 per cent, main city by 38 per cent; Bangalore periphery by 92 per cent, main city by 35 per cent, Coimbatore periphery by 50 per cent, main city by 24 per cent; Madurai periphery by 87 per cent, main city by 29 per cent (1961-71). This peripheral industrial growth only enlarges the metropolitan commuting zone, promotes urban-rural imbalance in the city-fringe, and increases the pressure on the already strained city in terms of urban services and amenities, and housing.

There is a high and statistically significant correlation ($\gamma=0.77$) between urban population and employment in manufacturing. As high as 60 per cent of urban growth is explained by 20 per cent of the working population engaged in manufacturing in 1961. The most industrialized regions (location quotient: 2.3) are the most urbanized regions e.g. Calcutta-Hooghly-Damodar Valley; Bombay-Poona; Kanpur-Lucknow; Madras-Chinglepet; Delhi-Meerut-Agra (Pathak, 1975). Analysis of the urban-industrial relationships at the State level (Karnataka 1951), where the urban system consists of cities, medium towns and small towns, also brought out that larger towns grew fastest and the larger towns, had more industry. Multiple correlation indicated that size-growth-industry showed the strongest relationship (Prakasa Rao and Learmonth 1961).

We may now analyse the relationship between the state-wise level of industrialization measured by total productive capital, total number of persons employed, total wages and salaries, total value of output and value added by manufacture (1959-1963) and per capita monthly total consumer expenditure which in a way reflects the level of living of the people (NSS : 15 to 19th rounds 1959-1964). It is found that the relative level of industrialization (in relation to population) is significantly correlated with per capita total consumer expenditure in the urban sector only ($\gamma=0.569$ in 1963). Such a relationship does not exist in the rural sector ($\gamma=0.284$ in 1963) (Tewari, 1976). The urban-industrial syndrome is clearly brought out by Factor 1 which explains 52 per cent variation with several variables emphasising the same viz. urban population (factor loading 0.907), gross output in industry per capita (0.944), industrial consumption of electricity per capita (0.928), average daily employment of factory workers per 1000 population (0.920), value added per capita (0.910), and Bank credit of commercial banks per capita (0.877). The high factor loading (0.728) for commercial crop acreage brings out the significance of commercial agriculture in response to urban market and industrial processing. The significant but lower factor loading (0.539) of the per cent of city population to total population only indicates the significance of the

TABLE 1.14 : Variables selected for statewise analysis

Variable	Factor Loadings (var. exp. 52%)
% of urban population to total population, 1971	0.907
% of Literates to total population: 1971	0.377
Area under selected commercial crops as % to gross cropped area, 1973-74	0.728
Per capita income from Agriculture, 1975-76	0.180
Av. daily employment of factory workers per 1000 population, 1975	0.920
Gross output in Industry per capita, 1976-77	0.944
Value added per capita, 1976-77	0.910
Industrial consumption of electricity per capita, 1977-78	0.928
Bank credit of commercial banks per capita, June 1977	0.877
Motor Vehicles per lakh population, 1975-76	0.691
Hospital beds per lakh population, 1976	−0.004
Growth of urban population, 1961-71	−0.441
% city population to total population, 1971	0.539

industrial component in the medium size class of towns (Table 1.14). The degree of urban-industrial inter-correlations is brought out by Table 1.15. Urban population, size of factory workers, value added, gross output and industrial consumption of electricity are highly and significantly

TABLE 1.15 : Urban industrial inter-correlations

Variables	1	2	3	4	5	6
% urban population	1.0	0.615	0.801	0.746	0.802	0.776
% city population		1.0	0.487	0.306	0.359	0.461
Average daily employment of Factory workers			1.0	0.927	0.916	0.808
Value added				1.0	0.977	0.852
Gross output industry					1.0	0.885
Industrial consumption of electricity						1.0

TABLE 1.16 : Factor scores* on urban-industrial factor

State	Score	Rank
Maharashtra	2.126	1
Gujarat	1.631	2
Punjab	1.244	3
Tamilnadu	0.779	4
West Bengal	0.774	5
Karnataka	0.574	6
Haryana	0.196	7
Kerala	0.043	8
Andhra Pradesh	−0.163	9
Madhya Pradesh	−0.509	10
Rajasthan	−0.557	11
Uttar Pradesh	−0.569	12
Jammu and Kashmir	−0.713	13
Bihar	713	13
Orissa	−0.801	14
Assam	−0.874	15
Himachal Pradesh	−0.889	16
Nagaland	−1.580	17

*Derived on the basis of principal component analysis.

inter-correlated. Statewise factor scores (Table 1.16) bring out that Maharashtra (2.126) is the most urban-industrialized State in the country, followed by Gujarat (1.631), and Punjab (1.244) if the first three ranks are considered. At the bottom of the urban-industrial scale measured by these selected indicators, are Nagaland (−1.580), Himachal Pradesh (−0.889), and Assam (−0.874).

The underlying processes : The urban-industrial syndrome

What underlies these correlates are the processes of urbanization and industrialization. If migration from villages to towns and shift from agriculture to non-agricultural occupations and land-uses constitute the basic process of urbanization, the process of industrialization consists of occupational and land-use shifts to manufacturing sector along with the associated complex technology in processing and development of inter-industry and regional links. What is often not fully recognised in this technological transformation is the transformation of the society from a highly stratified rural society to a cosmopolitan 'working class' society, though one must not infer from this that the caste system is rapidly disappearing.

Both urbanization and industrialization processes are interacting and the resultant patterns are agglomerative in space and structure. While there is yet no satisfactory explanation of industrial agglomeration, it is recognised that access to labour skills, market potential, economic and social infrastructure and scope for inter-industry linkages are the key elements (Alonso, 1964). Nodality is the first attribute of both urban and industrial agglomeration though all nodes are not urban-industrial agglomerations as all of them do not have the necessary resource and infra-structure base. In the developed countries, urban-industrial growth is circular and cumulative in the initial stages of urban-industrialization (Pred, 1965). Industrial-urbanization so well integrated in the industrial west even in the earlier phase of industrialization, is often unrelated in India. The urban-industrial economic growth syndrome is being supplemented or bypassed by the urban-commercial economic growth syndrome through new agricultural technology and agricultural surpluses, may be in a highly localized and in an incipient form as in Punjab/Haryana and East Coast Deltas.

To understand fully the implications of urban-industrial relationship, it is necessary to recognise the multiplier effects of industrial growth on the dependency ratio, transport and trade sectors, and in some cases, on the links with ancillary industry and even with household industry. These in turn increase the demand for service trades and employment. Thus employment is both direct and indirect. A paper mill with Rs. 48 crore investment and an annual capacity of 42,000 tonnes provides direct employment for just above 1400 workers and indirect employment for 5,000 workers.* For Bangalore metropolis, the basic-service employment ratio worked out to 1 : 0.886 i.e. for 1000 basic employees, the service employees will be 886. The worker dependants ratio worked out to 1 : 3.75 (Tewari, 1978). It must be mentioned here that employment multiplier tends to increase with the size of the city up to a certain level, and thereafter it starts declining over time. This is explained by a decrease in investment per unit of resources which leads to low employment multiplier for the bigger cities (Misra, *et al.* 1975). It is the "snowball" effect of the multiplier that contributes to population growth. Of the different urban growth inducing sectors, manufacturing is found to be a greater employment multiplier, and an increase in manufacturing employment accelerates urban growth but not indefinitely. The growth curve of industrial cities, irrespective of their population size and industrial type (e.g. textile or steel or sugar), is characterized by a sharp spurt, followed by a declining growth rate (Table 1.17) unless the occupational structure gets diversified to expand the employment base. Here it needs no mention that urban-industrial growth is determined by urban and industrial structural relationships. These are analysed in the following section.

Both urban and industrial sectors have distinct locational linkage and regional bases, and are not an undifferentiated mass. Just as city-size and type vary, industrial size and type vary. Locational options also vary. What is significant in the

*Project Profile: Rayalaseema Paper Mills, *Indian Express*, July 1st, 1981.

TABLE 1.17 : Industrial cities/towns

Industrial city/ town (selected examples)	Population 1971	% Decennial Growth							Occupational Structure: 1971			
		1901-11	1911-21	1921-31	1931-41	1941-51	1951-61	1961-71	Manufacturing	% to total Trade % Commerce	Working Transport Storage	Population Services
1. Ahmedabad	1,585,544	16.62	26.40	14.52	89.68	47.40	37.46	44.40	45.39	19.60	7.28	21.52
2. Kanpur	1,154,338	—11.95	21.21	12.62	99.92	44.75	37.66	31.32	31.74	22.0	7.30	29.28
3. Sholapur	398,361	—18.52	94.93	20.97	46.99	30.32	21.83	18.00	44.63	18.2	7.99	15.71
4. Jamshedpur	356,783	—	911.28	45.99	77.59	46.70	39.12	17.55	59.13	11.9	7.12	15.10
5. Bodhan	37,589	8.67	—40.14	68.22	175.98	15.68	37.52	21.53	28.18	13.4	4.74	11.32
6. Burnpur	28,924	—	—	—	138.29	35.16	13.72	37.58	74.13	5.3	3.93	16.07

urban-industrial syndrome is the co-association of economic and physical factors in varying combinations to induce certain types of industries to locate in towns of particular size and resource settings. Not all types of industries have the same degree of relationship to all size-classes of towns as all types of industries are not equally appropriate to all city-size classes. The engineering and chemical industries are more city-localized industries in contrast to the agro-based and mineral industries which are localized more in small and medium size towns and rural areas. Textile-based industries have a dual location pattern, with locations in towns of different size classes and also in rural areas (Table 1.18). Different industrial types have also different shares and different structure of backward and forward linkages* (Shanbhag 1977). The highly labour-intensive textile industry has the maximum share of the district's backward linkages (76%). In sharp contrast, the highly capital-intensive chemical industry and transport equipment have a maximal share of backward linkages in wages and emoluments 83 per cent and 98 per cent respectively, followed by the ferrous and non-ferrous metal industry 74 per cent which also has the maximum forward linkage 69 per cent with the district's output (Table 1.19). Thus it is the type of the industry which determines the share of backward or forward linkages. Distinct from these linkage patterns and locational clusters are technological clusters of industries (e.g. non-ferrous minerals and electric equipment block, textile-based, machinery-based and petroleum and chemical-based which have not yet developed to their full scale excepting in a few highly developed regions (Lakadawala, a *et al.* 1974). The inducements for the concentration of manufacturing industries in the large cities are known: information flows and contacts, and accessibility to markets, labour skills and modern urban facilities. The level of metropolitan benefits in the large cities is so high, compared to those in the small cities and medium towns, that in spite of attractive subsidies being made available nearer smaller cities, metropolitan industrial concentration

*Backward linkage is defined as the sum of all the input purchases of materials plus water, electricity and labour. Forward linkage is defined as the value of the output.

TABLE 1.18 : **Distribution patterns of industries in urban and rural areas of south India**

Factories based on	Percentage of total number of factories in							Number of Factories
	Million cities	Class I	Class II	Class III	Class IV-V	Rural areas	South India	
Agriculture ..	4.37	14.10	13.82	13.70	21.42	32.59	100.00	5,212
Textile ..	1.40	27.81	7.02	6.18	9.36	48.23	100.00	1,068
Forests ..	9.50	19.71	16.68	17.70	17.81	17.60	100.00	558
Minerals ..	4.91	13.67	7.13	12.78	18.43	38.08	100.00	407
Engineering ..	27.68	30.68	14.11	10.34	4.79	12.40	100.00	2,233
Chemicals ..	19.56	40.58	8.86	8.50	11.80	10.7	100.00	271
Number of Factories ..	788	2,013*	1,256	1,181	1,540	2,771	—	9,749

*Excluding million cities

Note: Data on factories relate to the year 1959 and urban centres to 1961.
Source: South India: Macro Regional Survey, Indian Statistical Institute, Mimeographed, 1962.

TABLE 1.19 : **Surendranagar district (Gujarat)* 1971-75—Sample industry groups: Linkages**

Industry group	Average no. of persons employed per unit	Average investment in fixed assets per employee Rs.	Average value of plant and machinery per employee Rs.	Mean share of district in backward linkage %	Mean share of district in backward linkage % wages+ emoluments	Forward linkage with district output %
Textile	204.00	2297	1447	76.46	38.64	—
Chemicals	9.40	28,466	18,444	20.06	82.55	0.87
Glass, Clay and Cement	25.60	11,161	5,704	32.17	53.68	16.72
Ferrous and non-ferrous metal	4.20	4547	2,619	5.69	73.84	68.90
Machinery (excluding electrical and transport equipment)	12.70	1,1549	8,588	27.34	61.16	31.76
Transport equipment	25.00	13,640	11,600	37.96	97.56	—
All Ind. groups	69 17	5,275	387	37.43	49.54	11.54

**Source*: Evaluation of the impact of the central investment subsidy scheme in Surendranagar district, Vinod Shanbhag—Centre for Environmental Planning and Technology, School of Planning, Ahmedabad (Unpublished), 1977.

still persists. The four metropolises—Calcutta, Bombay, Delhi and Madras—accounted for 78 per cent of industrial licences issued till 1971 (Ausaf Ahmed, quoted by Moonis Raza, *et al.* 1979). The same tendency of disproportionate concentration of industrial licences was observed in 1951 also. Of the total licences issued, 35 per cent were found in Calcutta and Bombay which comprised 14 per cent of urban population in 1951 (Bredo 1962). To what extent a million and a capital city located in a backward region can dominate in industrial concentration is best illustrated by Hyderabad urban-industrial agglomeration. Out of the 38 industries that are located only in towns in Telangana, 34 are located in Hyderabad. As many as 24 out of 34 industries are located only in Hyderabad and in no other Telangana town. Out of a total of 88 industrial licences issued to Telangana towns, Hyderabad captured 72 licences during the period 1956-64. Out of the 72 licences, licences for metallic, electrical and engineering industries numbered 28, and 24 for chemicals and fertilizers, followed by 7 for textiles.* Thus during the two decades 1951-1971, the metropolitan cities captured a major share of industries despite a dispersal policy. Urban-industrial Gujarat presents a different pattern with the million and capital city of Ahmedabad sharing its industrial dominance with the half-a-million city of Vadodara and the Class I and even the Class II cities. The growth rate in the share of industrial workers in Ahmedabad during 1961-71 was only 19 per cent in sharp contrast with 98 per cent in Vadodara and 104 per cent and 82 per cent in the Class I and Class II cities respectively. While Ahmedabad showed a decrease in the share of industrial workers, the other Gujarat cities showed an increase (Table 1.20).

Yet if the "tenet of appropriateness" is pursued, certain indicative groups of industries by city size** emerge (Mathur *et al.*, 1968):

Large City : Textile furnishing and processing-composite; industrial rubber beltings inorganic chemicals; Special steel-rolling with electric furnace;

**Data Source :* Office of the Chief Inspector of Factories, Hyderabad.

**For a detailed list, refer Mathur *et al.*

Iron and steel structures; Precision and special purpose machine tools; Surgical Instruments, Optics.

Medium City : Dehydration of fruits and vegetables; Knitting mills-woollen hosiery; Paper for packing; Iron and Steel rerolling; Bolts, nuts, nails, screws etc.

Small city : Canning and preservation of fruits and vegetables; Cold Storage, Paper board and strawboard Castings and sewing machine parts.

Ubiquitous : Flour mills; Bakery products; Edible oils-oil expellers; Metal, furniture and fixtures; Paints, Varnishes and Lacquers; Hume pipes and other cement products; Cast iron pipes, Utensils; Wheat threshers.

TABLE 1.20 : **Industrial and urban growth**

Size Class		Share of Industrial workers % 1961-71		Growth in share of Industrial workers % 1961-71	Growth rate in population % 1961-71
Ahmedabad	Million	42.8	36.4	18.8	44.4
Vadodara	Half a million	13.8	19.5	97.8	63.8
Class I cities	>1,00,000	8.4	12.3	104.1	86.7
Class II cities	>50,000	8.5	11.1	82.3	86.0

Data Source : Census of India, 1971.

It is this "tenet" that should be judiciously used by planners in industrial dispersal.

The above analysis clearly brings out that the urban-industrial syndrome cannot be fitted into one model, and regional variations indicate that there exist both agglomerations leading to regional imbalance, and also dispersal reducing the imbalance. Yet the scale of dispersal is not large enough to counter concentration.

Urban population size and population growth

During 1961-71, the average rate of urban growth increased with an increase in the urban size class. The larger the city size-class, the greater the growth rate. But during 1951-61, the size-growth relationship did not indicate such a progressive increase with the size class. While the largest size-class i.e. >1,00,000 was associated with largest growth rate during both the decades, the small town size class showed a higher growth rate (39%) than that of the medium town size class (35%) during 1951-61. Towns with less than 20,000 showed a negative rate during 1951-61, while this class of towns showed a positive though lowest rate during 1961-71.

There are sharp differences in growth rates, and between the two decades, if the city-size class (i.e.,>1,00,000) is disaggregated into sub-classes. Overall, the quarter million, the half million and the million cities grew faster during 1961-71, than during 1951-61. While the half-million cities recorded the maximum growth rate (85%) during 1961-71, the million cities recorded the maximum (53%) during 1951-61. Thus among the cities, the largest size class, the million cities did not record the largest growth rate during 1961-71 (Table 1.21). But if the million cities are differentiated into the main city and city agglomeration, the city agglomerations, located at the city periphery, grew faster than the main city in the case of four of the million cities (Calcutta, Delhi, Ahmedabad and Bangalore).

We get greater insights into size-growth relationships if growth rates are examined on individual city basis. The median growth rates for the cities during 1951-61 and 1961-71 were 3.1 per cent and 3.0 per cent respectively. The upper quartile values of growth rates were 4.5 per cent (1951-61) and 5.2 per cent (1961-71). Thus the cities grew faster during 1961-71, than during 1951-61. During 1961-71, high growth rates (>4% per annum) were associated with the million, half-million, quarter million and also small cities (1,00,000-2,50,000). As many as 6 out 9 million cities recorded

TABLE 1.21 : **Urban population size class—Urban growth rate**

Size class	No. of towns		% share total urban population		Annual growth rate	
	1961	1971	1961	1971	1951-61	1961-71
Million	7	9	23	25	5.3	5.4
Half-million	5	10	5	6	2.2	8.5
Quarter-million	21	34	9	11	4.7	6.9
1,00,000-2,50,000	72	95	14	13	4.5	3.3
Class I cities 1,00,000+	105	148	50	56	4.6	5.4
Medium towns 50,000-1,00,000	130	183	11	11	3.5	4.1
Small towns 20,000-50,000	459	582	18	16	3.9	2.9
Urban villages <20,000	1727	1723	21	17	—1.2	0.8

>4 per cent growth rate during 1961-71. But the highest growth rate (8 per cent) was recorded, not by the large cities but by the quarter million and small cities—2 out of 34 and 10 out of 94 cities respectively. The cities with such high growth rates, whether during 1951-61 or 1961-71 decade, were either industrial cities like Bhilai, Durgapur, Rourkela, or mining cities (Dhanbad) or capital cities: Bhopal, (Bhubaneswar, and Chandigarh). The growth rate of new industrial cities like Durgapur shot up to 39 per cent (1961-71) per annum. Such very high growth rates are typical of industrial towns irrespective of their size. Dandeli, a small town in Karnataka, recorded a growth rate of 22 per cent during 1961-71. Of the Karnataka towns even small and medium size towns recorded growth rates of more than 4 per cent (19 out of 30) and 6 per cent (4 out of 6). These are again industrial and irrigation project towns. Thus very high growth rates are type (function) specific and time specific and are not related to population-size.

Town type, population size and growth rate

Analysis of the relationship between town type, size and growth has both conceptual and methodological problems. First, there is the problem of the identification of town type, as no single method of classification is satisfactory for all purposes. Methods range from simple and arbitrary to multi-variate. Here the question is how to ensure that town type classification is not method dependent. Any town type would have evolved over a period, and to relate its growth during the latest one or two decades is strictly not correct. Average growth rate over time: (three or four decades) has the problem of changing growth-promoting factors. Type-size-growth relationships cannot be independent of the previous size of the town and the size-type-growth of the nearby towns, say within a radius of one or two hours travel time.

In a dynamic setting, a majority of towns tend to develop multiple functions, and hence have a diversified economic base. Manufacturing and service towns record the largest average size (>1,00,000) whereas agricultural towns record the smallest average size (<20,000). Diversified towns, mining/fishing towns and trading towns have a medium population size (30,000-40,000). Manufacturing towns show the highest population growth rates (40% per annum 1951-71), while diversified and agricultural towns record the lowest growth rates (3% per annum: 1951-1971). These are aggregate relationships for Karnataka towns (1971).

Classifying town types of Telangana, a sub-region of Andhra Pradesh, by the least-square linear regression technique (LSLR), and analysing type-growth relationships, over periods ranging from 3 to 6 decades (1901-1971), it was found that 11 agricultural towns were stagnant and 3 were growing; 5 household-industry towns were stagnant, and 5 were growing; 2 service towns were stagnant and 4 were growing; 1 mining town was stagnant, and 2 were growing. All these town types were medium (10) and small towns (56) (Waheeduddin Khan 1973, Venugopal 1970, and Prakasa Rao, 1966). An experiment conducted using both SD and LSLR to classify 71 towns of Telangana brought out that the method dependency increased as the functional diversity of the towns increased. The problem of selection of an appropriate technique of identification of town types remains unresolved.

Declining towns constitute a distinct category, and in a developing region, no town shows a declining trend over a longer period, as there are always development impulses through planning. Consequently, a declining town in one decade shows revival in the next decade. Decline over two or three decades is more an exception. Kolar Gold Fields, the gold mining town (Karnataka), showed a declining trend during two decades 1951-1971 from 1,59,000 to 1,47,000 to 1,19,000 but showed revival in 1981 with increasing population: above 1,44,000, through diversification of industries and the consequential increase in the employment base, and the associated multipliers. A study of declining towns in India brought out that during 1961-71, 129 towns experienced an absolute decline in population: 80 per cent of the declining towns were small towns: <20,000; 40 per cent were parts of urban agglomerations. Cantonment towns, defence towns, household industry towns, mining towns, and old port towns recorded declining population (Sita and Phadke, 1980). Out-migration due to decrease in employment opportunities, weak economic base both in the town and its hinterland, urban shadow effects, and fading away of feudal patronage which was sustaining the town's economic base, appear to be the main contributing factors for decline. Thus, decline in town population is type-specific, size-specific and time-specific.

This chapter has brought out the complexities underlying the urbanization process, patterns and correlates in India, and provides a framework for a detailed analysis of the Indian urban system in its inter-city, regional and intra-city dimensions in the Chapters to follow.

2

URBAN SYSTEM

IN THE whole settlement spectrum ranging from hamlet to megalopolis, only the central places constitute the hierarchic class system which is a fundamental, though controversial, postulate of the central place model. Associated with the hierarchy of central places are the hierarchies of tributary areas and transport routes. In a changing urban and socio-economic system, hierarchic system also responds to the changes and is thus dynamic. The position of an urban centre in the urban and regional setting provides its level of functional specialisation and associated hierarchic "order". Urban hierarchic structure gets restructured by the acquisition of higher order functions, or by devolution of functions or by the development of new functions (Holmes and Pullinger, 1973). The hierarchic structure is such that in the lower order of urban and regional hierarchic system, city-regional reciprocal relationships are more dominant, as in resource and market towns and their hinterlands, while in the higher orders, inter-urban and inter-regional relationships are more dominant. This hierarchic structure gets disturbed with diversification in resource use, change in the level of production and transport technology, increasing incomes and the changing cousumer and producer travel behavioural patterns. These are related to the region's stage of development. In the industrial and post-industrial stages of development, urban-industrial and regional systems are integrated. In the agricultural, pre-industrial and initial industrial stages of development, urban and regional and urban and rural and inter-urban systems tend to become dichotomous with functional and spatial gaps and overlaps. As a consequence, there are more deviations and distortions than conformity to Christaller-Lösch-Perroux models. In spite of the critique on the validity of the central place theoretical framework for the construction of settlement hierarchic models, the basic postulates of the theory may stand: the consumers' and producers' tendency for minimum aggregate travel and clustering of urban functions at threshold levels, with population-central functions non-linear relationship still hold good. The telescoping of functions, emergence of mobile trading units and the differential in the trip patterns of the different income groups, all contribute to dual patterns and disturb, if not destroy, the "classical" hierarchic structure. But it must be stressed here that a hierarchy does not exist in all regions. In regions with subsistence economies, limited development potential and with intra-regional transport inaccessibility, independent local centres develop without hierarchic structure. Hierarchy implies differential provision of central functions, and hence inter-dependence between different levels of central places. Christaller's hierarchic model consists of seven orders of central places arranged in a nested hierarchy (Table 2.1). "Nesting implies that higher level of settlements is congruent with settlements in the preceding lower level, and there is an incremental basket of services compared with the lower level of settlements." There is an incremental progression in the level of services from the lower hierarchic level to higher level. Where the function happens to be the same, its quantum and variety will progressively increase up the ladder. "Nesting" process involves the capture of the small trade areas by the larger by virtue of their greater power for competition and hence domination (Berry, *et al.* 1962). Changes in transport technology, business organization and consumer travel preferences disturb the idealized form of "nesting". An idealized conception of the seven-fold nested hierarchy is illustrated in Fig. 2.1.

There is a positive but non-linear relationship between the order of the central place, its centrality and the order of goods and services available at the central place. Higher order functions are associated with higher order places, and have greater variety and higher level of specialization. Consequently, their population thresholds are higher to ensure the

TABLE 2.1 : Christaller's Model*

Type	Number of places	Number of Complementary Regions	Range of Region (km.)	Area of Region (sq. km.)	Number of Types of Goods offered	Typical Population of places	Typical Population of Region
M	486	729	4.0	44	40	1,000	3,500
A	162	243	6.9	133	90	2,000	11,000
K	54	81	12.0	400	180	4,000	35,000
B	18	27	20.7	1,200	330	10,000	100,000
G	6	9	36.0	3,600	600	30,000	350,000
P	2	3	62.1	10,800	1,000	100,000	1,000,000
L	1	1	108.0	32,400	2,000	500,000	3,500,000
Total	729						

*Ref. Appendix A.

M — Market
A — Township centre
K — Country seat
B — District City
G — Small State Capital
P — Provincial head city
L — Regional capital city

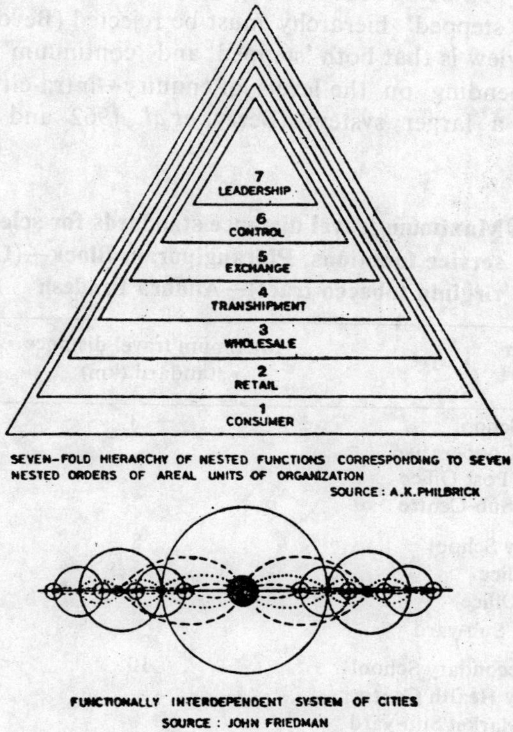

FIG. 2.1 : *Hierarchy-system of cities*

required profit levels. Likewise the lower order places have lower order functions. While the lower order functions are many and the consumer travel distances for 'convenience goods' are minimal, the travel distances are maximum for specialized and 'shopping goods'. Thus distance increases progressively from lower order places with lower order functions to higher order places with higher order functions (Table 2.2). Through policy intervention and subsidization, the level of social services could be kept high at lower population thresholds. Here welfare goals would outweigh profit motivations.

Whether the hierarchic class system is 'stepped' or a

'continuum' is being debated upon.* One view is that the notion of 'stepped' hierarchy must be rejected (Bevon 1977). The other view is that both 'stepped' and 'continuum' may be found, depending on the levels of enquiry—intra-city, a sub-system or a larger system (Berry, *et al.* 1962 and Rushton 1971).

TABLE 2.2 : **Maximum travel distance standards for selected service functions, Phirangipuram Block—(Cotton-virginia tobacco tract)—Andhra Pradesh**

Institution	Maximum travel distance standard (km)	Miles
Primary School	3	2
Credit Cooperative		
Branch Post Office		
Health Sub-Centre		
Secondary School	8	5
Post Office		
Retail Office		
Market Sub-yard		
Higher Secondary School	10	6
Primary Health Centre		
Large Market Sub-yard		
Technical School	15	9
Junior College		
Market Yard and Storage		
Hospital	20	13
College		
Regulated Market		
Fertilizer Wholesale Facility		

**Source*: Roy and Patil (1977).

The city of Bangalore and the Karnataka State are selected to test the form of hierarchic class system—intra-city and

*Christaller (1933) identified a stepped hierarchy of central places and Lösch (1943) in his extended work identified a 'continuum'. Brush (1953) identified a three-tier hierarchy and Vining (1955) argued for a continuum.

inter-city. Both the systems are found to be step-like as evident from the significant F-ratios.

Intra-city : Bangalore

Out of the 17,954 retail establishments (1971) in the city, 5,815 establishments listed in 15 shopping centres, classified into 104 retail trade types using National Industrial Code (NIC), constituted the data base for analysis.

Retail trade hierarchic structure is identified using (1) Guttman scaling, (2) Functional index, (3) Market potential model, (4) Retail gravity model (Huff), (5) Connectivity and (6) Consumer travel patterns. The derived hierarchy levels are tested using the F-ratio for their significance.

Guttman scaling

The technique scales the retail types of shopping centres to identify the different levels of shopping centres and points out the most ubiquitous and segregated retail types. The 104 retail types are grouped into a four-tier hierarchy of shopping centres (Table 2.3) with the coefficient of reproductibility as 0.9024.

The technique also indentifies, antique, carpet and novelties, photogoods and luxury items as the most segregated types; and general provision, medical, footwear, books and stationery and liquor as the types available in all the shopping centres.

TABLE 2.3 : **Hierarchy of shopping centres by retail types**

Hierarchic order	Shopping centre	No. of retail functions	F-Ratio
I	1. K. R. Market	73	
II	1. Majestic	67	
	2. Russel Market	66	11.24*
	3. M.G. Road	60	
III	1. J.C. Road	52	
	2. Jayanagar	52	
	3. Malleswaram	50	
IV	The remaining 8 centres	43 to 2	

*Significant at 1 per cent level. The hierarchy levels differ significantly.

Functional index

The centrality index technique of deriving the functional index developed by Davis (1967) is used here to derive the functional indices of different shopping centres and their hierarchic levels.

Based on the number of retail establishments under each retail type, the centrality index of a single establishment called 'location coefficient' is computed using the Davis formula. The four hierarchic levels are found to differ significantly. The scattergrams drawn with functional index versus number of retail establishments and retail types also clearly revealed the same four-tier hierarchy of shopping centres (Table 2.4). The dendogram drawn with functional ranks vs. functional index again revealed the same four-tier hierarchy of shopping centre (Fig. 2.2).

TABLE 2.4 : Hierarchic levels of the shopping centres by Functional Index.

Hierarchic order	Shopping centre	Functional Index	F-ratio
I	1. K.R. Market	3.832	
II	1. M.G. Road	2.369	
	2. Russel Market	2.044	96.5*
	3. Majestic	1.964	
III	1. J.C. Road	0.833	
	2. Jayanagar	0.687	
	3. Malleswaram	0.675	
IV	The remaining 8 centres	0.509 to 000	

*Significant at 1% level.

Market potential

The market potential, an abstract index of accessibility of an index of the intensity of possible interactions with markets is used to identify accessibility of different shopping centres and their hierarchic levels.

The market potential indices derived for the fifteen shopping centres clearly revealed the four-tier hierarchy of shopping centres, (Table 2.5). The hierarchic levels differ significantly.

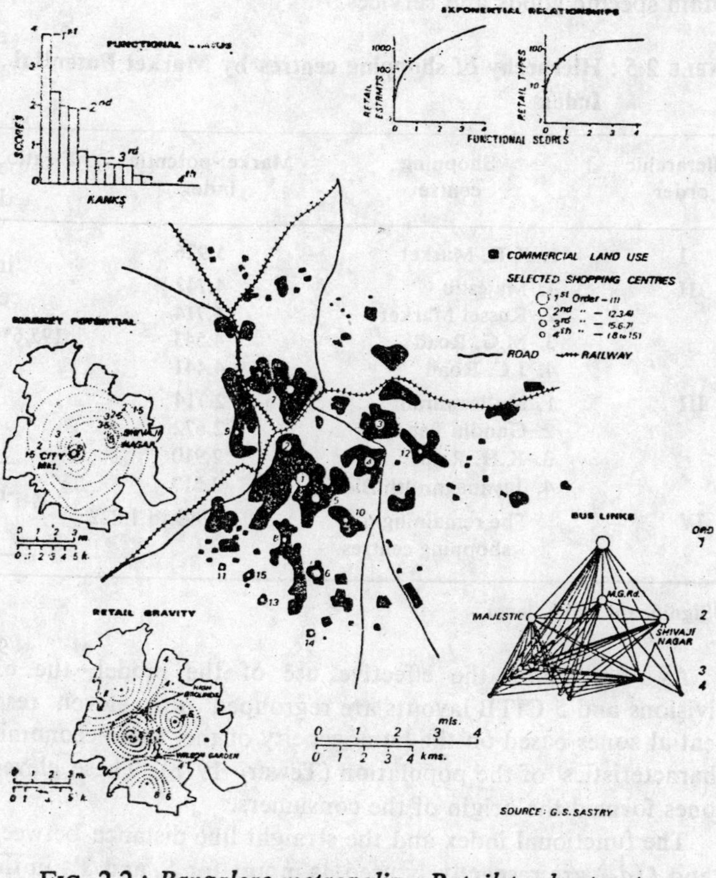

FIG. 2.2 : *Bangalore metropolis—Retail trade structure*

Retail gravity model

The retail gravity model developed by Huff (1967) is used here to identify the hierarchy of shopping centres. In a metropolitan region, with no restriction on the distance due to a rapid transport system, the travel behaviour of a consumer is more probabilistic than deterministic. In densely built-up urban areas, consumers have a considerable number of shopping centres of varying attractiveness available within their economic reach. The probability model developed by Huff (1962) describes the process by which consumers choose from among the acceptable alternatives, a particular distribution to obtain specific goods and services.

TABLE 2.5 : **Hierarchy of shopping centres by Market Potential Index**

Hierarchic order	Shopping centre	Market-potential index	F-ratio
I	1. K.R. Market	5.926	
II	1. Majestic	4.742	
	2. Russel Market	4.714	
	3. M.G. Road	4.543	195.6*
	4. J.C. Road	4.441	
III	1. Malleswaram	2.714	
	2. Gandhi Bazar	2.672	
	3. K.H. Road	2.910	
	4. Jayanagar 4th Block	2.517	
IV	The remaining 6 shopping centres	1.999 to 1.822	

*Significant at 1% level.

As a first step in the effective use of the model, the 63 divisions and 5 CITB layouts are regrouped into eleven residential zones based on the homogeneity of the socio-economic characteristics of the population (Tewari 1978). These eleven zones formed the origin of the consumers.

The functional index and the straight line distance between i and j (d_{ij}) are respectively used as inputs for S_j and T_{ij} in the model. The squared distance is assumed to work out the probabilities. A *Fortran*-Programme was developed on DEC-10 system to compute the probability distribution and expected consumers to the various shopping centres.

The total expected consumers to the various shopping centres clearly revealed the same four-tier hierarchy of shopping centres (Table 2.6).

TABLE 2.6 : **Hierarchy of shopping centres by Retail Gravity of Consumers.**

Hierarchic order	Shopping centre	Consumers attracted	F-ratio
I	1. K.R. Market	415,361	
II	1. M.G. Road	261,926	
	2. Russel Market	215,704	
	3. Majestic	213,701	93.6*
III	1. J.C. Road	92,444	
	2. Jayanagar	77,037	
	3. Malleswaram	75,237	
IV	The remaining 8 centres	61,630 to 200	

*Significant at 1% level.
The hierarchic levels differ significantly.

Connectivity

The number of bus links to different shopping centres in a city reflects the importance of the shopping centres and hence their level in the intra-urban shopping system. The number of bus connections to the various shopping centres worked out using the B.T.S. time-table formed the basic input for the connectivity analysis. The bus links clearly revealed a good connectivity pattern, but with varying intensities at different shopping centres. The number of bus links clearly identified the four-tier hierarchy of shopping centres. The linkage tree of 15 shopping centres drawn using the functional index number of bus links and spatial distribution of shopping centres also emphasized the four-tier hierarchy of shopping centres (Table 2.7).

The indices of all the shopping centres derived by using different techniques are detailed in Table 2.8.

Consumer travel pattern

It is known that consumers who visit shopping centres for various needs have varied preferences. Here consumers travel patterns, analysed according to four selected retail types, clearly identified the hierarchic levels of the shopping centres for the

TABLE 2.7 : **Hierarchy of shopping centres by connectivity**

Hierarchic order	Shopping centre	Number of bus links	F-ratio
I	1. K.R. Market	125	
II	1. Majestic	105	
	2. Russel Market	95	
	3. J.C. Road	84	
	4. M.G. Road	80	93.27*
III	1. Malleswaram	55	
	2. Jayanagar	45	
	3. Gandhi Bazar	41	
	4. K.H. Road	40	
IV	The remaining 6 shopping centres	35 to 4	

*Significant at 1% level. The hierarchic levels differ significantly.

selected four retail types—vegetables, provisions, textiles and jewellery. Vegetables revealed the most localized character with as many as 81 per cent of the consumers patronizing neighbourhood shopping centres. The average distance travelled by the consumers is least for vegetables (0.72 km). On the other hand, jewellery revealed maximum segregation. The consumer has to travel about 4 km. on an average. Provisions and textiles occupied intermediate position.

The desire lines drawn connecting the consumer origin and the shopping centre visited for the four types clearly revealed the four hierarchic levels of the shopping centres (Fig. 2.3)—the neighbourhood; the regional centre; the second order city centre; and the first order city centre.

The urban system of Karnataka

Urban Karnataka as a sub-system of the national urban system had 7.1 million population (24 per cent of total population) living in 230 towns in 1971. The growth of the urban population during 1951-71 was 60 per cent. Of the 230 towns/urban agglomerations in the system, one is a million city (Bangalore), two are quarter of a million cities (Hubli-Dharwar and

TABLE 2.8 : Number of retail establishments, retail types, functional score, market potential index, consumer gravity and bus links of selected shopping centres

Shopping centre	No. of retail establishments	Retail types	Functional score	Market potential	Retail gravity of consumers	No. of bus links
K.R. Market	1,769	73	3.832	5.926	415,361	125
M.G. Road	136	60	2.369	4.543	261,926	80
Russel Market	780	66	2.044	4.714	215,704	95
Majestic	618	67	1.964	4.742	213,701	105
J.C. Road	197	52	0.833	4.441	92,444	84
Jayanagar 4th Block	314	52	0.687	2.517	77,037	45
*Malleswaram	383	50	0.675	2.714	75,237	55
Rajajinagar	274	40	0.509	1.998	61,630	35
Gandhibazar	314	43	0.470	2.672	46,222	42
K.H. Road	61	32	0.456	2.910	45,122	40
Hanumanthanagar	142	30	0.207	1.914	15,407	23
Ulsoor	147	32	0.197	1.999	14,525	20
N.R. Colony	54	24	0.077	1.911	3,250	11
Jayanagar 8th Block	14	7	0.011	1.822	2,975	9
Street Corner	2	2	0.000	1.875	200	4

Mysore), 9 class I cities (more than 1,00,000) and 9 class II cities (50,000—1,00,000), sharing 59 per cent of the total urban population.

Though the hierarchy of urban centres is closely related to the population size, attempts are usually made to apply a variety of techniques for determining the hierarchic orders in an urban (settlement) system. While some methods utilise existing social and economic infra-structure in each centre, others are based on their fields of interaction. Some examples of these methods are—rank-size relationship, scalogram analysis, centrality index, functional scores, potential and gravity models network and linkage analysis. In this section an attempt is made to determine the hierarchic orders in the urban system of Karnataka using population, social and economic functions and bus connectivity of the 230 urban centres in the system.

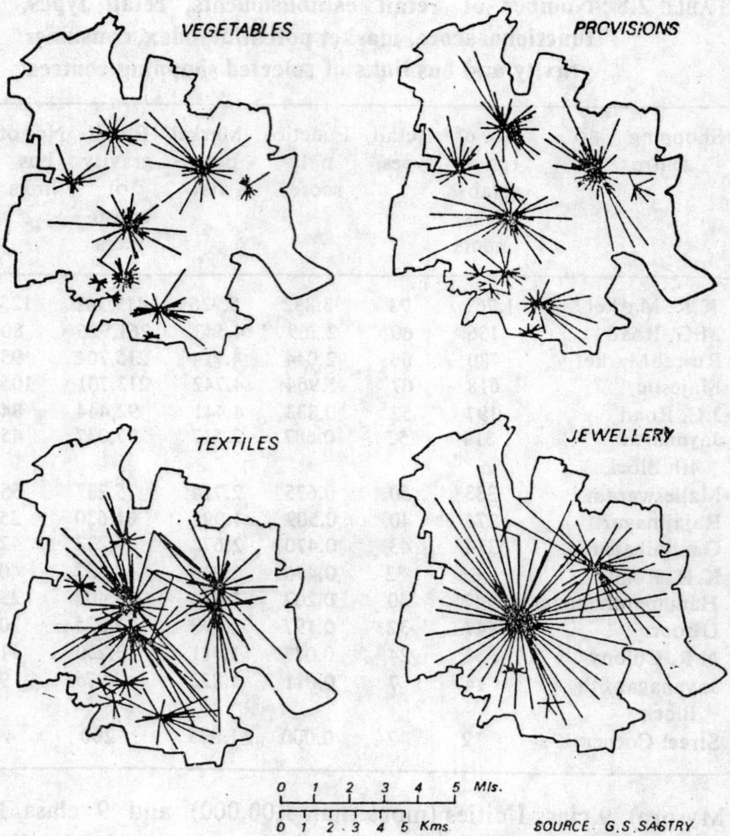

FIG. 2.3 : *Bangalore metropolis—Consumer movement patterns*

Rank-size relationship

The population of urban centres in Karnataka in 1971, varied from 764 (rank 230) to 1.654 million (rank 1). The rank-size relationships of the towns of more than 10,000 population in 1951 and 1971 showed that the distribution was nearer to the "Rank size rule" in 1951 ($q=-0.878$) than in 1971 ($q=-0.858$). The primacy of Bangalore has increased in the distribution and a step-like size hierarchy has emerged. The population of Bangalore in 1971 was 4.36 times the next ranking city, while in 1951 it was 3.37 times. The rank-size distribution in 1971 reflected a four-tier hierarchy of urban centres. Bangalore the primate city falling in the first-tier, Hubli-Dharwar and Mysore in the second tier, 14 centres in the third tier and the rest in the fourth tier of the urban hierarchy. The four breaks in the rank size graph occur after Bangalore, Mysore, Mangalore and Hospet. mangalore and Belgaum with population size of about 2 lakh are nearer to the lower group than to the Hubli-Dharwar and Mysore group. Significantly, Hubli-Dharwar ranked third in 1951, grew much faster than the second ranking city Mysore during the two decades and occupied second rank in 1971 (Table 2.9).

TABLE 2.9 : **Population and growth of towns of more than 50,000**

Town	Population		% growth 1951-71	1971 population rank	Growth rank
	1971	1951			
Bangalore urban agglomeration (UA)	1,653,779	822,228	101	1	6
Hubli-Dharwar	379,166	196,180	93	2	9
Mysore	355,685	244,323	46	3	19
Mangalore (UA)	215,122	131,521	64	4	14
Belgaum (UA)	213,872	117,827	82	5	11
Gulbarga	145,588	77,189	89	6	10
Bellary	125,183	70,322	78	7	12
Davangere	121,110	56,018	116	8	4
K.G.F. (UA)	118,861	159,084	—25	9	21
Bijapur	103,931	65,734	58	10	17
Shimoga	102,709	46,524	121	11	3
Bhadravati (UA)	101,358	42,451	139	12	2
Gadag-Betgere	95,426	65,509	46	13	20
Raichur	79,831	54,032	48	14	18
Mandya	72,131	21,158	241	15	1
Tumkur	70,476	35,999	96	16	8
Hospet	65,196	38,651	69	17	13
Bagalkote	51,746	32,285	60	18	16
Hassan	51,325	24,869	106	19	5
Bidar	50,670	31,341	62	20	15
Chitradurga	50,254	25,081	100	21	7

Functional index

The four-tier hierarchy in the urban system of Karnataka is also brought out by the functional scores. The index is calculated using 17 variables of functional importance of the centres (Table 2.10). The scores on the first principal component, explaining 73 per cent of the variation, is used as an index of functional (infra-structural) importance of the centres. The analysis shows that Bangalore gets a score of 14.08 when the lowest ranking centre gets the score of zero. The two centres of the second order, viz. Hubli-Dharwar and Mysore, score 3.82 and 3.22 respectively. The index scores of the 17 third order centres vary from 0.68 to 1.96. The rest of the 210 centres score between 0 and 0.53. The orders in the hierarchy have been determined by identifying sharp breaks in the distribution of the scores.

TABLE 2.10 : **Factor loading on first principal component of the variables selected for constructing functional index.**

Variable	Factor loading
Total municipal expenditure ('000 Rs.)	0.991
Higher secondary schools (No.)	0.988
Beds in medical institutions (No.)	0.986
Electric connections domestic (No.)	0.986
Electric connections commercial (No.)	0.979
Banks (No.)	0.976
Electric connections industrial (No.)	0.973
Cinemas, Auditoria, Drama halls (No.)	0.972
Library/Reading Rooms (No.)	0.955
Art, Science, Commerce Colleges (No.)	0.918
Medical, Engineering Colleges, Polytechnics (No.)	0.908
Non-agricultural credit societies (No.)	0.813
Protected water supply (litres)	0.654
Number of buses connecting (No.)	0.363
Agricultural credit societies (No.)	0.158
Number of routes converging (No.)	0.057
Total variation explained by the first component	73 %

A comparison of population ranks and functional score ranks of towns shows that while in the higher orders of hierarchy the two ranks are more or less identical, there are variations at the lower orders. Mandya which ranks 15th in terms of population size ranks 6th in functional score and conversely, Kolar Gold Fields ranking 9th in population size ranks 16th in functional score.

Connectivity

Although on a generalized plane, movements of vehicles, which is used as a surrogate for movement of people and goods, are biased one way or the other, as in the case of bus frequency linkages which are purported to represent movement of people, data on originating and terminating number of buses tend to underplay the connections of intermediary points, whereas the number of buses connecting the centres tend to overplay the importance of the intermediary nodes in the system. However, a cautious interpretation of bus frequency data, without claiming much more than what it stands for, is useful and least expensive way to analyse inter-urban linkages, particularly in the absence of data on other types of flows.

The linkages between urban centres are analysed through a study of the frequency of buses connecting the 230 centres of the State. The matrix of bus connections outline a complex network of inter-city ties. The numbers of buses connecting different centres are used to bring out the importance of urban centres and consequently their level in the hierarchy. The centres are grouped on the basis of dominant connections. A large frequency between pairs indicate a greater degree of association and vice-versa.

The identification of systems of urban centres follows a procedure similar to the one used by Nystuen and Dacey, generally referred to as primary linkage analysis (Nystuen and Dacey, 1961). The number of buses connecting each pair of urban centres could be recorded in a matrix form of $n \times n$ dimension. Although the primary linkage analysis is performed on the entire matrix of bus connection (230=230) only a matrix of 59×59 recording frequencies of bus connections between the 59 largest urban centres of the State is given here.* Each urban centre interacts with other centres, in the strength of bus connections. It is, therefore possible to develop a tree of connections between urban centres. Thus each urban centre would be connected to one other urban centre. The dominant nodes if any in the system would then attract a number of places whose largest frequency of buses is oriented towards them. In cases where only a few centres are connected independently with each other on the basis of maximum frequency, a further grouping of the nodes may be achieved by connecting the smaller system to another system on the basis of second largest links.

Fifteen groups of centres based on the dominant connections may be identified, centred on Bangalore, Mysore, Hubli-Dharwar, Hassan, Kolar, Mangalore Chickmagalur, Sirsi, Shimoga, Davangere, Bellary, Raichur, Gulbarga, Bijapur and Belgaum.

However, the fifteen groups of centres are not of same level of bus connection hierarchy. The smallest group is centred on Sirsi which attracts dominant association of 6 other centres. Sirsi itself is connected to the entire urban system of Karnataka by only 127 bus connections per day. At the apex lies Bangalore which is connected to the other centres of the state by as many as 1,428 bus connections per day. Within its group are found 70 other centres dominated by it directly and through such centres as Tumkur and Mysore. Within the Bangalore system, Mysore and Tumkur dominate 28 and 9 centres respectively.

By including second and third dominant connections to higher order centres, the entire tree of urban linkages may be outlined. The hierarchic orders of the centres based on total number of links between them by number of buses connecting, are clearly brought out by the linkage pattern. Four orders of centres are discernible :

I. Bangalore

II. Hubli-Dharwar and Mysore

III. Hassan, Kolar, Mangalore, Chickmagalur, Shimoga,

*Appendix.

Davangere, Bellary, Raichur, Gulbarga, Bijapur, Belgaum and Sirsi

IV. All other centres

The pattern of bus connections indicates that the dominance of Bangalore while obvious is not to the degree that would be suggested by simple gravity formulation (Prakasa Rao and Tewari, 1978). Many sub-systems do operate within the shadow of Bangalore. While the first and the second order centres' fields transcend their district boundaries, the third order centres tend to dominate their districts. This is particularly true of Hassan, Mangalore, Kolar and Chickmagalur. Non-hierarchical ties are apparently stronger in the Bangalore system. Consequently, nesting of centres is distorted. A number of urban centres with large population and bus connections fail to have strong ties with smaller towns located near them. Such small centres tend to interact directly with Bangalore and in some cases with Mysore. Mandya, an agricultural town with a population of over 70,000 located in the sugarcane-paddy core area and sandwiched between Mysore and Bangalore, is a typical example which is bypassed by other smaller centres located around it. Conversely, a few small centres because of their strategic locations on the bus network system not only have higher connectivity but also attract strong ties from other centres around them. Examples of this kind are represented by centres like Arsikere, Haveri, etc. The locational advantages with reference to bus connection network and the disadvantages of location near large centres distort the nesting of smaller centres within the fields of larger centres. Compared to the Bangalore system, the Hubli-Dharwar sub-system has lesser distortions, where although large centres have low bus connections, they come closer to a nested ordering.

The hierarchy in the urban system of Karnataka

Based on rank-size, functional scores and connectivity, the four-tier hierarchy of urban centres in Karnataka consists of one centre of order I, two centres of order II, 21 centres of order III and 206 centres of order IV (Table 2.11). The classification of urban centres in the first-two hierarchic orders remains similar by all the three methods used for the identification of the hierarchy. The composition of the III order

TABLE 2.11 : The hierarchy of the urban system of Karnataka

Hierarchy order	Urban centre	Order determined by rank-size graph/functional score/connectivity methods
I order	1 Bangalore	All the three methods
II order	1 Hubli-Dharwar	-do-
	2 Mysore	-do-
III order	1 Mangalore	-do-
	2 Belgaum	-do-
	3 Gulbarga	-do-
	4 Bellary	-do-
	5 Davangere	-do-
	6 KGF	Rank-size graph and functional score
	7 Bijapur	All the three methods
	8 Shimoga	-do-
	9 Bhadravathi	Rank-size graph and functional score
	10 Gadag-Betgere	-do-
	11 Raichur	All the three methods
	12 Mandya	Rank-size graph and functional score
	13 Tumkur	-do-
	14 Hospet	Rank-size graph
	15 Bagalkote	Functional score
	16 Hassan	Functional score and connectivity
	17 Chitradurga	Functional score
	18 Kolar	Connectivity
	19 Chickmagalur	Connectivity
	20 Udipi	Functional score
	21 Sirsi	Connectivity

determined by the three methods differs marginally at the lower end. The final list of urban centres of the third order includes all the centres classified in the order by any of the three methods: Mangalore, Belgaum, Gulbarga, Bellary, Davangere, Bijapur, Shimoga and Raichur are the eight towns which fall in the third order by all the methods, while KGF, Bhadravathi, Gadag-Betgeri, Mandya, Tumkur, Hospet, Bangalore, Hassan, Chitradurga, Kolar, Chickmagalur, Udipi and Sirsi are those centres which are included in the third order due to the high rank they score by at least one of the three methods.

A four-tier hierarchy is identified based on functional scores. These four levels differ significantly (Tables 2.12, 2.13 and 2.14).

TABLE 2.12 : Four-tier hierarchy identified based on functional scores.

Order	Town	Functional scores	F-Ratio
I	Bangalore	14.0765	
II	Hubli-Dharwar	3.8222	
	Mysore	3.2178	
III	Belgaum	1.9593	
	Mangalore	1.8077	
	Mandya	1.3634	516.0
	Davangere	1.2454	
	Bellary	1.0957	
	Chitradurga	0.9559	
	Raichur	0.9543	
	Shimoga	0.9396	
	Bijapur	0.9221	
	Tumkur	0.8165	
	Gulbarga	0.7960	
	Udipi	0.7653	
	K.G.F.	0.7421	
	Bagalkot	0.7250	
	Hassan	0.7138	
	Bhadravathi	0.6929	
	Gadag-Betgere	0.6821	
IV	Remaining 138 towns	0.5247-0.0891	

Note : Hierarchic levels differ significantly.

Settlement hierarchies

Settlement hierarchies are constructed for regions of different order and structure, e.g. States Andhra Pradesh and Karnataka; developed regions: agricultural—Muzaffarnagar district and Karnal taluk; agro-industrial—Coimbatore district; and plantation district—Nilgiris; and under-developed and low productive agricultural tract with millet economies—Miryalguda taluk. There are sharp differences in the number and types of variables selected. The most commonly used variables relate to the tertiary sector, economic and social infrastructure, communications, commuting, legal and administrative services and entertainment, mostly cinemas. In some cases even trips to marriages and religious places are included. Thus the 'bag' of central functions is highly mixed in terms of type, establishments and units of measurement. In some

TABLE 2.13 : **Four-tier hierarchy of towns identified based on population.**

Order	Towns	Population	F-Ratio
I	Bangalore	1653779	
II	Hubli-Dharwar	379166	
	Mysore	355685	
III	Mangalore	215122	
	Belgaum	213872	
	Gulbarga	145588	
	Bellary	125183	
	Davangere	121110	
	K.G.F.	118861	301.76
	Bijapur	103931	
	Shimoga	102709	
	Bhadravathi	101358	
	Gadag-Betgere	95426	
	Raichur	79831	
	Mandya	72132	
	Tumkur	70476	
	Hospet	65196	
IV	Remaining 141 towns	51746-10179	

Note: Hierarchic levels differ significantly.

TABLE 2.14 : **Four-tier hierarchy of towns identified based on bus connections.**

Order	Towns	No. of bus connections	F-Ratio
I	Bangalore	1428	
II	Mysore	999	
	Hubli-Dharwar	579	
III	Hassan	361	
	Shimoga	352	
	Belgaum	349	15.19*
	Kolar	238	
	Bijapur	234	
	Chickmagalur	231	
	Davangere	225	
	Gulbarga	216	
	Bellary	215	
	Mangalore	212	
	Raichur	203	
	Sirsi	127	
IV	Ramaining 143 towns	483-0	

*Significant at 1 per cent level.
Note : Hierarchic levels differ significantly.

studies, the non-policy variables like personal services—barber and tailor, and the ephemeral services like 'request-bus-stop' also are included. Techniques of analysis also differ from presence or absence of a variable to multivariate techniques. Each exercise attempts to develop a new technique or apply more than one technique to make the result method independent. These variations do pose problems in comparative analysis. The problem question is to what extent one can standardize at least some of the variables and techniques of analysis. Should we not eliminate from analysis all ubiquitous variables. Even the methods of survey vary from total inventory to sample survey. The validity of sample survey for working out hierarchies particularly from the grassroot levels can be debated. There are yet no simple and ready answers to these questions.

Table 2.15 indicates the number of hierarchic levels identified for different types and scales of regions.

TABLE 2.15 : **Number of Hierarchic Levels**

State	Number of hierarchic levels
Karnataka[1]	
Bangalore 1st order	4
Andhra Pradesh[2]	
Hyderabad 1st order	6
Sub-region (group of districts)	
Telangana[3]	
Hyderabad 1st order	5
Gorakhpur region[4]	
Gorakhpur 1st order	5
Micro region (district)	
Muzaffarnagar District[5]	5
Muzaffarnagar 1st order	
Nilgiris district[6]	4
Ooty 1st order	
Coimbatore district[7]	4
Coimbatore 1st order	
Tract[8]	
Karnal taluk	5
Karnal 1st order	
(Karnal: also district headquarters)	
Miryalguda taluk[9]	
Miryalguda: taluk headquarters	3

1. Prakasa Rao, *et al.*
2. Manzoor Alam, *et al.*
3. Prakasa Rao, V.L.S.
4. Jagdish Singh
5. Prakasa Rao, V.L.S.
6. Steine Folke
7. Parvati, C.
8. Bhat, L.S.
9. Sen, L.K. *et al.*

Karnataka State, Coimbatore district (agro-industrial) and Nilgiris district (hill-forest and plantation area) have the same number of levels, i.e. four levels. Telangana and Gorakhpur (less developed sub-regions: group of districts), Muzaffarnagar district and Karnal tahsil (developed agricultural areas) have five levels for each. Miryalguda taluk is a tract of small villages ranging in population size from 500-2000. The taluk headquarters town is a small town with a population of about 18,000 (1971), which is located at a distance of 18 miles from the district headquarters town with a population of 33,000. It is in this tract that a project (boom) town with a population of 56,000 and with urban infra-structure out of proportion to its threshold is located. This tract should be considered as 'atypical' and as a deviant from Christaller-Lösch norm. Thus the number of levels has no significance either in relation to the level of development or the size (geographical area and the number of settlements) and structure of the area (physical and economic). All along the settlement size spectrum, there is clustering of functions in certain discrete population sizes: villages—1000, 3000 or 5000, and cities—1,00,000-1,50,000; 2,50,000-5,00,000 and above.

This differential clustering of functions is implicit in settlement hierarchy. The population size of the settlement is highly and positively correlated with the number of functions and the rank of the central place is directly related to the scale of the functions. The relationship between population size and its functional scale is non-linear irrespective of the size of region, its structure and level of development. 'Boom towns' like irrigation project towns and transient mining towns do not conform to the discrete population-size-clustering relationships. These stand out as anomalies in the functional profile of settlements (e.g. as in Miryalguda taluk). Allowing for these disturbances, there is a recurring pattern in hierarchy, i.e. a large functional gap between the largest settlement and its next ranking settlement irrespective of sharp differences in the geographical size, regional economic structure and level of development (Table 2.16). These functional imbalances are related to the very physical and economic structural imbalances. Historical imprints and policy interventions contribute their due share.

TABLE 2.16 : Functional gap

Karnataka State	Population 1971	Functional score/index
Bangalore I[1]	1,654,000	14.08
Hubli-Dharwar II	379,000	3.82
Andhra Pradesh[2]		
Hyderabad I	1,796,000	5612
Vijayawada II	317,000	2700
Gorakhpur sub-region[3] (Backward)		
Gorakhpur I	231,000	20364.00
Basti II	50,000	3263.6
Coimbatore District[4] (Developed: agro-industrial)		
Coimbatore I	353,000	13.3
Erode II	104,000	4.5
Muzaffarnagar District[5] (Developed: agricultural)		
Muzaffarnagar I	88,000*	118
Shamli II	26,000*	57
Karnal Taluk[6] (Developed: agricultural)		
Karnal I	93,000	47394
Gharaunda II	13,000	9294

*1961 Population

1. Prakasa Rao, V.L.S. *et al.*
2. Manzoor Alam, *et al.*
3. Jagdish Singh.
4. Parvati, C.
5. Prakasa Rao, V.L.S.
6. Bhat, L.S.

In the non-linear population-size functional score curve, both urban settlements and rural settlements have distinct spatial patterns. In the higher levels of the settlement hierarchy (cities: 1,00,000 and more) with extra-regional functional links, the settlement pattern with the associated functional clustering tends to be 'axial' along the major transport routes with urban-industrial and functional clusters located at unequal distances like 'beads'. Here the settlement hierarchic structure gets dichotomised between 'axial' belts and interstitial areas and between urban and rural settlements. Some of the interstitial areas are highly productive and have high rural population densities with higher levels of development (Muzaffarnagar, Karnal and Meerut districts). The transport network and connectivity patterns are such that interstitial areas are well linked to the cities. In the highly productive and well developed interstitial areas, the settlement size classes of 1000-1500,1,500-2,500 and 2,500-5,000 are more frequent and capture the low order central functions and are more evenly distributed due to uniformly higher levels of land productivity. Here functional clusters are associated with these size classes. The interstitial areas where the resource endowments are low, and where there is greater isolation (Telangana, Bombay-Konkan) the functional clusters are of low order and are few and scattered. Here the axial belt—interstitial dichotomy and the associated hierarchic imbalance is sharp. Where a national metropolis is located in a less developed region, there is a double effect—the metropolitan shadow effect and the region's poverty effect that truncates the settlement hierarchic system, as for example in the South Kolaba region, where between Bombay and the lowest order central villages, the middle tier is functionally weak and lopsided, and is often bypassed (Deshpande *et al.*, 1979). Telangana, the least developed sub-region of Andhra Pradesh is another typical example of a truncated urban system with Hyderabad (1.7 million population in 1971) nearly eight times larger than the second ranking city, and with majority of the towns stagnant or slow growing, declining or growing at a decreasing growth rate. The intermediate level of towns, the middle section of the city-size distribution is weakly linked (Waheeduddin Khan 1973, Prakasa Rao, 1966). In the developed regions with high productivity and high population density also, the intervening opportunities are bypassed. To get an insight into the consumer travel behaviour patterns of the rural folk in a developed district, Muzaffarnagar district* is selected for study, and

*Muzaffarnagar district (Uttar Pradesh), with an area of 1683 square miles and a population of 1.4 million people, living in 920 villages (1961).

the results of the study are presented in the following section.

Mobility and choice of central places*

Consumer travel patterns : Purpose and mode of transportation

The frequency and purpose of trips for obtaining various consumer goods and services as revealed by the interview of 70 heads of families in Athain village are presented in Table 2.17. It appears from the Table that the most frequent purpose is for credit (banks and cooperative societies). The next is provision stores and medical services. The least frequented visits are for items like sewing machines and radio repair services. Frequency of trips for obtaining clothing goods, for repairs of cycles, and for recreation form an intermediate category. There are some differences in the travel purposes between different income groups (income indicated by the size of holdings). For credit, poorer agriculturists actually

*This section was written jointly by the author and Prof. R. Ramachandran of Delhi University, and the results were already reported in Regional Development Planning in India (Misra *et al.*, 1974). The research reported here is based upon field interviews of several individuals in a number of villages in Muzaffarnagar district, U.P. The objective is to gain first-hand knowledge of the mobility patterns and the consumer travel behaviour of rural people. Two separate and independent surveys were undertaken for this purpose. The first survey involved a detailed study of one selected Development Block (the Morna Block). Within this block, detailed questionnaires were distributed to the village level workers. In all, 80 heads of households were interviewed from 16 villages. In each village, heads of households were selected in such a way as to include the rich, middle class and poor farmers, agricultural labourers and representatives from non-agricultural occupations. The second survey involved only one village from the same block (Athain village). In this village, 70 heads of families were interviewed using a separate questionnaire. This questionnaire related essentially to consumer travel patterns. The results of these two field enquiries are discussed in the following pages; the discussion is organized into three parts dealing with: (1) the purposes and modes of transportation used, (2) the pattern of consumer travel in Morna block, and (3) the choice of central places by consumers.

TABLE 2.17 : **Purpose and frequency of trips for consumer goods from Athain village.**

Purpose	Frequency*	Rank
Banks and Cooperative Banks	2002	2
Courts, Tehsil offices and Panchayat Offices	408	13
Public utilities (Police, Post Office etc.)	785	7
Educational (Libraries and reading rooms)	93	19
Professional services (Lawyers)	137	17
Medical (other than the medical stores)	1626	3
Provision Stores	2105	1
Medical Stores	230	16
General Stores	441	12
Metal Ware (Blacksmiths)	710	9
Cloth and Apparel Stores	784	8
Tailors	836	5
Carpenters	800	6
Cycle Repair Shops	470	10
Automobile, Tractor repair shops	49	22
Engineering goods (Tubewell equipments, Oil Engine etc.)	69	21
Recreation: Cinema etc.	232	15
Tea Shops, eatables	70	20
Cart repair shops	273	14
Radio repair service	29	23
Sewing machines	14	24
Flour Mills	1060	4
Books and Stationery	133	18
Tobacco	462	11

*Frequency of visits during month preceding date of interview.

move to money-lenders and the rich to banks. For repair services, smaller and medium income groups move more frequently than large income groups. The frequency of visits is more in the larger income groups for luxury items.

The transitional stage in the transformation from traditional to modern is well brought out by the coexistence of the different modes of transport (Table 2.18). Bicycles are the most frequently used mode, followed by the bus; movement on foot ranks next to the above two modes of transport. The rubber tyre 'bogie' has almost replaced the traditional bullock cart and in so doing, increased the relative speed, but of course, not the distance range of 20 to 25 miles. Movement by tractor is an innovation, but a wasteful one, particularly for passenger movement.

TABLE 2.18 : **Mode of transportation used by consumer from Athain village.**

Mode of Transport	Proportion of trips per month
Bicycle	42.03
Bus	27.23
On foot	12.45
Bogie	10.56
Tonga	4.72
Car	1.63
Tractor	1.25
Auto Rickshaw	0.12

It needs no mention that the mode of transport, the distance and the purpose are inter-related, and there are definite groupings—cycle and on foot for most essential consumer goods and food items, money-lender and primary school within a distance range of 2 to 6 miles; bogie and tonga for repair service facilities, automobile spare parts and agricultural implements, within a distance of less than 20 miles (average 8 miles); and bus is naturally the important mode of travel for distances longer than 10 miles. The maximum distance travelled in the district is 25 miles, and this is for banking services; and for higher education, the average distance travelled for these purposes being 11 miles.

While from analysis of these data we have gained insights into the purposes for which rural people move to various central places and the modes of transportation used in this connection, it is in fact more important to find out whether or not rural people make definite choices of specific central places for given sets of functions. If these were confirmed then it would greatly affect the potential growth pattern among central places.

Consumer travel patterns in Morna block

Data on consumer travel in 16 villages in Morna Block offers evidence demonstrating that—(1) villagers do make definite choices of central places for particular types of goods that they ordinarily buy, and (2) that lower order central places can be differentiated in terms of purposes for which they are visited.

Morna Developmental Block is located to the east of Muzaffarnagar town, at a distance of about 10 miles. There are no census towns in the district, nor are there any wholesale markets. The Block is entirely rural in character. The nearest urban places are Jansath, towards the south and Muzaffarnagar town, towards the west. Although Morna village represents the Block headquarters, there are other villages that are equally if not better placed to serve as central places, such as Bhopa and Tissa.

Data on the frequency of visits to central places for the purchase of 37 items commonly used by villagers (these include such items as clothing, footwear, vegetable, ghee (oil), cycles, utensils etc.) were obtained from interviews of 80 heads of families living in 16 villages in the block. Out of the 37 items, response to 16 items was poor, and have been deleted from the analysis (Table 2.19). In all 10 central places were visited by all those interviewed for the purchase of 21 items. These central places were then ranked on the basis of the frequency with which they were visited. This revealed that Muzaffarnagar town, lying outside the developmental block is the most frequented central place. This is followed by Bhopa, Tissa and Morna, all located within the block.

Muzaffarnagar town and Bhopa are visited for obtaining all the 21 items, while other central places are visited only for a limited range of items—about 19 items in the case of Morna to only 2 items in the case of Gadla. The dominance of Muzaffarnagar town shows that there is clearly no natural focal point in the entire block and that the villagers tend to bypass the lower order central places in favour of higher order centres, even though the distance to be travelled is greater. This preference for higher order places is partly explained by the multiple trip pattern of visits to central places, and partly

TABLE 2.19 : **Frequency of trips to central places for obtaining consumer goods in Morna Block, Muzaffarnagar District.**

	Muzaffar-nagar	Bhopa	Tissa	Morna	Godwada	Bhokerni	Kakrauli	Khai-khara	Sikandar-pur	Gadla
(1)	(2)	(3)	(4)	(5)	(6)	(7)	(8)	(9)	(10)	(11)
Watch	25	3	0	0	0	0	0	0	0	0
Tooth Paste		3	0	1	1	0	0	0	0	0
Radio	26	3	0	2	0	0	1	0	0	0
Utensils	19	5	0	1	0	0	0	0	0	0
Clothing	50	9	0	5	2	1	0	0	0	0
Footwear	34	11	0	4	1	2	1	0	0	0
Towel	16	5	1	4	0	0	0	0	0	0
Cycle	18	6	4	2	0	0	0	0	0	0
Hair oil	22	7	4	4	1	1	0	0	0	0
Fountain pen	20	9	2	4	0	0	1	0	0	0
Dalda	21	8	8	3	1	0	0	0	0	0
Washing soap	23	12	1	5	2	1	0	1	0	0
Toilet soap	17	6	7	5	0	1	0	0	0	1
Cigarette	13	4	6	3	0	0	0	1	0	2
Tea powder	15	9	5	2	2	0	1	0	0	0
Torch	27	4	5	0	0	1	0	0	0	0
Fruits	14	10	3	5	0	1	1	0	0	0
Sugar	8	5	4	3	1	0	0	1	0	0
Bidi	12	12	7	1	1	0	0	1	0	0
Kerosene oil	7	15	6	4	3	0	1	0	1	0
Vegetables	7	12	6	5	0	1	2	2	6	0

by the attractions of greater variety in products and lower prices in high order centres.

The choice of higher order centres is not, however, consistently the same for all the 21 items (functions). The patterns of choice differ from one function to another. The similarity/dissimilarity between pairs of functions has been analysed employing the Kolmogorov-Smirnov test.* The results of this analysis are presented in Table 2.20. This analysis shows that significant differences exist between pairs of functions in terms of the mix of central places from where they are generally obtained. For example, the patterns of trips for obtaining watches, tooth paste, radio/transistors, utensils and clothing are similar, but these differ significantly from the pattern of trips for other items. The existence of groups of functions with similar patterns of trips is indicated in Table 2.20 although it is somewhat difficult to identify all of the groups of functions.

The same data set also provides the basis for examining differences among central places in the mix of purposes for which they are visited. Here the analysis proceeds by taking pairs of central places and examining the frequency of visits according to the ranked order of functions. Again the Kolmogorov-Smirnov test is applied to find out whether the patterns of purposes of visits for pairs of central functions significantly differ or not. The results of this analysis are presented in Table 2.21.

The matrix of similarity/dissimilarity of patterns of trips to central places reveals a marked grouping tendency, indicating that discrete levels of central place hierarchy exist in this area. Four orders of central places are clearly evident. Muzaffarnagar stands out as a centre which is different from all others, while Bhopa, Tissa, Morna, Godwada and Bhokerni form a single group of central places with similar trip patterns. Kakrauli stands out as a unique centre. At the lower end are a group of centres including Godla, Sikandarpur and

*The Kolmogorov-Smirnov test is a two sample non-parametric test involving an ordinal scale variable. The maximum difference between two cumulative frequency distributions is used as the test statistic. In this study, both functions and central places have been ranked to yield ordinal scale variables for the test.

TABLE 2.20 : **Matrix of similarity/dissimilarity of patterns of trips to central places in Morna Block for pairs of consumer goods*.**

Function No.	1	2	3	4	5	6	7	8	9	10	11	12	13	14	15	16	17	18	19	20	21
1.	X	X	X	X	X																
2.	X	X	X	X	X	X															
3.	X	X	X	X	X	X															
4.	X	X	X	X	X	X	X	X													
5.	X	X	X	X	X	X	X	X	X												
6.		X	X	X	X	X	X	X	X	X	X	X									
7.				X	X	X	X	X	X	X	X	X	X								
8.					X	X	X	X	X	X	X	X	X	X	X	X	X				
9.					X	X	X	X	X	X	X	X	X	X	X	X	X				
10.					X	X	X	X	X	X	X	X	X	X	X	X	X				
11.						X	X	X	X	X	X	X	X	X	X	X	X	X	X		
12.						X	X	X	X	X	X	X	X	X	X	X	X	X	X		
13.							X	X	X	X	X	X	X	X	X	X	X	X	X		
14.								X	X		X	X	X	X	X	X	X	X	X		
15.								X	X	X	X	X	X	X	X	X	X	X	X		
16.								X	X	X	X	X	X	X	X	X	X	X	X		
17.								X	X	X	X	X	X	X	X	X	X	X	X		
18.											X	X	X	X	X	X	X	X	X	X	
19.											X	X	X	X	X	X	X	X	X	X	
20.																		X	X	X	
21.																					X

*Patterns of trips for pairs of consumer goods were considered to be similar/dissimilar on the basis of Kolmogorov-Smirnov's tests using the cumulated frequency of trips for obtaining consumer goods from various central places (ranked in order to importance in the Block).

X Indicates similarity and blank indicates dissimilarity. See Table 2.19 for original data used in this test.

TABLE 2.21 : **Matrix of similarity/dissimilarity of patterns of trips f r the purchase of consumer goods between pairs of central places in Morna Block.**

		Central Plac									
		1	2	3	4	5	6	7	8	9	10
CENTRAL PLACES	1	S	S				S				
	2		S	S	S	S	S				
	3		S	S	S	S	S				
	4		S	S	S	S	S				
	5		S	S	S	S	S				
	6	S	S	S	S	S	S				
	7							S			
	8								S	S	S
	9									S	S
	10								S	S	S

Note : (a) S indicates similarity and blank indicates dissimilarity.

(b) Names of Central Places

(1) Muzaffarnagar (2) Bhopa (3) Tissa (4) Morna (5) Godwada

(6) Bhokerni (7) Kakrauli (8) Khaikhara (9) Sikandarpur (10) Gadla

(c) Patterns of trips for obtaining consumer goods from Central places were considered to be similar/dissimilar on the basis of Kolomogorov-Smirnov test of the frequency of visits for various purposes to each of the Central Places. See Table 2.19 for original data used in test.

Khaikhara, which are least frequently visited, and that only for very basic items.

Choice of central places and socio-economic status of villagers: That villagers discriminate between central places is clearly evident from the analysis of consumer travel patterns in the Morna Block. But there is another aspect relating to the choice of central places not revealed in the preceding analysis. This relates to differences in the choice of central places for particular goods as between the various socio-economic categories of farmers. Evidence is here presented to demonstrate that it is only the higher income groups that visit central places of higher orders, bypassing the lower order centres, while the lower income groups continue to be dependent on the lower order centres.

For the present analysis, data on socio-economic status of farmers and their consumer travel behaviour were obtained through an interview of 70 farmers and non-farmers in one selected village (Athain) in the Morna Block. The choices of central places open to Athain villagers were limited to two in number—Bhopa and Muzaffarnagar town. Bhopa, a lower order central place, only a mile away from Athain village, has a medical store, cloth shops, a radio repair shop, three tractor repair shops, and a number of shops dealing in food and other consumer items. Muzaffarnagar is 12 miles away from Athain, and is easily accessible by bus. Being the largest central place in the district, Muzaffarnagar offers a much wider range of goods and services. Furthermore, each function is represented by large number of establishments, thus offering greater choice to consumers.

For a number of goods and services, which are offered both in Bhopa and Muzaffarnagar, contingency tables giving the frequency of visits by villagers from Athain, categorized according to four socio-economic classes, were prepared (Tables 2.22 to 2.26). The goods and services considered here are—(1) cloth and apparel goods, (2) goods from general stores, (3) tobacco, (4) books and stationery goods, and (5) tractor repair services. These represent a mix of both traditional and non-traditional items. The socio-economic categories included three cultivator classes—rich, middle class and poor—and a non-cultivator category of agricultural labourers, carpenters, blacksmiths etc.

TABLE 2.22 : **Frequency of visits of villagers from Athain to central places for the purchase of cloth and apparel goods*.**

Category of respondent	Bhopa (Distance from Athain : 1 mile)	Muzaffarnagar (Distance from Athain: 12 miles)	Total
Cultivators** :			
Rich	—	410	410
Medium	10	117	127
Poor	55	120	175
Non-cultivators† (Service Class)	44	24	68
Total	109	671	780

*Chi-square value is 260.51, significant at 0.01 level.

**Cultivators are classified here on the basis of the size of holdings : rich cultivators own 10 or more acres, medium cultivators between 6-10 acres and poor cultivators less than 6 acres.

†The non-cultivator category includes :
(i) Agriculture labour, (ii) Carpenters and blacksmiths, (iii) Barbers, and (iv) Sweepers.

A detailed examination of Tables 2.22 to 2.26 reveals that in almost all cases, the rich and medium class cultivators tended to go to Muzaffarnagar for various goods and services, thus in effect bypassing Bhopa, a lower order centre. The poor cultivators tend to go to both the centres in almost equal proportions. There is, however, some preference for Muzaffarnagar in the purchase of cloth and apparel and general store items, but the reverse pattern exists in the purchases of books and stationery items and tobacco. The non-cultivators, on the other hand, obtained most of the goods and services from Bhopa itself. In the case of the goods and services considered here, the relationship between socio-economic status and choice of central place is statistically significant. The richer classes tended to go to higher order central places for all goods and services, while

TABLE 2.23 : **Frequency of visits of villagers from Athain to central places for the purchase of goods from central stores*.**

Category of respondent	Bhopa (Distance from Athain : 1 mile)	Muzaffarnagar (Distance from Athain : 12 miles)	Total
Cultivators**			
Rich	—	206	206
Medium	35	112	147
Poor	15	40	55
Non-cultivators† (Service class)	39	5	44
Total	89	363	452

*Chi-square value is 186.40, significant at 0.01 level.

**Cultivators are classified here on the basis of the size of holdings : rich cultivators own 10 or more acres, medium cultivators between 6-10 acres and poor cultivators less than 6 acres.

†The non-cultivator category includes :
(i) Agriculture labour, (ii) Carpenters and Blacksmiths, (iii) Barbers, and (iv) Sweepers.

TABLE 2.24 : **Frequency of visits of villagers from Athain to central places for the purchase of Tobacco***

Category of respondent	Bhopa (Distance from Athain : 1 mile)	Muzaffarnagar (Distance from Athain : 12 miles)	Total
Cultivators**			
Rich	—	106	106
Medium	16	69	85
Poor	88	73	161
Non-cultivators*** (Service class)	105	10	115
Total	209	258	467

*Chi-square value is 216.15, significant at 0.01 level.

**Cultivators are classified here on thé basis of the size of holdings: rich cultivators own 10 or more acres, medium cultivators between 6-10 acres and poor cultivators less than 6 acres.

***The non-cultivator category includes :
(i) Agriculture labour, (ii) Carpenters and Blacksmiths, (iii) Barbers, and (iv) Sweepers.

TABLE 2.25 : **Frequency of visits of villagers from Athain to central places for the purchase of books and stationery goods*.**

Category of respondent	Bhopa (Distance from Athain : 1 mile)	Muzaffarnagar (Distance from Athain : 12 miles)	Total
Cultivators**			
Rich	16	42	58
Medium	29	6	35
Poor	25	5	30
Non-cultivators*** (Service class)	11	—	11
Total	81	53	134

*Chi-square value is 47.29, significant at 0.01 level.

**Cultivators are classified here on the basis of the size of holdings : rich cultivators own 10 or more acres, medium cultivators between 6-10 acres and poor cultivators less than 6 acres.

***The non-cultivator category includes :

(i) Agriculture labour, (ii) Carpenters and Blacksmiths, (iii) Barbers, and (iv) Sweepers.

TABLE 2.26 : **Frequency of visits of villagers from Athain to central places for repair of tractors*.**

Category of respondent	Bhopa (Distance from Athain : 1 mile)	Muzaffarnagar (Distance from Athain : 12 miles)	Total
Cultivators**			
Rich	5	23 (Bijnore: 5)	33
Medium	—	8	8
Poor	—	—	—
Non-cultivators*** (Service class)			
Total	5	31	41

*Chi-square value is 1.26, not significant at 0.01 level.

**Cultivators are classified here on the basis of the size of holdings: rich cultivators own 10 or more acres, medium cultivators between 6-10 acres and poor cultivators less than 6 acres.

***The non-cultivator category includes :

(i) Agriculture labour, (ii) Carpenters and Blacksmiths, (iii) Barbers, and (iv) Sweepers.

the poor go to lower order central places for the same goods and services.

The analysis of consumer travel behaviour of villagers throws up several important insights—(1) that villagers discriminate between central places in the purchase of various consumer items, (2) that central places differ in mix of purposes for which they are visited, (3) that the richer sections of rural society tend to bypass the lower order central places and invariably go to higher order central places for various goods and services, and (4) that the choice of central places for the purchase of goods is significantly influenced by multiple purpose visits and differences in price levels.

Thus urban system is both behavioural and structural and may be defined as a set of urban centres of different hierarchic orders interlinked by sets of relationships within each hierarchic order and also between hierarchic orders (Table 2.27).

TABLE 2.27 : The hierarchy of urban systems

Hierarchy of urban system	Urban centres in the hierarchic order
National urban system	1 National capital and other regional metropolitan cities
	2 State metropolitan cities
	3 Regional cities
	4 District/market towns
	5 Resource towns and service centres
Meso-regional (state) urban system	2 State metropolitan cities
	3 Regional cities
	4 District/market towns
	5 Resource towns and service centres
Sub-regional urban system	3 Regional cities
	4 District/market towns
	5 Resource towns and service centres
Micro-regional urban system*	4 District/market towns
	5 Resource towns and service centres
Resource and service centre system*	5 Resource towns and service centres
Religious and tourist centres constitute special systems	

*Also includes villages and provides the link between rural settlements with higher order urban system.

The sets of complex interrelationships are functional linkages—physical, economic, social, administrative and political. The linkages between urban centres that bind them into a system are through interaction of people, goods, services and ideas. These interactions rooted to the structure and character of the originating and terminating centres weave complex networks that indicate the relative order of the centres, their ties in the system and their fields of interaction. It is the increasing specialization of city functions that contributes to hierarchy of linkages. The structure, volume and frequency, and distances involved vary.

Urban system of India : An overview

The Indian urban system is characterized by a polymetropolitan apex with the four multi-million cities Bombay, Calcutta, Delhi and Madras, standing as "islands of urban potentials", with state metropolitan capitals, regional cities, district/market towns and small towns/large villages constituting the different levels of the urban hierarchy. The different hierarchic levels are distinctly identifiable due to large functional gaps existing between them. The fact that population sizes of the urban centres (2636 in 1971) in the country's urban system vary from less than 400 for the smallest town to over 7million for the largest metropolitan city, clearly indicates the extent of associated functional gaps between the lowest and the highest hierarchic levels. The four first order metropolitan cities have population ranging between 4 million and 7 million (1971).

Second order cities in India take the form of state capitals which are also cities with high primacy and concentrations of high order administrative, manufacturing and service activities. These centres mostly fall in the population range of 750,000—3,000,000. The third order cities are in between the state capitals and district headquarters in population range of quarter-million to three quarter of a million and have developed to provide higher order functional linkages between sub-regions of the meso-regions (States). The fourth order cities which are district headquarters and important market centres really provide the integration between urban system and the regional resource base. These centres can be broadly classified into the population range of 50,000 to 250,000. The fifth order centres are resource towns/service centres with less than 50,000 population which mainly act as lower order marketing and service centres to the surrounding rural areas. The Indian urban system consists of multiple specialized systems—industrial, commercial, governmental and cultural (religious and tourist). The co-association of these different specialized systems is stronger in the million and capital cities. The regional urban system has a closer fit with the administrative hierarchic system—State, Division, District and Tahsil. Deviations are more an exception, e.g. District headquarters cities and Tahsil headquarters towns having lower functional and infra-structural scale than industrial and trading centres in the region.

The metropolitan apex

Based on population size, metropolitan functional index, airline connectivity and the number of inter-city flight connections per week, Bombay, Calcutta, Delhi and Madras are found to dominate the urban system (Table 2.28). In population size, Calcutta (9 million), Bombay (8 million), Delhi (5 million) and Madras (4 million) continue to be the largest four cities in 1981 also (provision figures 1981 census).

TABLE 2.28 : **Metropolitan functional index***

	Population in '000*		Functional index cumulative rank	Airline connectivity rank
	1961	1971		
Greater Bombay	4152	5971	97	I
Calcutta	5737	7031	85	I
Delhi	2359	3647	79	I
Madras	1945	3170	74	I
Ahmedabad	1206	1742	55	IV
Bangalore	1199	1653	44	II
Hyderabad	1249	1796	43	I

*Including urban agglomeration.

Source: Chandrasekhara and Sundaram (1970), W.E. Reed (1970).
Metropolitan Indicators : Telephone calls; outward and inward Sept. 1963; Air traffic : number of passengers 1966 ; Rail traffic: goods and passenger 1963-64; Flow of funds Dec. 1967, State Bank of India.

Bombay and Calcutta stand out as industrial and commercial metropolises. Bombay with largest stock exchange and the headquarters of Reserve Bank of India is recognised as the financial capital of India. Delhi as a metropolis, and as national capital, has its distinct role to play. Madras has the lowest metropolitan rank among the "Big Four" but is nearer to Delhi in functional scale. The functional gap between Madras and the next ranking Ahmedabad is large. The four metropolises are characterized by a high concentration of production units and industries. Out of 533 production units owned by the 75 economic giants, 54 per cent are located in the States of Maharashtra, West Bengal and Madras with the three port cities capturing the major share. If there was any decentralization of industrial units, it was through Indian entrepreneurial enterprise in contrast with the foreign business group (*Data Source*: Ashok Mitra 1968). On the industrial front, 78 per cent of industrial licences are concentrated in Bombay, Calcutta, Delhi and Madras. Out of these, Bombay captured the maximum—34 per cent, followed by Calcutta—23 per cent (Ausaf Ahmad). These four metropolises play a major role in the organization of the country's space-economy as the outlets of international trade of dependent enclaves and assembly points of primary produce by suction mechanism as it were through the hinterland, with other cities acting as satellites to feed the metropolises. The function of these metropolises is to receive freight from poorly developed areas and ship the freight to areas with higher levels of development, (Moonis Raza and Amitabh Kundu 1979; Neera Ramachandran 1979). Thus the metropolises play the role of major distributors and redistributors of economic goods and dominate the primary sector as evidenced by the excess of exports over imports of primary products produced in rural areas. Here, not only the apex cities but also the other million cities participate in the distribution of economic goods, both primary and manufactured (Satyesh Chakraborty 1978). Where the freight consists of high value goods e.g. electronic equipment, handicrafts and warm garments, the mode of transport tends to be air-transport. Bombay, Calcutta, Delhi and Madras dominate in sharing air traffic flows (Das 1977). Distinct from this role of organizing the space-economy, each metropolis has its structural dimension which is changing. In Bombay, during 1962-68, service employment increased faster, by 30 per cent, in contrast to factory employment which increased by 10 per cent (Bombay Municipal Report, 1974). But what is crucial as the lag between the increase in jobs and increase in population. For example, jobs in Calcutta metropolitan district increased by 0.2 million during 1961-71 while population increased by 1.4 million. A significant proportion óf industrial and service sector employment is 'informal' with low wages and cheap raw material. The 'informal' component in both sectors accounts for 82 per cent of establishments and 30 per cent of employment (Sivaramakrishna 1978). It is this component that breeds slums. But metropolises also have an increasing share in quaternary services, innovative industries, shopping complexes, high rise office complexes and super luxury apartments. Here the beneficiaries who belong to high income groups are drawn from the whole nation. This polarized and dual structure is typical of both metropolitan and non-metropolitan cities but it is the scale that becomes important in categorizing the metropolises separately. Ranking next to metropolises are regional cities, market towns, resource towns and service towns with stronger regional and local links with varying structure. These variations are discussed in the next chapter.

APPENDIX A

CENTRAL PLACES IN SOUTHERN GERMANY

Walter Christaller, Translated by C.W. Baskin, Prentice Hall 1966, pp. 140-141

1. Institutions of administration
   - (a) Lower types : Standesamt (marriage, birth and death office in the Rhineland), town police station, Burgermeisterei (mayor's office), Steuererhebestelle (branch office of internal revenue).
   - (b) Middle types : County offices, lowest courts, county tax offices.
   - (c) Higher types : Provincial government, next higher courts, labour offices.
   - (d) Highest types : Central offices of the State Government and the highest court.
2. Institutions of cultural and religious importance
   - (a) Lower (elementary) schools, middle (junior high) schools, public libraries, the seat of the lowest religious administration.
   - (b) High schools, country school administration, and church dekanate (bishop's seat).
   - (c) and (d) University, scientific institutes, state libraries, museums, theatres.
3. Institutions of importance in health and sanitation
   - (a) Physicians, Veterinarians, Dentists.
   - (b) Apothecaries, country doctors, country hospitals.
   - (c) Specialists, scientific institutes, large hospitals, sanitoria.
4. Institutions of social importance
   - (a) Hotels, Cinemas, local newspapers.
   - (b) The above, but of greater importance.
   - (c) Night clubs, stage productions, big newspapers, sports stadia, radio stations.
5. Institutions for the organization of economic and social life
   - (a) Independent artificers, guild, consumer co-operatives local social clubs.
   - (b) Country organizations of the above and also lawyers, notaries public.

(c) State organizations of the above and chambers of commerce, of trade, of agriculture, and of artificers.

6. Institutions of commerce and finance
   (a) Shops of all types, loan offices, warehouses with large inventories (agricultural brokers), weekly markets.
   (b) Special shops, chain stores, consumer co-operatives, savings and loan associations, banks and their branches.
   (c) Department stores, wholesalers, brokers (not agricultural), foreign trade agents and agencies from other German lands, stock exchange, branches of the national bank.
7. Professional institutions
   (a) General carpenters, repair garages, breweries, mills.
   (b) Special carpenters, large bakeries, slaughter houses, gas works, electric (steam) plants.
   (c) The above, but of greater complexity.
8. Importance as a labour market
   Each according to the number and size of the economic activities and the strength of the labour force (i.e. the demand and supply of labour).
9. Institutions of transportation and communication
   (a) Railroad stations, bus terminals, highway intersections, post offices (or more important, post agencies).
   (b) Stops for express trains, railroad junctions, post offices of middle rank, central telephone offices.
   (c) Terminals for express trains, offices of the directors of railroad districts and post office districts.

3

URBAN AND REGIONAL INTERRELATIONSHIPS

THEORETICAL FRAMEWORK

THE CENTRAL PLACE, the Growth Centre and the Diffusion theories provide the theoretical framework for the analysis of Urban and Regional Interrelationships.

The following statements/questions emphasise the need to review these theories in retrospect and prospect.

1. The Central Place Theory is of "relatively residual validity" with increasing incomes, better accessibility and dispersed specialization (Berry 1971). Does this mean that the theory has validity in regions with low level of incomes, inaccessibility and concentrated specialization ? In fact in Christaller's theory, the first requirement is the very character of the region—poor in natural endowment and thinly settled agricultural area which is "most nearly self contained" (Ullman 1941). Thus his central place theory is region-specific.
2. Critical comments on central place theory range from total refutation to complete acceptance of the theory (Munnich, 1974).
3. Do central places form a hierarchy or a continuum ?
4. The postulates of the central place theory (the centralistic principle, reciprocal and functional relationships, population thresholds, and hierarchy) are valid but not its theorems/properties (hexagonal geometry, fixed number of central places and hierarchic levels and

'nesting' following the rules of 3, 4 and 7, physical proximity and homogeneity in population, purchasing power and transport surfaces) (Rushton 1971).

5. With increasing emphasis on efficiency and equity in social services, it is necessary to evaluate the functioning of the existing delivery systems through appropriate Location-Allocation Models (LAM), and suggest alternative location models. In this context, behavioural postulates and locational decision making acquire greater significance than spatial postulates (Location of Services in India Project; Rushton, McNulty, Tewari 1980-82).
6. How to integrate central place theory which is static and deductive with growth centre and diffusion theories which are inductive and dynamic ? The caveats and qualifications in integrating the three theories for Policy Planning and getting insights into economic growth and development process are many, and are still unresolved (Richardson 1973).

Central place theory

The distribution of settlements, ranging from farmstead to metropolis though uneven, is not disorderly. Central place theory hypothesizes this orderly pattern of distribution of settlements (not all types of settlements), and demonstrated its validity with reference to the macro region of Southern Germany in the 1930s. What is often not emphasised is the first requirement, i.e. the very character of the area/region where the theoretical ideal becomes the best fit. Such an area/region is a poor (in natural resource endowment) and thinly settled agricultural area which is "most nearly self contained" (Ullman 1941). Attention to this basic requirement was rightly drawn by Munnich, 1974 : quoting Neef 1950* when he referred to the area specificity of the theory : "Thinly and evenly settled areas with a predominantly agricultural population." Next in importance to region specificity is the central place principle. The fundamental principle of the

*E. Neef. 'Das problem der Zentralen Orte, *Petermanns Geographische Mitteilungen*, 94 (1950).

central place theory is the "centralistic principle". While settlements vary in size, number and functions, the "centralistic principle" is to be sought in the location of economic, social and administrative structures and their visible and not so visible forms of expressions. The principle becomes evident in the location of the settlement with reference to its hinterland, and even in the location and form of structures like church or temple, town hall, school, university, the secretariat in a capital city, and market place within a settlement. Thus the centralistic principle has intra-settlement and inter-settlement i.e. regional dimensions. Regional importance versus local importance and ubiquitous versus non-ubiquitous distribution of services determine the importance of centrality. Centrality (C) is the relative importance of a place or the surplus of its regional importance over its local importance (L) a discrete unit, consuming central goods and services : $C+L=N$ (Nodality). Thus centrality and nodality are distinct but related concepts (Preston 1971). Though it is difficult to measure centrality, in view of the vague and varied notions of central place, centrality is basic to the theory. While in the regions of low level of development and natural resource endowment, geographic centrality, a function of physical proximity acquires significance, in the better developed and better endowed regions, it is the more accessible functional centre which becomes important even with eccentric location. The availability of a surplus good for the complementary area of the central place and the attractiveness of a place for goods and services are the other common measures of centrality. Both surplus and attractiveness are not static and hence centrality itself is not static. Consequently centrality can increase or decrease. An ideal location is one where the geographic centre and the functional centre coincide. But location becomes more complex where "relative" location has more than one attribute e.g. contact zone and frontier locations. A settlement could be central to its catchment area, and yet function as a satellite to a metropolis. What underlies centrality and the centralistic principle are the reciprocal structural and behavioural relationships between central places and their hinterlands which are discrete spatial units. This constitutes the logic of central place theory. The three principles—the market, transport/traffic and administrative (political/administrative separation) which determine the organization of the central place systems are valid even today. The chance of simultaneous operation of the three principles is greater in the lower order central places. The potential value of central place theory got lost mainly because of the emphasis or initially overemphasis, on the theorems—rigidity in the numbers of central places and hierarchic levels with nesting following the rules of 3, 4 and 7, hexagonal geometry, treating hinterlands of central places as closed areas, the role of physical proximity, and the very concept of homogeneity in population distribution, purchasing power and transportation surface, all in a static framework. Locational analysis drawn into locational planning exercises are rightly stressing that the power of the central place theory lies in its concepts/principles and logic, and not in its theorems (Rushton 1971).

That central place theory relates basically to the spatial distribution and optimum location of the tertiary sector leading to a competitive equilibrium over space, and is not able to deal with the dynamics of regional development and with non-uniform economic landscapes like industrial and mining landscapes is repeated and reiterated many times. Wholesale trade has also not been drawn explicitly into central place theory. This does not exclude attempts to introduce a dynamic element into central place theory (Isard 1957). Likewise, border regions are "fragile" in Christaller's scheme as complementary regions are cut up by international frontiers (Hansen 1978). The administrative principle has not received due attention in developing countries with their colonial, political and economic legacies. This principle has probably greater relevance in India where the administrative framework moulds the development patterns to a great extent. If central place theory is considered deficient as a basis for optimum location of non-uniform economic activities, classical location theory of the optimum location of the firm is considered equally deficient, since the theory is concerned basically with the location of the individual production unit as a point location to the exclusion of other related activities (Alonso 1964). Like Christaller, Lösch set himself to the task of explaining why and where towns grow. Like Christaller's basic distinction between urban and rural, Lösch recognized the fundamental cotradiction between agriculture as a production-oriented activity dispersed in space, and industry with its production and processing of industrial goods, concentrated in space. Here, concentration is the consequence of specialization and large scale production. The locus of the industry is the city with its external economies. In Löschian landscape, towns are "punctiform agglomerations of non-agricultural locations". Here production/processing units serve much larger areas. In Löschian system, the structural distinction between towns as producers of industrial goods and consumers of agricultural commodities, and villages as producers of agricultural commodities, and consumers of industrial goods is well maintained. Here is a clue to the advocates of integrated development. But with greater technological mobility and better transport accessibility, industrial units with their links with higher order centres are getting dispersed into villages. Yet the processing function of the industry distinguishes it from production function from the soil of village. Lösch's economic region/landscape is the market area which is a part of a market network. Here, spatial structure includes three main types of economic regions—market areas, regional networks and regional systems. Each regional system has a large town as its centre; every large town is not the centre of a regional system. In the landscape so constructed, there is an equilibrium of locations under certain assumptions. There need not be hierarchical progression of central places and the associated central functions. Spatial organization of the regional economy in a cotton-dominant area for example, is associated with cotton growing farms, cotton gins located in cotton producing areas, a network of presses, oil mills, transport points, collection depots and cotton mills. The flows of raw, processed and semi-processed cotton goods link the rural and urban and yet cannot remove the structural distinction between the village, a part of the production area, and the town with its service and processing function (Lösch 1954). Lösch's postulation of uniform distribution of consuming population with different scales of concentration of industrial activity and employment base at various production centres has been critically commented upon (Isard 1972). The Lösch model like Christaller's model, is static and is also based on unrealistic homogeneous surfaces—population, raw materials, transport, consumer tastes and preferences. In spite of criticisms, the chapters on Christaller's and Lösch's models are not completely closed. The relevance of these models in a revised form, the availability of excess or normal profits to the traders and entrepreneurs, and consumer and producer travel patterns to proximate or farther but higher order locations are being reinterpreted in the context of changing mobility patterns and transport technology, new forms of business and service organizations and policy interventions. The applicability of the central place theoretical framework to intra-city structural analysis of the distribution of the tertiary sector is being reemphasised. The earlier debate on the hierarchic structure—step like or continuum is being revived (Bevon 1977).

Central place theory and regional planning

The validity of central place theory as a guide for regional planning ranges from complete acceptance to total refutation. The central place principles have been used as a guideline for relocation policy, and the Theory was enacted as an integral part of regional planning policy in Germany (Munnich 1974). In the north-eastern Polders, in the initial years, the location of settlements, population size, linkages, hierarchy and allocation of market and service functions were determined by central place principles. Here the land type and land-use and the socio-economic level of the polder community provided the base (Prakasa Rao, 1963). During the initial stage, the polder was not drawn into the metropolitan system of "Randstad". But today the whole polder region/polder community functionally has become a part of "Randstad" regional system. Thus there cannot be one framework to guide the locational and regional planning policy for all time to come, and periodical revision in response to the changing scale and pattern of regional development becomes necessary. With relatively higher population densities, increasing incomes, and with better accessibility, and with centres protecting themselves through product specialization as against protection of distance, as in the developed countries, central place theory has "relatively little residual validity" (Berry, 1971). In the less developed regions like the low population density, hill-forest areas, and endemic drought and dry farming areas, or even in the high population density irrigated agricultural areas which are not yet drawn into the spiral of metropolitan-industrialization, the central place principles provide a rationale for selective location and efficient division of space and functions. Missing elements can be incorporated, new techniques can be developed, more refined data can be collected and processed but the logical construct and the rationale underlying the principles cannot be questioned. Even the nearest centre hypothesis which is being rightly questioned is valid for low income groups for convenience goods of low order (Prakasa Rao, 1976). This is valid in both the developed and less developed regions.

The central place theory has drawn attention to town and country and inter-town interdependence in terms of functional and behavioural dimensions, and the need for rigorous understanding of the principles underlying the locational and functional patterns of settlements in regional and resource settings. With the increasing emphasis on integrated planning, it is being recognized now that the approach to central place analysis should be not only from urban to rural but also from rural to urban (Galpin, Sanderson and Kolb quoted by Johnson, 1970), thus underscoring the sharp urban-rural distinction of the classical and static models. In this context, Galpin's concept of "rurbanism" through a "partnership" between farm-village-rural community—small town becomes most relevant. "Rurbanism" and the associated "social topography" and regional structure are not just the products of rural and urban statistics. The size and structure of "rurban community"—"agro-urban community", is ecologically distinct. The distinctiveness lies in the combination of urban and rural technologies and institutions, and urban/market-oriented rural land-use. As an ideal construct, it has the advantages of both urban and rural; "rurban" is one step in urban-rural continuum. The spectrum is along rural community—village-rurban community—urban fringe—urban community-city. In the "rurban" ecological "interface", settlements develop reciprocal relationships with the local resource base and function as "agro-towns" responding to the urban market and yet also absorb the urban spill over, and provide a commuting and dispersal base for the central city.

It was the search for an approach to analysing the interrelated and hence intricate economy rooted in an urban-industrial base with its more dynamic and heterogeneous surface that led the regional scientists to develop more specific industrial complex analysis as an alternative or as a complement to partial locational analysis, and the more general input-output analysis with its static and unrealistic postulates (e.g. constant production costs and static supply channels) which is also not able to take into account economies of scale and urbanization economies (Isard 1972). Industrial complex analysis also has its limitations and impracticable elements. One view is that production complementarities are overstated, and the scope is limited only to technologically well developed and hence linked industries. There are problems associated with working out projected linkages based on present norms, and in ensuring and sustaining linkages. Thus both industrial complex analysis and input-output analysis raise false hopes (Stuart Holland 1977), if they are applied too blindly and as a substitute for informed judgment, instead of a guide towards judgment.

It is mainly to fill in the gap created by Christaller Lösch models in dealing with dynamic urban-industrial growth that the attention of both regional scientists and planners is drawn to growth pole concept, in turn not without limitations.

Growth Pole concept

The theoretical bases and applications of growth pole concept have been systematically and critically appraised (Applaraju and Safer 1976, Mosely 1974, Misra 1972, Derwent 1969 and Boudeville 1966). It is clear that the 'growth pole' in economic space as a field of forces as enunciated by Perroux (1950) is an aspatial economic concept, while the 'growth centre' concept is spatial and has a location in geographic space. The 'growth pole' when translated to geographic space becomes 'growth centre'. Here, when reference is to locational or spatial arrangement the term 'development' pole is used (Boudeville 1966).

This basic distinction is too often neglected (Derwent 1969). Whether this neglect makes any difference from the operational standpoint is being debated, considering the varied functions that are assigned to growth centres. With the recognition of geographic space, it is necessary to recognize that geographic space is varied—homogeneous, nodal or polarized and planning space/region (Boudeville 1966). Richardson (1973) uses the term programming region. Geographic space is also structured—agglomerative, axial along transport corridors, and dispersed. Mixing up of basic notions and the consequential confusion led to confusion in translating economic space to geographic space. The degree of confusion, sometimes semantic, and ambiguity that surround the growth pole concept are well brought out by tabulating 13 examples from developed and less developed countries (Mosely 1974). Much of the confusion has its roots in—(1) 'the plethora of names and notions' relating to the very terms growth pole and growth centre, (2) variations in regional setting, (3) the structure of growth components, (4) the associated population size ranging from a small town or a large village to a metropolis, (5) hierarchic framework, (6) the scale of agglomeration economies, (7) the power of the centre in promoting and dispersing development, and (8) its promise and potential in developing optimal patterns. Apart from these varied interpretations, it is pointed out that the role of diffusion in development is overemphasized without giving due weight to spatial and structural barriers to development (Gaile 1980). In developing countries, in India particularly, there is a slow diffusion of messages, with a high rate of 'noise' and loss due to 'low level of connectivity with high distance decay', and long networks necessitating information flow through numerous nodes (Blaikie 1976).

Even the role of external economies in localization is overestimated. The possibility in internalization of production economies (product innovation through internal research) is not given due recognition. The relationship between the size of the growth pole and external economies is being questioned (Holland 1977). While interpreting localization and flows, and the role of 'distance friction', the transport cost is emphasized without recognizing that there is a shift from the traditional elements of localization to urbanization and transfer economies (access to urban infra-structure as a whole as a 'gestalt', and market and information fields). It is in the context of these complexities that the relationships between growth pole, growth centre, and central places need to be examined. The central place hierarchy and the normatively derived hierarchy of growth foci cannot be mixed mechanically on the basis of the principle of correspondence (Hermensen 1972).

It is rightly asserted that 'growth pole' needs further conceptual clarification in the context of reinterpretation of the concepts of growth and development, and the new types of growth sectors which are recognized (e.g. an agro-industrial complex, a market complex of first order, a tourist or a religious centre of first order, the quaternary sector particularly the office sector). In all these, the structure, scale, linkages and multipliers differ. The divergence between economic growth and development has become very clear both in the developed and developing countries. Yet the dictum that economic growth cannot take place evenly in geographic space, and growth is highly localized at certain 'epicentres' with different degrees of intensities, spreading differentially in different directions, has not lost its validity totally. Here the scale and structure of the growth sector are important. If the 'development pole', e.g. an industrial city in a lagging region, is unable to diffuse benefits to the adjoining tract, it is because of the tract's incapacity or low capacity to provide the needed linkages and derive benefits. Yet an industrial city, e.g. a steel city, by its very production structure has more technological multipliers than socio-economic multipliers, and by its very capital intensive nature has low labour absorption capacity. Consequently the development impact on the adjacent region is minimal.

Development itself is being redefined, and there is a shift of emphasis even from 'distribution' to 'cultural impact' and capacity to derive benefits from diffusion (Seers 1978). The essence of development, economic or social or both, is related mainly to the benefits to the present generation. This is a shortsighted view in the context of conservation of natural resources and integrated natural resource use particularly in the hill forest areas, watershed regions and endemic areas for natural hazards. Such regions need more service centres and intermediate level growth centres and not primate cities or industrial complexes except where resource potentials justify and national strategy demands. Then there are different categories of growth centres—rural service centres, agro-towns, market cities, industrial complexes and metropolitan complexes. While the notion of polarized development underlies the industrial and metropolitan complexes, the notion of dispersed development underlies the market cities and service centres. 'Dispersed concentration' or 'decentralized concentrated dispersion' is yet another pattern of the process of economic growth (Richardson). In this spectrum of development and settlement types, while a hierarchy exists, what form it takes in future-a-multi-tier, primate or 'binary'—will depend on the future development strategies, patterns of development and population growth.

With the multiplication of the categories of growth foci, it becomes more difficult to apply Perroux's and Boudeville's concepts and consequently get insights into the structure and process of development and evolution of settlement hierarchies. It must be recognised that if central place theory is a partial theory of "spatial and static equilibrium", growth pole theory is a conditional theory of regional growth relevant only to certain regions and certain sectors. Even the hierarchical diffusion model of Berry cannot capture the intricate linkage patterns in national urban systems (Hansen 1967 and 1978). But then models are selective, quite deliberately concentrating on what seem to be crucial variables in a particular context. They may be heuristic devices, to add to understanding and may or may not be capable of operational functions.

The growth centre project*

With increasing concern to ensure minimum welfare to population at least through improving accessibility to basic goods and services keeping equity and efficiency criteria in focus, the

*This section is drawn extensively from: (1) The Pilot Research Project in Growth Centres : Second progress report, 1972, and (2) Fisher and Rushton's paper in 'Man, Culture and Settlement'.

Fourth Five Year Plan initiated a "Pilot Research Project" in growth centres in 1972. Forty 'blocks' located in different regions of the country were selected for study. This gave official sanction as it were to formulate growth-centre strategies for optimal organization of services in space. The pilot project had its roots in the experience gained in the earlier Community Development Projects begun in 1951, mainly to develop a community approach in overall developmental work in the villages. In this effort, plans for functional integration between different sectors—education, transport and markets did not succeed, evidently because of uncoordinated and independent implementation of programmes by each sector. The growth centre strategy was designed to help the Indian Planning Process from the grass roots i.e. from the level of villages, blocks and districts. Growth centres were treated as service centres in the lower orders of the settlement hierarchy. The social service function is largely a welfare function at least in the initial stages of development. The moment the growth centres—the small towns and large villages—are expected to function as development nuclei for future socio-economic development of their respective hinterlands, the confusion starts, and the problem becomes more complex. The growth centre project recommended three steps—(1) general service centre plan, (2) sectoral development plan for education and industries, and (3) an integrated plan reconciling (1) and (2). In the settlement hierarchic system, the identified growth centres were expected to bridge the functional gap between the district level towns and individual villages (Fisher and Rushton 1977).

The main thrust of the whole project was to work out an optimal locational pattern (arrangement in space) of service facilities and related investments. Such a pattern was considered as important as the quantum and quality of services. In the exercise on allocation of scarce resources, due weightage was given not only to the conceptual framework central place, growth/development pole, multi-level planning—but also to appropriate methods for allocation to specific places to maximize the impact equitably and efficiently.

It would have been highly rewarding and illuminating if the empirical results for all the blocks had been available within a comparative and regional framework. Differences in regional setting, landscape structure and levels of development would have given a valuable insight and guidance in evaluating the significance of distance friction. The same 10 km. average distance and 40 km. maximum distance for the same service mean different things in different landscapes e.g. the inaccessible hill-forest landscapes with largely immobile tribals at one end and the most accessible and highly commercialized agricultural landscapes with most mobile progressive cultivators at the other end. In a plural structure society, there is a case for multiple distance standards with critical distance ranges. The distance factor tends to become rigid for the low income groups while its flexibility increases with increasing incomes. In the developed regions and the regions of rapid development, the intervening service centres get bypassed if they are located in the urban fields of larger cities.

The contribution of the Pilot Project lies primarily in working out appropriate methodology to select locations for investments to develop service facilities. The development of methodology was the main assignment given to the project. There is a shift from searching for spatial and geometrical characteristics of the settlement system to the development of appropriate methodology to suggest alternative locations. While it is necessary to maintain a balance between the power of theory, of the empirical base and methodology, given the first two, appropriate methodology has a crucial role to play. The locational efficiency of spatial organization of the different service systems can be tested by Location Allocation Models (LAM), which would allow the translation of central place theory into applied analytical models for different socio-economic contexts (McNulty and Rushton 1980).

Junagadh experiment

The main purpose of this experiment was to evaluate the location patterns of services in one district of Gujarat, the Junagadh district, and attempt to quantify the resulting savings from the adoption of modern methods of identification of optimal locations and allocation of services to those locations, and also to work out the cost of not planning. Agreeing that every method has its advantages and disadvantages be it graphical or by computer it was recommended that computer methods could be used primarily in the refinement of manual methods, and also as a supplement in evaluating the existing locations and deriving optimal locations.* Very rightly, the limitations of merely visual map analysis for identifying inefficient location patterns were indicated.

The Table 3.1 summarizes the results of the locational efficiency of six selected services. Efficiency is found to be maximal or inefficiency to be minimal in the location pattern of police stations and block headquarters. Locational inefficiency is maximal in the case of banks and posts and telegraphs as measured by the longer distances travelled than the optimal

TABLE 3.1 : **Integrated rural area planning in India—Spatial efficiency of selected services in the Junagadh District.**

Facility	Distance in Kilometres				Per cent inefficiency of existing averages[2]
	Existing		Optimal		
	Max.	Average	Max.[1]	Average	
1	2	3	4	5	6
Banks	40.7	6.77	22.70	4.75	42.25
Police Station	36.20	7.55	30.50	6.89	9.6
Block Headquarters	40.7	9.78	34.20	9.35	4.6
Posts and Telegraphs	40.7	7.45	26.40	5.04	47.5
Vet. Dispensary	43.1	12.46	45.10	11.21	11.2
Hospitals	42.4	14.55	45.10	12.00	21.00

1. These are maximum distances implied by optimal average distances, not optimal maxima (though these maxima could be found using the same computer programme).
2. $\text{Col. } 6 = \frac{\text{Col. } 3 - \text{Col. } 5}{\text{Col. } 5}$

Source : Fisher and Rushton.

ones and hence desirable distances. The range of locational inefficiency in the district is high, varying from 4.6 (Block headquarters) to 47.5 (Posts and Telegraphs). These specifications provide a more accurate basis for working out the costs of

*For details of these methods, refer to P. Roy and B.R. Patil (eds.) 1977, *Manual for Block Level Planning*. The Macmillan Co. Ltd., Delhi.

provision of services within specified distance and cost norms, and also working out priorities. These results need to be recast taking into account the functional hierarchic structure of settlements, clustering patterns of services travel behaviour patterns and organizational patterns within the overall development patterns of the district within the development framework of the state and the nation.

Both in developed and developing countries, there are still more unknowns than knowns in understanding the process of development. The achievement of growth centre strategies even in advanced economies is 'far from impressive'. Many of the assumptions concerning growth transmission and hierarchical diffusion are mistaken, and in some cases are even inaccurate. It is not enough to know the flow patterns. To understand the structure of the links, it is necessary to identify the most significant propagators of flows—goods, services, capital and information (Pred 1976). On the theoretical front "there are many caveats and qualifications in any exercise in integrating central place theory, growth pole theory and diffusion theory with policy implications" (Richardson 1973). A further complication is the fact that new dimensions are becoming important e.g. the role of organizational links, decision making and locational preferences in development. If a five-year period is too short for a growth centre to pay off as a policy instrument, a 15 to 25-year period time horizon as emphasized by Richardson (1976) is too long. In a country like India, natural and political hazards and the very population growth are powerful enough to lead to policy failure over such a period.

While such is the state of the art relating to the theoretical framework for integrating urban and regional dimensions, it is necessary to seek insights into the structure of urban regions and the interrelationships between urban structure and regional structure. This is attempted in the following sections.

Urban Rural interface

The sharp division between urban (town/city) and rural (farmstead/village) is becoming increasingly less and less perceptible today with the development of technology, transport and communication systems. With the urbanization of the countryside and ruralization of the towns, the spread of "suburbia", and the growth of 'rurban' settlements and suburban villages, it is becoming difficult to draw the boundary where the 'urban' stops and the 'rural' begins. Thus a "Rural-urban Continuum" is tending to emerge, but more in the post-industrial countries/ regions than in the pre-industrial countries/regions and the "third world".

The contacts between the town and the country are varied and are getting multiplied and are both direct (commuting and wholesale and retail trade) and indirect (e.g. radio and newspapers, and also policy making). These urban to rural and rural to urban contacts involving the movement of people, goods and services are in the form of ebb and flow, or perhaps crest and trough. There is action and reaction and interaction between urban and rural. It is the intensity of urban-rural interaction that determines the pattern of continuum or dichotomy in land-use and occupational structure, distance friction, demographic characteristics, life styles, and neighbourhood social and political attitudes. Thus the interacting components are physical, economic, social and political and there are distinct regional patterns.

The principle that the city is the product of its region, and the region is served and transformed by its city, illustrates the reciprocal and dynamic nature of relationships between the city and its region. It is this reciprocality that constitutes the logic of central place theory and integrates urban centres with the region. This principle of city and regional relationships can be also restated as : "the region creates the city, and is recreated by the city". This is the basic principle of urban-regionalization, where urban influence is both centripetal and centrifugal. Both urban and regional structures are changing, and constitute a set of interrelated sub-systems nesting in an upward hierarchic manner from the lowest order sub-system to the national system.

In developing countries like India, not only the urban-rural distinction but also urban-rural dualism persists that is, in a sense there are two nations and regional types of urban-rural interrelationships which are highly varied, consequent upon the sharp regional variations in the levels of socio-economic development, urban infra-structure, resource endowments, and population densities.

Metropolitan regions and the lagging rural regions are the two polar ends of the urban-rural regional profile. The intensity and pattern of urban-rural relationships vary in different regions with different levels of development. In the developed countries, the urban-rural profile takes the form of a tidal wave (Wolfe 1969) in which the rural is stamped by the urban or an integrated and fused metropolitan core and inter-metropolitan periphery (Friedmann and Miller 1965). In developing countries like India, the profile is characterized by dichotomy and crest and trough. The metropolitan cities stand out as peaks with high population densities and 'population potentials' in the expansive sea of low levels of development. As a consequence of both planned and unplanned physical sprawl of the rapidly growing cities and city fringes, and the increasing interaction between the city and its adjoining rural areas due to changing patterns of development and extension of transport and communication networks, the urban-rural interaction profiles are changing. Urban gradients are sharp, and also show a sharp break. There is a distance decay in the interaction patterns also in the metropolitan regions. The metropolitan cities, particularly the million-cities, have distinct city fringes, a transitional zone, and an 'ecotone', a zone of conflict mainly in land-use and administration. The city fringe has the maximum intensity of interaction with the city but there are inaccessible and isolated pockets of low development in the interstitial areas away from the developing corridors, and yet located near the city boundary.

All urban centres do not have urban fringes and cannot develop hinterlands. Project construction and mining towns cannot develop hinterlands as they do not serve as focal centres to their surrounding areas and get served by them. An irrigation project or a mining town even with a population size of the order of 80,000, with 70 per cent as labour and transient service sector, and in spite of acting as a service centre for its surrounding area cannot develop a hinterland. Here the service function of a town for its hinterland needs to be distinguished from reciprocal socio-economic relations between the town and its region. In contrast, a market city of the same population size develops a distinct hinterland. Urban hinterland P differ in extent, structure and intensity of interaction, all the three being related to population size, function and situation of the regional urban centre.

The city-region

The concept of the city-region which is recognised as a world-wide phenomenon, has its roots in the very complementary relationships between the city and its region.* The city region differs in extent, structure, and intensity, all three being related to the population size, functional scale and the city's situation as a regional centre. The terms—the city fringe, the city edge, the city periphery, near the city, the city outskirts, the city's environs, the city's adjoining area are interchangeably used. Planning area, Conurbation Area, Metropolitan Area, Standard Urban Area are delimited to accommodate the sprawling city and the future growth of the fringe, and for area notification for land-use controls and zoning. The metropolis provides commercial, educational, medical and cultural services to its region. In turn, the city region supplies the daily consumption needs e.g. milk, fruits, vegetables, fuel etc. to the metropolis. In addition, the city region, is the potential area for the spillover from the metropolis and for the location of industries and sub-metropolitan centres in a predominantly rural environment. The city region of a metropolis has a definite structure—the urban tract, the inner built-up area, the core, the intermediate zone; the periphery; the fringe and the rural periphery. With rapid developments in transport and communication technology, the 'urban realm', consisting of different "groups of people communicating with each other through space", seems to be taking the place of the city-region. Here the shift is from a place framework to a "non-place" framework of city growth, like organizational and administrative aspects (quoted by Wise, 1966). The many and changing approaches to the city-region concept can be noted as: a built-up physical plan, bound together by transport net;

*"The most conspicuous contributions of geographers to the study of cities do not lie in explaining sites and growth, however, but in putting the city into its regional setting" and mapping, measuring and analysing the city-regional relationships (Emrys Jones, 1970).

an economic region with increasing area and functional specialization; as a society, bound together by common interests; a working system of central places;—a complex of functions rather than a constellation of places; a region of continuing change with inflow and outflow of people; an outward-moving fringe with communities interlinked to the city economically and socially (Wise, 1966). There are different views on the zonation of the fringe. One view is that the fringe has no definite structure (Gist and Fave, 1965). In contrast to this, the fringe is identified as a distinct interface of urban and rural traits (Kirk, 1975), a zone of transition and rapid change and transformation (Wherein, 1942; Andrews, 1942), a marginal zone in rural and urban land-uses and urban accessibility (Fiery, 1946), and an interpenetrating zone of urban and rural land-uses (Kurtz and Eicher, 1958).

The city-region in India

The need to adopt a regional strategy for city development has been recognized and the State Governments through their respective Directorates of Town Planning delineated metropolitan development areas which included the metropolitan city and its surrounding area. These areas have been officially designated as urban or metropolitan development areas under independent authorities. The rapidly industrializing cities also have drawn surrounding areas into their legal jurisdiction by extending their city limits and by 'area notification'. For census tabulations also, agglomerations adjoining a city and the adjoining interdependent rural areas are delineated as urban agglomerations and Standard Urban Areas (SUA). But the SUA has not gained official or academic recognition. City-regions have been delineated and studied for metropolitan and market cities in the country by various scholars both for understanding of the city-regional structure and form, and to provide a regional base for formulating city-regional development strategies.

Some of the studies are reviewed in the following section.

Comparative study of city regions (Ellefsen 1962)

The complexity of the structure of the city-region and urban-rural relationships along the regional profile from the city through its fringe and the adjoining rural area into the peripheral rural area is brought out by a comparative study of five cities—Delhi, Madras, Hyderabad, Bombay and Baroda. The impact of the city on its region is inferred from the responsiveness of selected characteristics—population density, sex-ratio, literacy, concentration of non-agricultural population and population dependence on commerce in particular, accessibility to the city, and increasing distance from the city. The intensity of urban impact on the region is related primarily to the degree of accessibility to the city, which is found to be even more important than increasing distance. The sharpness of the gradients (rate of decline from the city) is taken as an index of the degree of impact and this is found to differ from city to city depending upon its functional scale. Yet there is an overall pattern of distance decay. In this analysis, a distinction is made between urban-rural inter-dependence along the accessible axial routes, a two-way channel (one characteristic of the Western city though the degree of influence and the structure differ), and urban impact on the villages adjacent to the routes through rural responsiveness, and finally the isolated interstitial villages, remote from the urban path. Thus accessibility to the city is a key factor in urban impact, though possibly in terms of accessibility rather than distance as the crow flies. If the adjoining rural areas are not drawn into the diffusion of some of the urban social and credit services, it is more because of the existence of traditional/indigenous forms—medicine, finance and trading—which act as deterrents than the lack of rural responsiveness. Literacy, population engaged in commercial sector, and other non-agricultural occupations which reflect the urban impact and the associated way of life, all show a sharp break in gradient at the city's edge, which is a transitional zone. The urban-rural profile from the city takes the form of a four-tier zonation—"the suburban wards, the fringe belt, the ribbon belts and the interstitial villages". The 'city fringe' is small in extent, and the development of urban land-uses and retail trade structure is "small and sporadic". Both the fringe and the nearby and even far off rural areas are loosely linked, and consist of 'single factor regions' e.g. producing food, milk, vegetables, fruits and flowers for the urban market.

Madras city region (Hyma 1971)

A structurally differentiated three-tier zonation of the city fringe is identified for Madras—(i) the urban fringe; (ii) the urban shadow zone, the intermediate zone, and (iii) the outer rural fringe. The compactness and the contiguity of the fringe is broken by the axial or ribbon belts—the corridors along the converging roads and railways. The major corridors are the north, west and south-west, likened to three spines of a star shaped city. The axial belts and interstitial areas cut through the three tiers, outwards from the city boundary, but with decreasing intensity. The inner fringe has 12 villages, and 11 villages are adjoining the three corridors of growth; 3 large villages with a population varying from 5,000 to 8,000, and 9 suburban towns with a population varying from 15,000 to 37,000. This is the most intense commuting zone by mass-transit trains and buses, and is urbanized both in terms of land-use and employment. Areal differentials between urban land-uses and industrial land-uses are not well marked; rural land with almost disappearing rural land-uses is dominant in the zone. This zone lies well within the city's postal service zone.

The intermediate zone with 53 villages is characterised as the region where urban pressures for conversion of rural areas are increasing and this is contributing to land sub-division for land speculation. The corridor-interstitial pattern continues with high concentration of non-agricultural occupation. This is also the zone of varied administrative units—municipal and panchayat towns, cantonments and rural panchayats, pressing for their respective development claims in different directions.

The outer rural fringe, the third tier with 58 villages, is more rural than urban, and the population size of villages varies from 200 to 2,000, and is mainly interstitial with dominant rural areas. This is the zone of declining agriculture, low intensity of urban impact, and increasing growth of non-agricultural population mainly in retail and wholesale trade. Factory locations are highly scattered.

Hyderabad city region (Alam and Khan, 1972)

The metropolitan region of Hyderabad extending to a radius of 40 miles from the central city has a distinct zonal structure—the metropolitan core, the peri-urban zone and the rural hinterland. The metropolitan core, extending within a radius of 6 to 8 miles from the city core, is a zone of high population density (1,000 per square mile), and the town groups are located in this zone. There is concentration of fruits and vegetables in this zone. Here, urban development is dominant. Extending to a radius of 16 miles lies the peri-urban zone with its axial development and high population density along the highways and the interstitial areas with multiple cropping of commercial crops dominating. The rural hinterland, with low density of population (300 per square mile) and with mainly food crops dominating the cropping pattern, extends up to 40 miles radius. In this low population density zone are located islands of multiple cropping and dairying with higher population densities, an evidence of the extension of the metropolitan impact on the outer peripheral-rural areas. This is also the zone of pastoral and forest areas. The region within a radius of 40 miles from the central city is designated as the region of "Metropolitan Dominance".

Based on correlation analysis of population growth (1951-61), percentage of non-agricultural workers to total workers (1961) and population density per square mile (1961) on the basis of six 5-miles circular belts around the city, and using the Mahalanobis Distance Function to establish the city's influence through the above mentioned variables, the zone of maximum impact, i.e. 5-10 miles was delimited. The zone of 10-20 miles was identified as one having greater impact than the zones 20-25 miles and 25-30 miles, but lesser impact than the zone of 5-10 miles. Location of public sector and private sector industries, residential layouts and educational institutions, and fruits and vegetable supply areas (localized in relatively more fertile areas), pull the city's area of influence along the converging State and National highways and also into the adjoining interstitial areas. As a result, there is an unequal corridor and isolated interstitial growth in different directions (Directorate of Town Planning, Hyderabad, 1972).

Delhi metropolitan region (Nangia 1976)

The region with maximum impact of the city is limited to an average distance range from 7 miles to 18 miles from the city centre (old Delhi railway station). These distance limits are really the inner and the outer limits of the "boundary girdle bunch". The axial routes—corridors of 4-mile bands along the converging transport routes from Delhi to Ghaziabad (east), Sonepat (north-west), and Faridabad (south-east) extend the zones of influence with a two-way urban-rural interaction. The city area i.e. the built-up area and the adjoining rural area within the city's legal limits, partially or totally swallowed by the city, the urban fringe, the zone of maximum commuting to the city, and the rural periphery constitute the three distinct structural zones. The corridors cut across the fringe and the rural periphery. There is a distance decay with sharp breaks, in both structural patterns and intensity of interaction through daily commuting and flow of goods and services.

Urban villages, large in population size (an average of about 2,500), high growth rate (60% 1951-61), higher population densities (1,800 per square mile 1961) and imbalance in sex ratio (827 females per 1000 miles 1961), and at least a 25 per cent of the population engaged in agriculture, characterize the rural area within the legal city limits. This is also the zone of high tertiary activity (57%), particularly trade, commerce and transport. The urban fringe extending unequally between 7 miles and 18 miles from the city centre, with sharp axial-interstitial dichotomy is the zone of industrial and commercial sectors, industrial estates, airport, sewage and pumping stations, transport terminals, milk collecting centres, and recreational spots. It is in this fringe that some of the villages have acquired the status of towns owing to industrial location. This is also the zone of fast developing urban market-oriented agriculture. High growth, larger population size, high population density, greater imbalance in sex ratio are the characteristics of the axial belts : the corridors with a distance decay pattern. This is the zone of maximum axial and interstitial urban-rural dichotomy. The rural periphery, adjoining the urban fringe is interspersed with pockets of urban settlements in the midst of rural tracts with 70 per cent of the population in agriculture and where a number of villages have shown a negative growth (1951-61). The sex-ratio is higher compared with the city area and the fringe. The axial belt-interstitial dichotomy is less distinct in this zone.

Bangalore city region (Prakasa Rao and Tewari 1979) (Fig. 3.1) Within a radius of 4 miles from the city centre (Vidhanasoudha) lies the zone of highest concentration of non-agricultural population. The national highways and the major roads extend the areas of high concentration of non-agricultural population, and also high population growth (1961-71), e.g. the Bangalore-Madras highway and Bangalore-Tumkur highway. In the first and the second two-mile bands surrounding the city-corporation

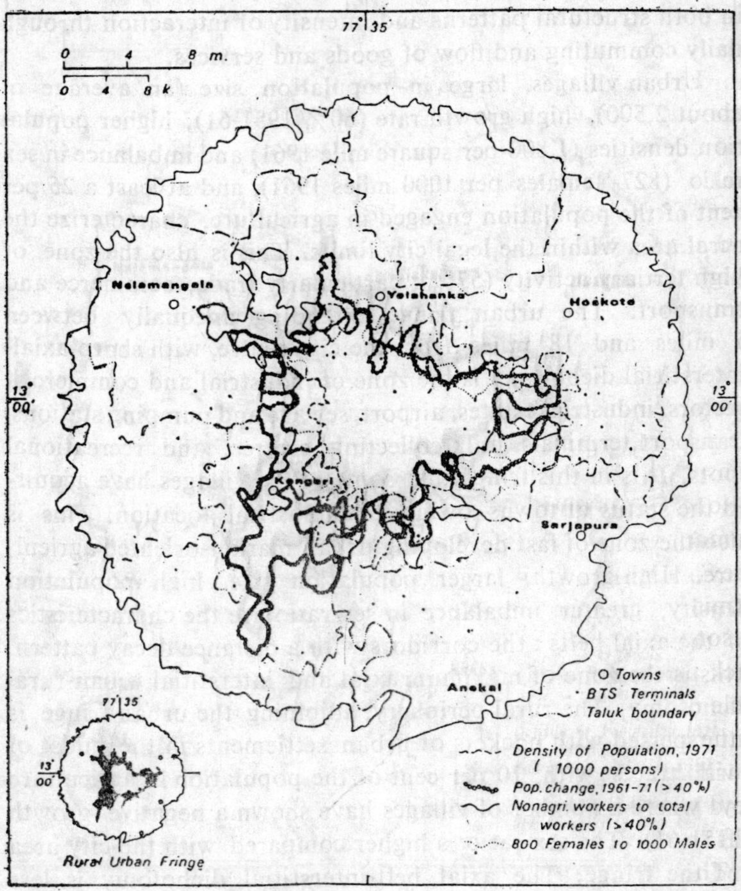

FIG. 3.1 : *Boundary Girdle—Bangalore city region*

boundary lie dispersed concentrations of fruits and vegetables, localized in first class agricultural lands and near perennial sources of water supply. The ratio of non-agricultural population to agricultural population and the percentage of the area under fruits and vegetables to total cultivated area are the most correlated variables in the two sets (population and land-use) with all other variables. There is distance decay in the concentration of non-agricultural population and fruits and vegetables. In contrast, the area under forests, permanent pastures and miscellaneous trees increases with distance.

It is in the first four-mile zone, and along and adjoining the axial belts, that land-use structure and patterns are changing. Land-use in the first class agricultural lands is becoming more intensive, and cultivation is extending into second class lands. Marginal lands are being used for construction activity and brick kilns, in response to the expanding built-up area. Fields where formerly dry crops such as ragi and horsegram were grown are now growing tomatoes, carrots, french beans and cauliflower for the city market. Farmers are preferring hybrid maize, paddy, irrigated ragi, chillies and mulberry, using modern methods of cultivation, discarding old methods. In contrast to this change, there is stability in betel-vine culture with its inherited and tradition-bound cultivation practices and attitudes, a carry-over through many decades. But on the marketing front, betel-vines are transported using modern transport and cold storage systems. The export market, both national and international, is expanding. Areca-nut, coconut, plantain and ginger are the crops grown along with betel-vine. The shift from grain farming to horticulture and vegetables farming has brought about a marked re-adjustment of the seasonal workload of the farmers. The earlier alternation of slack period with peak period of work in the farmers' work cycle is now giving place to around-the-year work cycle. Many of the agriculturists interviewed were keenly aware of their loss of village labour to city-oriented occupations, and felt that they had enough work in the field, and there was no need to shift to the city for jobs (Rukmini Srinivas, 1981).

The commuters' zone with maximum number of commuters is limited to a radius of 4-5 miles from the city centre. The frequency of buses shows a distance decay pattern. The exceptions are those relating to the bus frequencies to industries and technical institutions located in the city fringe. Both the boundary girdles and the distance-decay girdles of population and land-use variables indicate four critical distance zones in the city-region; 8-9, 9-14, 14-18 and 18-29 miles from the city centre. The zone of overlaps extends from 8 to 12 miles from the city centre. The adjoining zone of 2-3 miles from the corporation boundary is the zone of high urban intensity. A limit of 10-15 miles is set to locate the satellite or industrial townships.

Market city region (Parvathi, 1977) (Fig. 3.2)

Pollachi, a medium size town with a population of 68,700 (1971), located in an irrigation command area, develops a

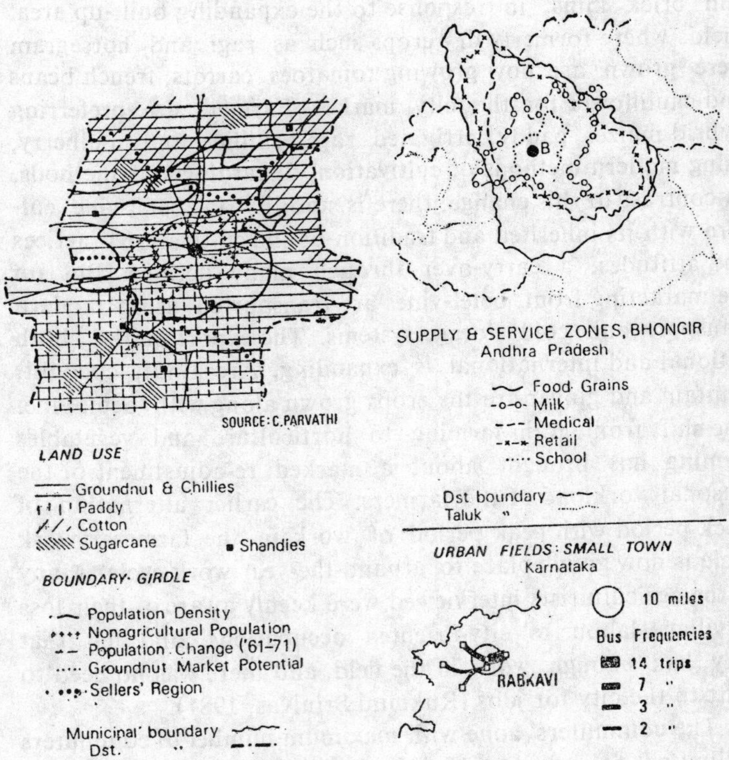

FIG. 3.2 : *Market regions and urban fields*

distinct "market city-region" both in structure and form. This market town is essentially a groundnut town located in the core area of groundnut production. The total quantum of market arrivals is of the order of 1,00,000 tonnes per annum. Pollachi is a collection and distribution centre for the Annamalai forest and plantation area, and is also a service centre of a higher order to the Annamalai area. The location of the town has triple attributes—(i) nodality, (ii) contact zone location between the forest and plantation region and the millet and oil seed zone of the Coimbatore plateau, and (iii) inter-state border location between Kerala and Tamil Nadu. In terms of "relative location" with reference to the other adjoining market centres, Pollachi is located in the "shadow zone" of Coimbatore, while two market centres are located in the shadow zone of Pollachi itself. It is difficult to fit such a complex location point into the geometry of classical or even modified central place theory.

Pollachi has its firm roots in its "shandy" (weekly market), which is the "image" of the town. The intense trade area of the shandy is limited to a radius of 15 miles, the bullock-cart distance zone. The boundary girdles of rural population density, percentage of non-agricultural to agricultural population, rural population growth 1961-71 and the "market potential" of groundnut delimit the market region. The city master-plan boundary also inter-weaves with the boundary girdles. The isopleth values bring out the gradient character and intensity. While the distance decay continues up to 12 miles from the city centre, the limit of the market region could be fixed at 6 to 8 miles. It is within the distance zone of 2 to 4 miles that there are a number of industrial villages where industries are established by the Pollachi entrepreneurs. In one village, the industrial land-use is as high as 46 per cent of the total geographical area. In this village, a textile mill is located with a small colony of mill workers. Some workers and staff also commute from Pollachi to the industrial villages, "reverse commuting". There is a high concentration of non-agricultural population (68%) within a radius of 4 miles. Here is the first step toward industrialization of the countryside in the vicinity of a market town. Super, imposed on this market region is the zone of "rural commuters" to Pollachi for multiple purposes.

This zone extends up to a radius of 20 miles. The plantation villages are linked through 34 buses. The regional city of Coimbatore, located within half an hour travel time is linked by 106 buses per day.

What is often not explicitly recognised in delimiting a market region is its relation to both sellers and buyers engaged in trading, which constitutes its very urban-economic basis. The terms "sellers region" and "buyers space" at once reveal the bounded nature of the former, constrained mainly by proximity/distance to market and the open-ended nature of the latter, where proximity/distance has lost its significance. In the "sellers region", 80 out of 130 villages in different distance zones send their produce to Pollachi market. Petty traders walk or cycle (1 to 6 miles). The 1969 traffic census revealed that 12,066 bullock-carts carted produce to the market during the peak season and 1,212 carts during the normal season. The bullock-cart is the main mode of transport within a distance of 10 to 15 miles, and tampo a new mode, is used within 16 to 18 miles. The small scale of the load transported and short distance are not economical for lorry transport. This "sellers region" is the supply hinterland, with the villages as the supply areas.

Unlike the "sellers region", the "buyers space" is structured by outward movement of goods from Pollachi to multiple centres which are consuming and also redistributing centres—Erode, Salem and Bangalore. The ports on the west coast (Cochin) and the east coast (Madras) act as terminal markets from where goods are exported in semi-processed or fully processed form. "Buyers space" is unbounded and more unstable, yet functionally better organized and integrated through market organization and transport and communication networks. The regional and extra-regional links are controlled and operated by brokers, commission agents, wholesale traders, processors, banks, export firms and lorry companies. The "buyers space" of Pollachi extends up to Delhi, Rohtak, Bombay, Cochin, Madras and Calcutta. Thus the market region of Pollachi has developed from not only local and regional production base but also from extra-regional links.

The market channel linking the rural (producers) and urban (consumers) takes the form of a "spindle" with producers and consumers/exporters at the opposite ends of the spindle (Fig. 3.3). The functionaries and processing units are at the middle. The channel structure linking rural and urban is multiple with a number of overlaps and interfaces between production-market systems, functionaries and processing units and consumers/exporters. The length of the channel, the distance to the consuming centre, and the size and structure of processing units are related to the nature of the commodity e.g. cotton, groundnut, turmeric, coffee, cholam or tomato to mention a few. The channel structure is simple in the case of cholam, and complex in the case of commodities like cotton or groundnut or turmeric. The market channel of the plantation crops (e.g. coffee) is equally complex but is better organized with cooperatives, pooling agents, and a marketing board, and the links are more national and international. Here inter-city links are more important than urban-rural links. The settlement hierarchic levels also differ for different commodities. Cotton has four levels (village market, agro-town, market town, market city) while turmeric a more localized and more institutionalized market crop has only two levels (market town and market city). The differences in levels are related to differences in viability as a bulking point.

The channel structure consists of producers, village markets, shandies, mandies, regulated markets—cooperative societies, petty traders, commercial agents, brokers, decorticators (in the case of groundnut), wholesalers, retailers and consumers and exporters. The linkage pattern is illustrated in the flow chart (Fig. 3.3). There is duplication of functions, and institutional linkage between the rural producer and the urban consumer is partial or weak. This results in intermediaries stepping in and capturing a larger share of the price spread through a higher margin. In the price of tomatoes, where the market margin is not high, the share of the intermediaries is 50 per cent compared to the 29 per cent share of the farmers. In contrast to this, in cooperative supermarkets the farmer's share is 80 per cent compared to 9 per cent to intermediaries.*

**Source*: An economic enquiry into the problems of production and marketing of Tomatoes in CBE Tract, Dept. of Agricultural Economies, Tamil Nadu Agricultural Unit, Coimbatore, 1974.

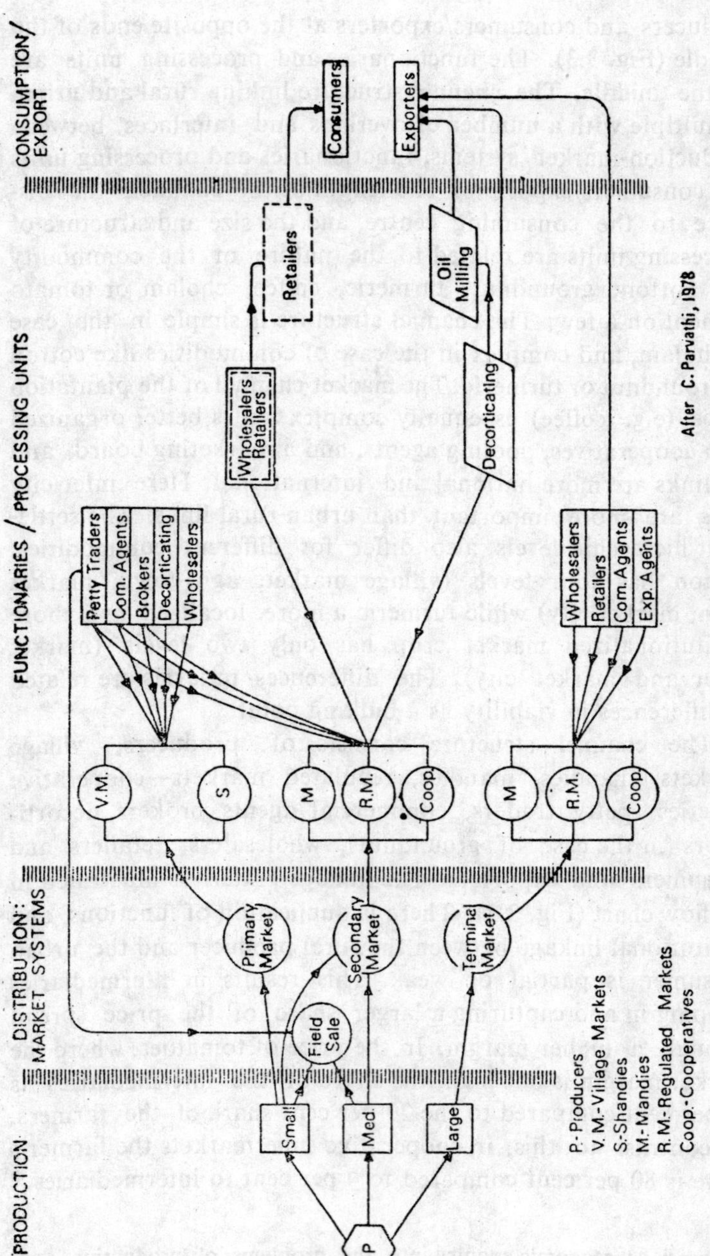

FIG. 3.3: *Market systems and channels—Groundnuts*

With the increasing complexity of the market channels as in the case of cotton or groundnut, wasteful duplication of functions between different functionaries increases the role of intermediaries, and consequently their margins.

It must be emphasized here that the structure of the market channel and through it, the rural-urban links are ever-changing particularly in regions with higher levels of agricultural development. Modern communications, innovative market systems, higher order central functions in lower order central places on selected days and multipurpose trips leap-frogging intervening central places of lower order, all modify the functional spatial systems.

The above review brings out that variables selected in regional delineation, and the very terminology used for different zones within the city region varied (Table 3.2). Methods of delineation also differed. There is nothing even approaching standardization. Consequently the sensitivity of the zonal structure, number of zones and the extent of the zone of metropolitan impact are not comparable. One common result that has emerged is that the metropolitan city is developing a fringe, a transitional zone, and a zone of both urban-rural conflict and interdependence. Both in structure and form, the market city-region differs from that of the metropolitan city region. It is the accessibility to the city which is the key factor in the spread of urban impact, and not the distance factor. There is an overall distance decay in the intensity of urban impact but with axial and interstitial urban-rural dichotomy, which is sharper in the case of metropolitan cities.

Urban structure and regional structure

Resource towns provide the best examples where urban structure and regional structure are interrelated, and one reflects the other. The town's functions are more oriented to its region than to its neighbouring larger city. Cotton towns, sugar towns, tobacco towns, spice towns and coffee towns are the best examples to mention a few.*

*Like Bydgi, Haveri (Chillies); Mercara (Coffee); Sirsi, Yellapur (arecanut/pepper); Mandya (sugarcane); Arisikere (coconut); Nippani (tobacco); Gadag-Betegiri (all these towns are in Karnataka State).

TABLE 3.2 : City region—Zonation

Zonation	Variables
1. Delhi-Madras-Hyderabad-Bombay-Baroda: (Ellefsen 1962)	
1. The City	
(a) Inner wards	Population density
(b) Sub-urban wards	Non-agricultural occupation
2. Belt Sector	Literacy
3. Ribbon Sector	Sex ratio
4. Secondary roads Sector	Commerce
5. Interstitial village sector	
2. Madras (Hyma 1971)	
1. The City	Urban land-use
2. Urban Fringe	Vacant land
3. Urban shadow zone	Residential land
4. Rural Fringe	Decline in agriculture
	Land sub-division
	Factory location and employment
	Non-agricultural workers: 75%
	Squatter settlements
	Daily bus service
	Telephone links in villages
	Postal services and administrative status of settlements.
3. Hyderabad (Alam and Khan 1972)	
1. The metropolitan core; radius of 6 to 8 miles from the city core.	Daily Newspapers University Education
2. The peri-urban zone radius of 16 miles	Regional accessibility and Traffic-shed.
3. The rural hinterland radius of 40 miles	Frequency of bus services
	Traffic flow and Trafficshed (Bus and Train)
	Supply zone of vegetables
	Milk supply
	Supply of fruits
	Grape cultivation
4. Delhi (Nangia 1976)	Density of rural settlements per 100 square miles
1. The City	Average population

TABLE 3.2—*contd.*

Zonation	Variables
2. The Rural-Urban Fringe 7-18 miles from the city	Size of settlement Population growth rate 1951-61
3. The Peripheral rural area	Occupational structure: Primary, secondary, tertiary Population Density Sex ratio Location of distinct Fringe uses like airports industrial estates, and sewage network and pumping stations, Bus service frequency, postal delivery zones.
5. Bangalore (R.L. Singh 1964)	
1. "Primary umland" including the city	Vegetable supply Milk supply
2. "Secondary umland" covering medical and newspaper zones	Bus service: passenger traffic Medical service Newspaper circulation.
Bangalore (Prakasa Rao and Tewari 1979)	
1. The City: core, intermediate, periphery	Population density, 1971
2. Urban-rural fringe (8 to 12 miles from the City Centre)	Ratio of non-agricultural to agricultural workers, 1971
3. Peripheral rural area	Population growth, 1961-71 Sex Ratio 1971 Daily bus trips Area under forests Permanent pastures and miscellaneous tree crops. % to total area Net sown area % to total area Net irrigated area% to net sown area Area under fruits and vegetables % to total cultivated area.
6. Bombay (Deshpande *et al.*, 1979)	
1. City 2. (a) Inner (b) Outer 3. (a) Zone of industrial spillover (b) Perishables supply zone	No explicit mention of variables.

TABLE 3.2—*concld.*

Zonation	Variables
4. Zone of indirect urban impact. (Sita and Padke 1979)	
1. Off shoots of the urban core	Population growth rate 1961-71
2. Rural-Urban fringe	Sex Ratio
3. Outlying rural area	Percentage of non-agricultural workers to total workers 1971.
7. Pollachi (Parvathi 1977)	
The city	Population density 1971.
The fringe	Population growth 1961-71
The rural periphery	Non-agricultural population 1971
	Daily bus frequency
	Commodity arrivals

There is a close correspondence between the seasonal rhythm of regional production and town rhythm and the seasonal cropping cycle (harvest season), the town life-cycle (peak of commodity arrivals in lorries and bullock-carts, commercial transactions with wholesale traders, retail traders, intermediaries and farmers) and processing activity with mills working in more than one shift. The peak season-slack season break is also disappearing partly owing to changing cropping rhythm from seasonal to time-bound perennial cropping and with improvements in transportation facilities. This rural-urban seasonal and cyclic rhythm gets modified giving place to more continuous and mixed work schedules with the development of other urban functions like industrial and tertiary. This sets the stage for a further "take off" leading to diversification in the town's economic structure and an increase in its functional scale from a resource town to a regional city.

The tobacco town of Nipani with a population of just above 35,000 (1971) (located in the tobacco tract of Karnataka) is a product of its resource. The town is choked in the smell of it with residents of the town inhaling the air filled with tobacco dust. Most of as many as 17,000 women, mostly Andhra Muslims, commute daily from a distance of 6 miles from Nipani, and are employed in tobacco pounding. The fortress-like tobacco godowns, the rising gallery of colourful multistoried houses of traders with middle class households living in the centre of the town in small lanes and alleys, the market place as the functional core of the town, the chawls in dilapidated houses where beedi-workers live and with heaps of rejected beedi stocks piled up at the doorsteps, all reflect the functioning of the town with its roots in tobacco production, beedi making as a household industry and tobacco trading, and echo the exploitive capitalistic structure of the town's economy (*Economic and Political Weekly*, 1978).

In the following section, the urban-structure regional structural relationships are examined in selected regions—a coastal horticultural belt (North Canara), a resource-rich hill forest region (Malnad), a region with a diversified resource base and urban-industrial axis (Bangalore-Mysore axis) and a development corridor converging on a metropolis (Meerut).

The very changing structure of commodity arrivals in the market towns not only indicates the changing demand for the commodities but also reveals the changing structure of land-use in the villages in the market city-region. The increasing arrivals of fruits—mango, banana, citrus, pineapple and jack-fruit in the market towns of Sirsi, Siddapur and Supa of North Canara district in Karnataka, only indicate the changing land-use structure from cultivable wastes and other marginal lands in the coastal belt of the district to horticulture, thanks to the incentives of the horticultural department, and the local farmers (marginal and small farmers) positive response.

The resource-rich Malnad region in Karnataka with its export-oriented production base (Areca nut, Coffee, Pepper, Cardamom and other Spices) the value of which runs into crores of rupees annually, remains poorly developed in urban infra-structure and transport network. The income generated is clearly not reflected in the level of development of the region or of the towns.

The urban settlements of Mandya district located in the paddy-sugarcane tract of Southern Karnataka consist of the district headquarters and the sugar city of Mandya with a population of about 72,000 (1971), and 9 small agricultural towns which are really large villages of which 7 are taluk headquarters towns with low order and sub-standard urban services and amenities. Mandya's economic base is rooted in the city's sugar factory with its ancillary industries and its gate-cane area. Consequent upon the very capitalistic structure of the sugarcane economy, Mandya developed its urban and economic links more with Bangalore and Mysore than with the small towns in the district. The mid-location of the city on the Mysore-Bangalore transport axis, and its transport network patterns are such that it is more accessible to Mysore and Bangalore than to the district's urban and rural settlements. By virtue of its location in the traffic-shed between Mysore and Bangalore, and due to the functional dominance of Mysore and Bangalore, the city could develop its hinterland only to a limited extent. There is a sharp imbalance in development between the Mysore-Bangalore axial belt with larger (>2000 population), rapidly growing and more prosperous villages rooted in the paddy-sugarcane economy, and the unirrigated millet economy with smaller villages of the periphery with its relative inaccessibility and low order taluk headquarters towns with administration as their main function. Field studies brought out clearly that the rural capitalists in the paddy-sugarcane area developed economic links with urban capitalists in Mandya, Mysore and Bangalore to participate in the game of economic development along with the businessmen and entrepreneurs. While the rich and the upper middle-classes bypass even Mandya in preference to Mysore and Bangalore, the lower middle classes bypass smaller towns in the district, in preference to Mandya for urban services and amenities. The poor rarely move out of their villages. At best, they move out to the nearby small towns for low order services and amenities. Consequently, neither has Mandya the population threshold for higher order functions, nor do the smaller towns have the population thresholds for middle level urban functions. Therefore, the district's urban structure is truncated, and reflects the sharp axial-belt-periphery socio-economic imbalance and large urban-functional gap. The functional score of Mandya is 1.4 while the scores of Bangalore and Mysore located within two hours travel distance from Mandya are 14.1 and 3.2 respectively. The functional scores of the small towns are less than 0.2. This imbalanced urban structure of the district is a consequence of the imbalanced socio-economic structure in the paddy-sugarcane zone (Bhooshan *et al.*, 1979).

While paddy-sugarcane has its distinct core area* in southern Karnataka, there are a number of other core areas--ragi, groundnut, fruits and vegetables and mulberry. It is this association of core areas which indicates the type of links in the urban system and the functional character of towns in the region. The nature of linkages in the system is reflected in the nature of regional produce—paddy, ragi and jowar originating from the farming areas to reach the consumers through nearby market centres; sugarcane processed through the nearest sugar factory to be pooled at the regional and state levels; fruits and vegetables transported to large urban centres via intermediary towns without further links; the cocoons reaching the nearby markets centres directly from the villages and distributed to silk producing centres to be linked up to the regional, national and international markets.

The information to study such linkages is limited. The available data pertain to regulated markets.** Doubtless vast areas and centres do not come under this regulation, where the private unregulated marketing system operates particularly in weekly markets, and even at the doorsteps of the progressive cultivators as a recent trend indicates. Apparently spatial gaps and overlaps would characterize the region. Since the market town is the main channel through which rural people obtain basic goods and services in return for their products, the role of such towns is crucial for the region.

The importance of the market function of the towns is brought out by the market arrivals of the different regional products (Tables 3.3 and 3.4). Many of the towns, which had the lowest status in terms of bus frequency linkages emerge as important market centres. Depending on the commodity,

*Core area is identified on the basis of crop concentration, its stability over years, and the associated processing and marketing units.

**There are 106 regulated markets in Karnataka of which 8 are located in the three districts Bangalore, Mandya and Mysore. The idea underlying the regulated market system is that the sale and purchase of certain "notified commodities" should be supervised by a committee charged with the responsibility for ensuring orderly and fair marketing practices.

TABLE 3.3 : Market arrivals (1976-77) of selected commodities at the eight regulated markets in Bangalore, Mandya and Mysore Districts.

Market Centre	Market arrivals in tons				
	Rice/Paddy	Ragi	Jaggery	Arecanut	Fruits and vegetables
Mandya District					
Mandya	334,960	3,950	276,640	—	—
Mysore District					
Chamarajnagar	8,850	6,700	—	11,040	4,260
Kollegal	212,130	11,080	55,950	—	490
Krishnarajnagar	20,810	1,670	360	370	—
Mysore	146,350	61,000	20,440	31,130	7,750
Nanjangud	26,720	900	1,570	1,810	230
Bangalore District					
Bangalore	11,640	346,290	90,820	480	1,100,440
Channapatna	3,640	15,830	3,580	7,070	1,000

TABLE 3.4 : Total transactions (1976-77) of reeling cocoons in the cross breed area markets (Urban) in Bangalore and Mysore and Mandya districts.

Market	Cocoons in Quintals
Bangalore District	
Ramnagaram	44,274
Vijapura	20,728
Kanakapura	20,074
Channapatna	12,388
Mysore District	
Kollegal	21,739
T. Narsipur	11,540
Nanjangud	1.730
Chamarajnagar	7,544
Mandya District	
Mallavalli	281

different centres attain importance in the marketing system. Mysore and Chamarajanagar dominate the groundnut market, Bangalore organises the fruits and vegetables and ragi marketing system, Ramanagaram and Channapatna dominate the cocoon markets. The fields of interaction, therefore, also shrink and expand according the magnitude of market arrivals and the production base. Paddy and ragi tend to be widespread within the region with a number of important centres, whereas groundnuts and fruits and vegetables show concentration within the region and in effect few centres have large hinterlands. Similarly, the cocoon marketing system, integrating the mulberry producing area operates in parts of the three districts where the market centres are located, rather in a close proximity to each other. But the apex decision body, the Silk Board, is located in Bangalore.

Meerut is a medium-size city (population of about 3,68,000 in 1971) located on one of the active development corridors converging on Delhi, and in an agriculturally developed tract with its highly commercialized wheat and sugarcane economy. Located at a distance of 40 miles from Delhi, Meerut is drawn into the Delhi metropolitan system, with a potential to develop both as a "counter magnet" to Delhi along with the other industrial centres like Ghaziabad, Mohannagar and Modinagar, and as a 'regional city' to serve primarily its highly fertile and rapidly developing hinterland. The city like many other developing cities, changed its functional role from a simple service centre to its local hinterland, to commercial centre, industrial centre, regional administrative centre, and a regional centre for specialized services particularly technological and credit inputs. One of the positive consequences of this functional dynamism is the growth of entrepreneurship with ability to invest, innovate and diffuse. Meerut, like the other cities in this part of the country, is fortunate in its 'refugee' population of migrants, which provided the "ignition element" for city development unlike the refugee migrants to Calcutta, who bloated the informal sector and the ranks of the unemployed. Some of the industrial firms are drawing quaternary services into their fold. It was partly the rich and prosperous hinterland, and partly the state's development policies through its selective location of industrial estates and industrial complexes that gave the impetus for the urban dynamism of the city. The city's proximity to Delhi which provides ready market for its industrial goods has contributed its due share, though the major thrust for industrial development appears to have come from its rural hinterland where agro-based industries and agri-business predominate. The city has a mix of industries—textiles, sugar mills and allied industries, metal and metal products, machinery including agricultural implements, sports goods, and chemicals and synthetic products, to mention a few. What is significant here is the rapid growth of the tertiary sector—wholesale and retail trade, agricultural servicing and repairing, the banking sector and diversified personal and community services. It is this associated development of industrial and tertiary sectors that contributes to the urban "multiplier". Of equal importance is commercialization of agriculture with the consequent increases in market surpluses, and this has increased the intensity of interaction between the city and its hinterland, and with Delhi (Sundaram 1974).

The analysis of the urbanization pattern and correlates (Chapter 1), the Indian Urban System (Chapter 2) and Urban and Regional inter-relationships (Chapter 3) clearly brought out the sharp inter-urban and inter-regional variations, and urban and regional deviations from the national metropolitan system with its core-periphery and axial interstitial dichotomy in development. The sharp discordance between the metropolitan system and the regional-urban system also became evident. The urban hierarchy is found to be stepped with sharp breaks in functional score, suggesting sharp functional gaps. Associated with these gaps are spatial gaps. With a case study of Karnataka, the importance of inter-city linkages at higher levels in the urban system and of town-hinterland links at lower levels in the integration of the system is established.

With the emphasis of the Sixth Plan (1980-85) on welfare dimensions, the need to disperse urban infra-structure particularly social infra-structure has become greater, but here, equity needs to be judiciously balanced with efficiency taking into account the very pyramidal structure of the urban infra-structure. The different aspects relating to social infra-structure planning are discussed in the chapter that follows.

4

SOCIAL INFRA-STRUCTURE DEVELOPMENT AND URBAN POPULATION THRESHOLDS

SEMANTICS

THE TERMS infra-structure, amenities, services and facilities are often interchangeably used to denote the provisions made to satisfy some of the basic needs of the people. These needs cater to a variety of requirements from the basic life-sustaining needs like safe drinking water, health and nutrition services, sanitation, housing and sewage disposal to 'felt needs' like educational facilities including libraries, shops, hotels, restaurants and recreational facilities, public transport facilities, electricity as a consumer good and police protection. The term 'social infra-structure' which is more comprehensive in nature and includes a variety of amenities/services/facilities is gaining greater currency. Since the provision of many of these facilities has become the responsibility of governments and also since these facilities are interrelated with each other for purposes of planning, package programmes are needed.

A distinction may be made between "felt needs" perceived by the people and "professed" or professionally defined needs suggested by urban-based specialists (Cheyne and Lloyd, 1975). The range of these needs includes the traditional weekly markets in the tribal and hill forest areas at the one end of the scale of infra-structural hierarchy (see Appendix I) and the modern shopping complexes with cinemas, discotheques and beauty saloons in the metropolises at the other end. Banks, co-operative societies and market infra-structure claim their due place in the list. Such a range of facilities combines both social and economic components. However, the two components cannot be compartmentalized.

Thresholds and related concepts

The decision to provide social facilities in specific locations calls for an analysis of the characteristics of an individual facility and its priority over a range of 'felt and professed needs' of the people. The provision of these facilities in a free market situation requires a minimum aggregate demand i.e. threshold to support the facilities in a given location. It follows, therefore, that the various facilities will have differing minimum aggregate demand requirements, and the required minimum aggregate demands will progressively reduce with increasing levels of development and increasing levels of income of the population.

The term 'threshold' itself has three different connotations in urban literature (Moseley, 1974). In terms of economic development, 'threshold' marks the 'take-off' point at which the economy attains self-sustaining growth; to the planner, threshold marks a break in a process or urban development which necessitates major capital investment before further development can take place; with reference to urban (or for that matter rural) infra-structure, threshold connotes the minimum support population necessary for sustaining an amenity or a function.

The minimum number of people required to support a facility would include not only the size of the population of the place where the facility is (to be) located but also the number of people living in the surrounding areas who are willing to travel a given distance (i.e. the range) to avail themselves of the facility. Consequently the 'range' of the facility cannot be isolated from the 'threshold'. The logical ties between these two concepts (range and threshold) are well brought out with the framework of Central Place theory, which provides the conceptual base for many of the locational problems associated with infra-structure (Chapter 3).

The range of the good and population threshold are the basic concepts. If social infra-structure is ubiquitously distributed over the settlements, population threshold loses its meaning. But in social infra-structure which is not ubiquitous, there is the "centralistic principle" both within a settlement and between settlements. This principle is to be sought in the location of services to which the users move. In regions with higher levels of development and better transport network, it is the more accessible functional centre even with eccentric geographic location which becomes important. With changing levels of development and owing to policy interventions, the hierarchy gets disturbed. The travel behaviour patterns of both consumers and producers also change, often leading to the bypassing of intervening opportunities. In an exercise in realignment of the theoretical base for efficient and equitable development of social infra-structure, the research theme is to link Central Place theory and Location Allocation Models*.

Associated with the problems of location of infra-structure is the distance factor. Distance norms are not only area-specific but also time-specific and are reviewed periodically, may be, synchronizing with development plans. With declining small towns and declining or disappearing small villages (below 200 persons), with the intervening settlements located within a critical distance range of 15 to 20 miles getting bypassed by the high income and middle income consumers, with closing down of market centres in some areas (e.g., Raichur district) and with new centres springing up (project towns and industrial centres) in other areas, regional systems are in a state of constant change. In spite of these changes, the "distance factor" is still significant particularly in the regions where small and medium farmers dominate, and the level of development is low. There is a progressive increase in distance from the low order functions to the high order functions (Table 2.2) which is already referred to (Chapter 2). The very pattern of consumer travel behaviour is changing in favour of larger settlements where superior and varied services are available owing

*Pilot Research Project (1969-74) of the Government of India. International Project on Locational Efficiency of Rural Service Delivery Systems (Rushton, McNulty, Tewari, Universities of Iowa and Mysore and the Indian Institute of Management, Bangalore, 1980-82).

to larger thresholds. The bypassing of intervening settlement located in the shadow zones of larger settlements and within critical distance zones is leading to redistribution of consumer demand for services. Mobile service systems and specialists (e.g. medical) from higher order centres opening regularly one or two day clinical units in the smaller and market towns are the emerging patterns of dispersal of urban services, (Parvathi, 1977). The analysis of consumer travel behaviour in a Block in a developed agricultural district in the upper Gangetic Plain (Muzaffarnagar district) threw up several important insights (Chapter 2).

Problems of measurement

Both the measurement of individual facilities and social infra-structure in general, on the one hand, and the measurement of thresholds for these on the other, pose a variety of problems.

How can a common denominator for measuring and evaluating different components of social infra-structure, which vary in number, unit of measurement, type, level and capacity be worked out? Some components are location-specific like education and health facilities, while others are not, for example, water and electricity, where the network system becomes more important in measurement. In the case of basic needs, the objective is to make them available to every individual and in every locality. Here measurement relates to the necessary minimal level. In India, the level is "near zero" starting point for the majority. When once this level is crossed, comparative measurement poses problems. Different levels can be equated from the lowest to the highest:

Primary School	—	University
Health Centre	—	Specialized Hospital
Provision Store	—	Shopping Complex
Route Terminal	—	Multiple route nodes

Methods of measurement are varied, and range from simple to complex. Mere availability (Yes) or non-availability (No) is too simple a measure for too complex a set of functions. A somewhat star-shaped symbol taking the form of a "windrose diagram" for each settlement can be used to assess the degree of attainment of selected services. These are measured along the radii of the symbol, centred over each settlement. The size and form of the symbol can be taken as a basis for comparative evaluation (Fig. 4.1).

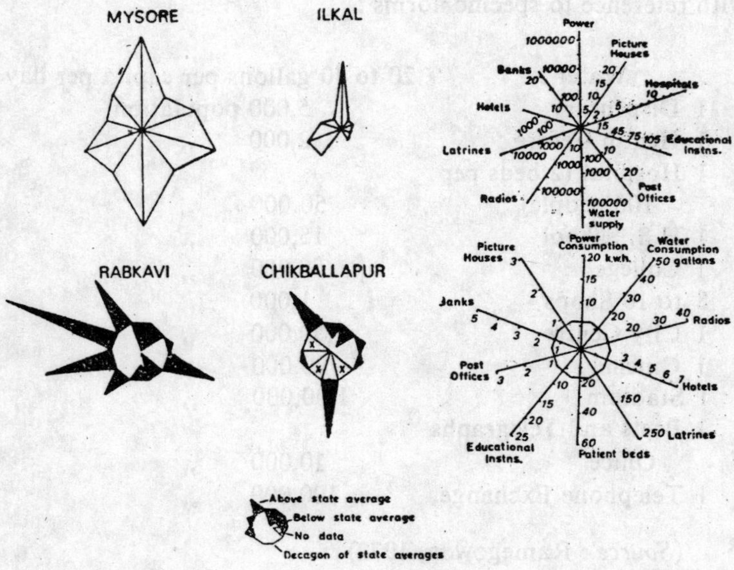

FIG. 4.1 : *Urban services and amenities*

The Figure indicates the absolute deviations from the state average represented by the decagon. The main advantage is that different services and amenities can be represented in one diagram. A comparative evaluation of the situation in urban services and amenities between towns and between one region and the other is possible since the scale for each element remains the same for all the diagrams. Contiguous areas in similar situations, as suggested by the similarity of shapes of symbols and their distribution, are clearly brought out.

The limitations of this type of measurement are: the scale along the radii is arbitrary, hence, a change in the scale changes both size and shape of the symbol; the units of measurement along the radii are different e.g. in gallons for water, absolute number for hospitals, schools, hotels, etc., and units for electricity. These different units need standardization, and should also be weighted (Prakasa Rao, 1964).

Adequacy or inadequacy in services can be measured also with reference to specific norms :

Water :	20 to 40 gallons per capita per day	
1 Dispensary :	5,000	population
1 Health Centre :	2,000	,,
1 Hospital (2 beds per 100 people)	50,000	,,
1 H.S. School	15,000	,,
1 College	50,000	,,
8 to 10 Shops	1,000	,,
1 City Centre	1,50,000	,,
1 Cinema	20,000	,,
1 Stadium	1,00,000	,,
1 Posts and Telegraphs Office	10,000	,,
1 Telephone Exchange	100,000	,,

(*Source* : Ramegowda, 1972)

To work out locational priorities in the development of social facilities, 'norms' are necessary. National norms such as one primary health centre for every 80,000-1,00,000 population, one self-health centre for every 10,000 population, a primary school within 1.5 km. or less of a village, a middle school within 5 km. of a village (Sen *et al*., 1971) very rarely fit local and regional realities. We do not yet have an inventory of norms for different regional and local situations in the country. The average number of schools or hospitals per 1000 people is often taken as a norm and those below the average are given priority. When once this target is reached, the norm will change. Thus the whole question of norms has to be examined and revised periodically.

Techniques of determining population thresholds based on the entry point (Christaller 1966) and the median population of settlements having the function suffer from the disadvantage of under-estimation in the one case and over-estimation of the threshold in the other. (Sharma *et al.*, 1977). A combination of the two (Reed and Muench 1938, Haggett and Gunawardene 1964, Ramachandran 1976), yields more accurate estimates. But inherent in this method too, is the tendency to over-estimate threshold values in the case of higher order functions. This, however, can be counteracted by disregarding the threshold values of functions which are not present in at least half the settlements above the threshold size (Sharma *et al.*, 1977). Based on the premise that the population size of a centre is a function of the complexity of goods and services offered, an exponential function of the form $P = A(B)^n$ has been used to derive population thresholds (Berry and Garrison 1958, Sen *et al.*, 1971).

All the above techniques, however, rest essentially on one assumption—the premise that the population of towns or villages is essentially homogeneous in nature and portrays similar consumer behaviour characteristics.

Population thresholds : Inter-State variation

The assumption that the threshold is dependent upon the order of the function presupposes a similar threshold size for a particular function irrespective of its location in space. But the realities of regional distinctiveness, cultural traits, the heterogeneity and the level of development of the area, all make this assumption untenable. Such distortions are brought out in the empirical analysis that follows.

Based on public sector and/or private sector involvement, urban services are also classified into three groups: (a) the basic services with almost no private sector involvement—water supply, drainage, roads and street lightings; (b) the supplementary services with both public and private sectors—education and medical; and (c) the special urban services—transport, housing and communication. While both sectors are involved in transport and housing only the public sector is involved in communication (MMDA 1978).

With increasing involvement of governmental agencies in

the provision and planning of 'social infra-structure' the problem includes 'non-economic' dimensions. Much of the provision of amenities which fall within the range of 'social infra-structure' are subsumed in a number of 'welfare programmes' aimed at 'specific target groups' and 'target areas' (backward areas). Consequently social infra-structure development implies not only making available the basic infra-structure but also providing for its more equitable distribution among the different socio-economic groups and over geographic space.

The stance of the government towards social infra-structure development is essentially non-commercial. The very term social implies a non-commercial stance (Williams and Anderson 1975).

Once, a non-commercial stance is taken for the provision of social infra-structure, the minimum aggregate demand needed to support the infra-structure in a given location loses its importance to a great extent. In other words, the thresholds are lowered artificially by investment by the government in the infra-structure. The lowering of the thresholds, then, becomes a function of the priorities of the government based on equity and 'felt needs'. This is manifested in the proclaimed targets of the government to make infra-structure available to a greater number of people at smaller distances. Consequently norms are fixed by the government from time to time that outline the government's intention for providing a facility for a given unit of population irrespective of its population threshold.

In the light of the preceding discussion the following questions can be raised. At what point does a town become capable of supporting a particular facility? Does the population threshold change with the general level of development? In other words, do we expect higher thresholds in backward areas indicating lower demand levels? Can we conclude that with increasing levels of development and facilities becoming ubiquitous, thresholds become progressively lower? To what extent does the stance of the local government relating to the provision of social infra-structure get reflected in the population thresholds?

A few selected infra-structural facilities are chosen for three States of India—Punjab, Karnataka and Orissa. The three states are at various levels of development as brought out by a composite index of development (Punjab: 1.2442; Karnataka: .5739; Orissa: 0.8005).*

The five facilities that are considered include those which are essentially public as well as private enterprises : (1) Medical/Engineering Colleges, (2) Polytechnics, (3) Arts/Science Colleges, (4) Hospitals, and (5) Banks. The population thresholds for these functions are computed following Reed and Muench (for ready reference the method is illustrated in Appendix II). The threshold values are tabulated in Table 4.1. A study of table brings out the following points :

1. There is a progressive increase in population threshold from Banks to Medical/Engineering Colleges in all the three states.
2. While the order of these facilities remains the same as indicated by the population thresholds, the threshold size itself varies in different States for a given facility.
3. Colleges have roughly the same population thresholds in all the three States.

TABLE 4.1 : **Population thresholds of urban facilities**

Facilities	Karnataka	Punjab	Orissa
Medical/Engineering College	86,000	1,08,000	75,000
Polytechnics	66,000	86,000	48,000
Arts/Science Colleges	24,000	25,120	25,500
Hospitals	8,600	12,590	5,000
Banks	2,625	5,012	8,000

*These indices are derived on the basis of a principal component analysis using the following variables for the major States of India: percentage of urban to total population, percentage of city population to total urban population, growth of urban population, percentage of literates to total population, average daily employment of factory workers per '000 population, per capita gross output in industry, per capita value added, per capita industrial consumption of electricity, per capita bank credit of commercial banks, area under selected commercial crops as a percentage of gross cropped area, hospital beds per lakh population, motor vehicles per lakh population.

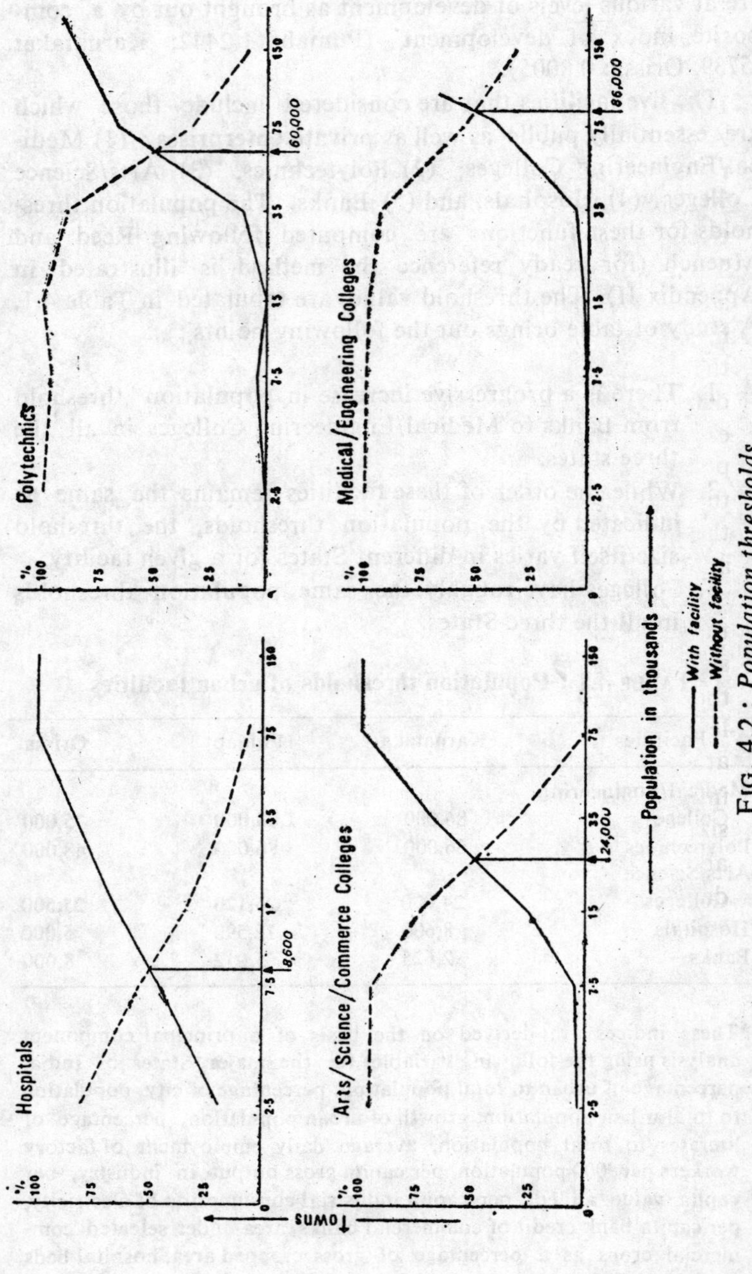

FIG. 4.2 : *Population thresholds*

4. There is no relationship between population threshold and level of development of the State.*

Population size and infra-structure : Intra-State variations

A closer look at the thresholds of these facilities in Karnataka reveals that there are small settlements that have a facility while there are larger ones without the facility. These situations are not rare but quite common as brought out by Table 4.2. Such anomalies occur owing to the non-commercial stance of the government, specific area development programmes, the influence or shadow effect of the large urban centres that encourage bypassing of smaller centres, the population density of the surrounding areas etc. To demonstrate the existence of these anomalies we have a closer look at the population size of the urban centres and the level of infra-structural development in Karnataka. The infra-structural scores of the urban centres are derived through principal component analysis using seventeen facilities.**

It is possible to compute the expected level of infra-structural development, given the population size based on regression analysis. High positive deviations of observed scores from the expected value will represent towns that have a higher level of infra-structural development than their sizes warrant at a given time, whereas high negative deviations indicate lower infra-structural development than warranted by population size. The size of the urban centres in Karnataka explains about 80 per cent of the variation in levels of infra-structural development.

*The lower threshold values (with the exception of colleges) for different facilities in the relatively less developed State of Orissa can perhaps be explained by the deliberate social interventions of the state. This, however, needs to be tested.

**Total municipal expenditure, Higher Secondary schools, Beds in Medical institution, Electric connections domestic, Electric connections commercial, Electric Connections industrial, Road light points, Banks, Cinemas, Auditoria, Drama Halls, Libraries/Reading rooms, Arts/Science/Commerce colleges, Medical/Engineering colleges, Polytechnics, Non-agricultural credit societies, Protected water supply, Number of buses connecting, Agricultural credit societies, and Number of routes converging (Prakasa Rao, *et al.* 1978).

TABLE 4.2 : **Anomalies in size and facilities in Karnataka**

Facility	Threshold	Number of towns	
		Above threshold without facilities	Below threshold with facilities
Medical/Engineering college	86,000	5	5
Polytechnic	66,000	4	8
Arts/Science college	24,000	9	34
Hospitals	8,600	43	15
Banks	2,625	14	3

Accessibility to social infra-structure

There is a conflict between efficiency and equity in social infra-structure development. Efficiency is ensured through population thresholds while equity is ensured through accessibility to services. Accessibility to users measured in route, cost and time distances is crucial in social and infra-structure planning but distance sensitivity is lost in the case of specialized services and Government controlled goods. In India, national distance norms and average distances have no meaning only because of the sharply contrasting natural landscapes e.g. the desert, the hill forest, and the riverine plains with a dense stream network. In fact, there is a range of distances with critical cut-off values. The very pattern of settlements e.g. dispersed, as in the Kerala coastal plains, variations in the spacing of settlements in different land systems, and the emerging urban corridors further underscore even regional distance norms. Accepting that the distance norms should be local, the question is how to delimit the locality or tract to work out norms. Districts or Blocks are taken for fixing norms. But even at this level, there cannot be a blanket decision. Each district or block needs to be tested rigorously with reference to geographical size and form, the pattern of distribution of settlements, transport network, and the often neglected edge problems (e.g. administrative and natural boundaries). The position of the administrative unit in the regional and functional hierarchy determines its degree of closure. It is the character of the edge which is critical e.g. an unbridged stream or the crest of a hill range. These become more critical in areas of low population density where the traffic does not bear heavy investment in removing transport breaks. Where needed, two or even three blocks should be combined to work out distance norms. Here the search should be for multiple boundary accordance at local level (Prakasa Rao and Tewari 1980). Delimitation problems get compounded in the "contact and transitional" regions.

Social infra-structure development planning (SIDP)

The goal of SIDP is to (1) reduce inter-town, town and village and inter-village disparities in the levels of social infra-structure, (2) up-grade infra-structure from near zero level to the Minimum Needs Levels for target groups and target areas, and (3) reduce the total distance (i.e. the sum of all distances between each person and each facility) between the users and the services. It needs to be recognized here that neither all places, nor all users can be made to reach all services. Thus priorities need to be worked out which change with levels of development and the associated income levels and aspirations of the users. The users should decide their priorities though often the reformers and the planners decide their priorities though often the reformers and the planners decide what the users should have. Proposals for public fountains, parks and mobile services for city slums, and multistoried structures for slum dwellers without reference to occupational structure are typical examples of the "professed needs" in contrast with the "felt needs" of the users.

Centralized planning at the national and state levels associated with implementation by local authorities with no decision-making power as in India, leads more to failures, which are manifested in the form of anomalies like under-utilized or unutilized versus overstrained infra-structure. This is a characteristic of all the developing countries, a result of decentralized implementation under centralized direction and decision-making (Cheyne and Lloyd, 1975). Mere decisions at the National or State level to reduce imbalances in social infra-structure, and shift in emphasis to the "grassroots" level without decentralized decision-making and financial devolution are no solutions. The questions, who will plan and who will implement, crop up again and again. What compounds the problem at both urban and rural levels is "the multiplicity of agencies involved in developmental work, each with its rules and regulations which often become 'clogs' in the wheels of administration and planning. The very dichotomy between urban/municipal administration and rural/panchayat administration in its turn leads to multiplicity of authorities resulting in functional and jurisdictional overlaps. In metropolitan regions, there is fragmentation of authorities. In a multi-level government administration, the system functions effectively only when upper levels of Government are willing to share power with lower levels" (Dutta, 1976). All these lead to conflicts between "developers", and act as constraints in integrated planning of social infra-structure.

At the planning level, the very development strategies of social infra-structure need to be examined critically. It is recognized that different components of infra-structure should be planned as a "package"—health, sanitation, safe drinking water, housing, education, and family planning. For the poorest of the poor, the utility of the "package" infra-structure gets highly discounted. Often the benefits of the "package" reach the "better off" of society. At the policy level, policy formulations like the National health policy linking up health development targets with rapid economic growth, full-scale employment, liquidation of literacy, raising adverse sex-ratio and the like only indicate the mixing up of long-term and short-term aspects of health planning. In physical planning of public utility services at the metropolitan scale for example, step by step incremental planning with "known effect for known effort" instead of long-term and capital-intensive investment in large scale and ideal solutions, is advocated as the most appropriate strategy for countries like India (Koenigsberger: quoted by Cheyne and Lloyd, 1975).

As in all sectors of development, inadequate finances become a key constraint in SIDP. Here the axiom "He who pays the piper calls the tune" should not apply but in practice it appears it applies. While the necessity to tap local finances by the local authorities is recognised, both the *modus operandi* and response do not seem to be facilitating the effort. Thus, in spite of the best will, finance becomes the bottleneck. The shift from "cost-norms" to "social-norms" in planning social infra-structure adds to a further strain on the budget. In this context, it is necessary to reiterate that priorities perceived by the users need to be given weightage over priorities fixed by the planners. The question is, where does the plan for "one bulb for one house" for the weaker sections stand on the priority list of social infra-structure vis-a-vis safe drinking water, health and sanitation and house, to mention a few ? The magnitude of the financial outlay even for minimal services will be astronomical, and no other organization but the public sector will be in a position to provide the necessary social infra-structure. When financial outlays (Rs. 42,000 million: Fifth Plan) are related to the population size of the country (548 million in 1971, with an expected annual increase of 12 million in 1971-81), it becomes evident that any amount of outlay on even minimal infra-structure will be a drop in the ocean. Added to this, the rate of growth in demand for services always outpaces the rate of growth in investments – (MMDA Report 1978). Increasing population, an increasing gap between demand for services and rate of growth of investments, and deterioration of services, because often, maintenance costs are not provided for, all conspire to add to the crisis situation in infra-structure. Thus the very population size becomes a constraint, and its rapid increase further deepens the crisis.

APPENDIX I

Order of settlements and variety and levels of functions

	Administration	Education	Health	Public utility
Lower Types	Police chowki, Panchayat	Balwadis/primary schools	Primary Health centre	P.O.
Middle Types	District Court, P.S. with jail Specialized Officers	Different types of nursery schools, Secondary schools, Tech. school	Doctor Dentist, Health Centre, Clinic, Drug store	Electricity, Municipal Water supply, Post offices telegraph, Telephone services
Higher Types	Mayors Office, High Courts, Jails, Special Government Service H.Q.	Secondary Schools, Colleges, Tech. Schools, Universities	General Hospitals, Specialized physician, large Drug Stores	Electricity, Municipal facilities, communication
Highest Types	Seat of State/ National Government, Supreme Court, H.Q. of Govt. Departments, Embassies	Universities, Tech. Institute, National Research Institutes, Scientific Academies	Specialized Hospitals, Medical Research Centres	Full range of Municipal facilities, Telex

Commerce (Shops)	Finance	Transport	Recreation
Weekly markets small	Village money-lender, Bank extension scheme	Unsurfaced Roads	Tea-shop, Travelling Theatre, Folk dances
Retail shops, specialized Retail shops, Wholesale markets (mandis), gas station	P.O. Banks, Pawn-shops, Finance Companies	Surfaced roads, R.S. for local slow trains	Cinema, restaurants, hotels
Large retail shop, Retail of large consumer durables, large wholesale & distribution warehousing	Banking, Insurance, Brokerage	Highways, Important Rail road, stations, Airport	Auditorium, Cinemas, Hotels, Night Clubs, Museums
Luxury retail shops, Departmental stores, Import/export, houses	Domestic and Foreign Banks, Financial H.Q., Chambers of Commerce, Trade Associations	Direct Super train links, International Air links, Shipping	Theatre, Ballet, Museums, Art galleries, Orchestras

APPENDIX II

Method of deriving population thresholds suggested by Reed and Muench (Fig. 4.2)

Thresholds can be derived through computations as well as graphically. Graphically derived thresholds for some of the facilities discussed in the text are illustrated in the following groups. The percentage values of towns having a facility and the percentage of towns that do not have the facility are plotted for various arbitrarily defined size classes of towns. In the graphs that follow, the *x*-axis represents size classes of towns based on census categories and the *y*-axis represents percentage of towns. Two lines are drawn (solid lines) representing percentage of towns having a facility and (broken lines) percentage of towns without the facility. The point of intersection of the two lines gives us threshold values of the facility (Ramachandran 1976).

In each of the arbitrarily defined size classes the number of settlements with and without a function is recorded. Cumulative frequencies of functions present at each lower level (*Ps*) and absent at each higher level (*Ag*) are then calculated. The percentage of settlements with the function in each size-class is given by $\frac{Ps \times 100}{Ag + Ps}$. The median population threshold (for which the percentage is 50) is estimated through inter-polation such that threshold$=a+bc$, where: a=mid point of size class which records just less than 50, c=interclass distance and

$$b = \frac{50 - \text{percentage just below } 50}{\text{percentage just more than } 50 - \text{percentage just less than } 50}$$

INDIAN CITY

5

CITY STRUCTURE, CITY SPRAWL, AND POPULATION DENSITY

INTRODUCTION

THE CITY in its totality is a part of the city-region system, which in its turn is a part of a system of cities. Thus, the city system has intra-city, city-regional and inter-city dimensions. Both city-regional and inter-city dimensions have their imprints on intra-city structure. City structure is complex and comprises sets of entities—objects, activities, infra-structure and land—inter-dependent and interacting among themselves and with their environment. To understand the structure in its totality it is recognised that various components of the structure need to be analysed within a common conceptual framework. Study of city structure requires an understanding of the processes and patterns underlying the structure and the nature of mechanisms involved.

The households of similar socio-economic status and similar activities tend to cluster at various locations within a city, and locations are determined by historical, social, economic and administrative factors. All these contribute to stratification in structure which changes over time owing to the very dynamic character of the city.

The three basic models of spatial patterning of households are those formulated by Burgess (1928), Hoyt (1939), and Harris and Ullaman (1945). Mann (1965) emphasized that the three structural patterns are not mutually exclusive and the end result is a tripartite structure. Sjoberg (1966) generalized the model with reference to the 'pre-industrial city' as one of 'rich centre and poor periphery' with a single centre. Here the socio-economic status of households is the basic explanatory variable. The other major model is the colonial city model. McGee (1971) describes the Indian city as dual structured, like all the colonial cities in developing countries with its "Bazaar-peasant economy" and "Firm-type capitalist economy". Other morphological studies on Indian cities also bring out this dual structure with traditional core and the industrializing and tertiarizing belts or strips along the transport axes. Smailes (1969) refers to another type of dualism—indigenous and anglicized, with reference to morphological elements of the city.

In reality, the Indian city structure is more complex than its simple "dual structure". Cities with an historic past like Hyderabad, Varanasi or Delhi have more complicated structures with discontinuous telescoping of political, cultural and economic systems belonging to different historic periods. There is structural unconformity which is best expressed as a city of 'pre-industrial society' living in a 'post-industrial city' with a slow rate of transformation (Ginsburg, 1969). The Indian city with its traditional elements, reminiscent of both pre-industrial city and colonial city elements is characterized as a 'collection of period pieces' (Jones, 1966). The very growth of the Indian city is interpreted as a function of high pre-industrial fertility and low post-industrial mortality (Davis, quoted by Dwyer 1974). In fact, in the early decades of this century, the Indian city was more an 'eater of men' (Spate and Learmonth, 1967). But this aspect of the city's demographic structure is changing with better control over mortality.

Some of the cities still retain their overall pre-industrial structural characteristics if socio-economic status of the city's households is the determining criterion. Commercial cities perhaps tend to conform to the pre-industrial city model of 'rich centre—poor periphery' like Vijayawada (population 3,17,000 in 1971), located at the apex of the agriculturally prosperous Krishna delta in the east coast plain of India (Prakasa Rao and Ramachandran, 1971), and Pollachi (population about 70,000) located in the rapidly commercializing groundnut tract of Coimbatore plateau in the south central plateau of South India (Parvathi, 1977). In other commercial cities, however, while the city-periphery is tending to become richer with its new residential extensions, the city centre (the core) still retains its economic prosperity and high socio-economic status.

To examine to what extent does the pattern of the ecological structure of Bangalore city follows the classical model, the structure in the historical past of the city and spatial distributions of selected socio-economic characteristics were analysed. The analysis is presented in the following sections. The analysis is based on a socio-economic survey of Bangalore city conducted by Prakasa Rao and Tewari, and draws heavily on the published report of the survey (Prakasa Rao and Tewari, 1979).

East-west zonation

Bangalore, the capital city of Karnataka, with its population of 2.9 million (1981) ranks fifth in the city system of India. The Fort near the City Market in the west, and the Barracks near the Ulsoor Tank in the east, were the two foundations of Bangalore city. The kernels of the city situated only 4 miles apart but founded with a time-lag of more than two and a half centuries—the Fort built in 1537 and the British Garrison and Barracks established in 1809. The neighbourhood of the Fort and the neighbourhood of the Ulsoor Tank developed under two different *raisons d'être*. The defensive strong point apart, the Fort city was oriented to the philosophy of a city and temple builder, an agriculturist turned warrior, under whose patronage developed a township of wholesale and retail traders, and of highly skilled artisans particularly families of cotton weavers (Hasan 1970, Rao 1930). In contrast to this, the neighbourhood of the Ulsoor Tank was developed to cater to the requirements of the British Troops and British Officers who were pulled out of Srirangapatnam and settled near the tank. Thus, a military cantonment developed along with a civilian settlement of mainly retail traders and service classes adjoining the Ulsoor village. While the Fort neighbourhood developed as a typical native town with its bazaar, traders, and artisans, the Ulsoor neighbourhood developed as a cantonment with its artillery and cavalry barracks, parade ground, Infantry road, the Mall, fine and spacious bungalows, bars and night clubs. In addition, polo-playing and racing developed in keeping with the "cantonment culture". Thus, the cantonment became the home for the British-Oriental Anglo-Indians (in the sense of Eurasians) and Indian Christians.

Both the nuclei expanded; the Fort neighbourhood expanded east, north and south, and the Ulsoor neighbourhood expanded west, north and south, invading the open spaces and fertile agricultural lands. The east and west developed under two independent administrative units, with independent development programmes for nearly eight decades till their merger in 1949. Thus the development goals of both the municipalities were to provide minimal urban amenities and housing; the initial disparities in congestion, growth rates, and levels of urban amenities led to an east-west zonation. With the development of the Russel Market and westward expansion of the cantonment, the nucleus of the west shifted to the Russel Market locality, while the development of the City Market near the Fort contributed to further intensification of the growing nucleus of the west. The east-west zonation certainly had its intermixing and integrating social-cultural elements in the two nuclei—temples, churches and mosques near both the City Market and the Russel Market though the east had more churches and mosques and the west more temples. Even the street names such as Dharmaraya Koil Street and Meenakshi Koil Street in the pre-dominantly Muslim and Christian areas near the Russel Market, and Sultanpet near the City Market, a predominantly Hindu area, only echo the existence of the different religious communities.

Although, the east-west differentiation in terms of economic characteristics is not so marked, it is quite significant in terms of social composition of the populations in the two parts of the city. According to the sample survey* (Prakasa Rao and Tewari, 1979) while the west had higher percentage of Brahmins (almost 4 times that to the east), the east had a higher percentage of Christians, Muslims and Scheduled Castes (almost twice that to the west).

*Sample size : 1745 households.

The core-intermediate—periphery zonation

In this section, the spatial patterns in the city structure are examined with reference to the core, the intermediate zones and the periphery. The core consists of areas (census divisions, 1971) centred around the City Market, the Russel Market, and the Vidhana Soudha (an area that though a part of the city in the early 20th century was developed as a central administrative complex only in the early fifties). The peripheral zone consists of all the census divisions on the periphery of the corporation boundary. The divisions between the core and the periphery were allocated to the intermediate zone.

Sharp differences existed between core, intermediate and periphery of the city in terms of density, and residential housing and living conditions (Table 5.1). The population density in the core (149 persons per acre) was more than five times that in the periphery (28 persons per acre). The density of houses also declined in the same ratio from core to periphery. The other characteristics which showed a similar declining pattern from core to periphery were percentage of workers in trade & commerce, percentage of population in low income and middle income groups, percentage of Muslims, and percentage of rented houses. The percentage of population in the high income group, percentage of Brahmins, rent per dwelling, percentage of households who used gas/electricity for cooking, percentage of households who owned a refrigerator, and percentages of households with independent toilet facilities were higher in intermediate and periphery zones than in the core. While the city core acquired a special character by its centripetal pull and dominance over the periphery mainly owing to the high concentration of work-places, financial institutions, higher order shopping areas, educational institutions, transport terminals, hospitals, and recreational and cultural centres, the periphery was characterized by higher levels of housing and living conditions than that in the core and intermediate zones.

Factorial ecology of Bangalore city

Based on the household sample data (1974) and the 1971 census, 20 variables were selected to analyse the degree of spatial variations in the 63 sub-areas (census divisions) of the city. The selected variables were categorized into four groups:

social, economic, family, and migrant status-tenure-density (Table 5.2). All the variables, except density of persons and houses, were taken from the household sample. The values were calculated as proportions of the total in the division. The distributions of the selected variables were then examined to find out the degree of spatial segregation of the households who share common characteristics.

TABLE 5.1 : **Selected characteristics by core, intermediate and periphery zones.**

Characteristics	Zone		
	Core	Intermediate	Periphery
1971 Census data			
Density of Population (Persons per acre)	149	109	28
Density of houses (per acre)	20	19	4
Percentage of workers in trade, commerce, transport communication and storage to total workers	42	30	25
1974 Survey data			
Percentage of low income group (less than Rs. 300) to total population	37	34	27
Percentage of middle income group (Rs. 300—1000) to total population	55	53	48
Percentage of high income group (Rs. 1000 and above) to total population	8	13	25
Percentage of Brahmins to total population	6	17	19
Percentage of Muslims to total population	17	10	9
Average rent per dwelling (Rs.)	45	58	91
Percentage of rented houses to total houses	67	65	57
Percentage of households who used gas/electricity for cooking	7	14	25
Percentage of households who owned refrigerator	2	5	10
Percentage of households with independent toilet facility.	61	74	80

Based on coefficients of variation of the spatial distributions, the resident-migrant ratio (203%), proportions of the scheduled caste (150%) and Muslims (145%) showed a high degree of segregation in space, while average household size (15%) and sex ratio (18%) showed least segregation. The coefficients of variations (CV) for proportions of Christians and Brahmins were 143 per cent and 113 per cent respectively, which also showed a high degree of segregation.

In the economic characteristics, the proportion of workers in high status occupations such as professionals, administrators,

TABLE 5.2 : **Coefficient of variation in the spatial distribution of the selected variables.**

Variables	Coefficient of variation (%)
Per cent Muslim population to total population	145
Per cent Brahmin population to Hindu population	113
Per cent Christian population to total population	143
Per cent Scheduled Castes and Tribes to Hindu population	150
Per cent professional, administrative and related workers to total workers	82
Per cent clerical, sales and related workers to total workers	40
Per cent service, production and related workers to total workers	36
Per cent workers in manufacturing to total workers	42
Per cent workers in wholesale and retail industry to total workers	69
Per capita income	45
Income per household	37
Rent per dwelling	63
Household size	15
Females per thousand males	18
Per cent women workers to total workers	78
Number of children in age group 0—9 per 1,000 females in age group 15—49 (fertility ratio)	37
Persons per acre	83
Houses per acre	87
Per cent rented houses to total houses	29
Residents per hundred migrants	203

executives and related workers showed the highest segregation (CV: 82%). The least coefficient of variation in the economic characteristics, 36 per cent, was in the distribution of service, production, and related workers. The income per household and per capita income, which indicate an overall mean income level, showed a low degree of variation (37% and 45% respectively).

In the family characteristics, the spatial distribution of per cent of women workers to total workers showed the maximum variation (78%).

As a group, social characteristics showed maximum segregation, and family characteristics the minimum.

Both the scheduled caste and slum population showed the same generalized pattern of segregation and association in space especially near the mill areas, though all scheduled castes do not stay in slums and all slums do not have only scheduled castes. Only the core areas which are essentially commercial areas and are highly congested have neither slums nor scheduled caste populations, just for want of residential space within the reach of this low income group. Thus, the scheduled castes and slum population were concentrated in the peripheral and intermediate zones, and revealed interrupted zonal patterns.

At the other end of the caste-hierarchy scale, Brahmins were concentrated mainly in the older northern peripheries, all located in the new intermediary zones. Muslims were concentrated in the census divisions located in the core near Russel Market, while Christians were mostly in the north-eastern census divisions located in the intermediate zones.

The spatial distribution of administrative, executive, and managerial workers showed their concentration in areas in the northern and southern periphery. The other group which showed high coefficient of variation in the distribution was workers engaged in wholesale and retail trade industry and such workers were in high proportions in census divisions located in the core.

The areas of low socio-economic status with higher level of congestion and lower levels of urban amenities had more residents than migrants, and the high socio-economic status areas had low population densities, higher level of urban amenities, and a low resident-migrant ratio.

Bangalore city is a metropolis of middle class households. According to the 1974 survey, 59 per cent of households belonged to the middle income group (Rs. 300—Rs. 1000). The per capita income in the city was Rs. 133 per month and the average household income Rs. 657. Household income showed close relationship with religion, caste, education and occupation of household head. The concentration ratio in the income distribution with respect to education was the largest out of these for all the four characteristics (Figs. 5.1 and 5.2).

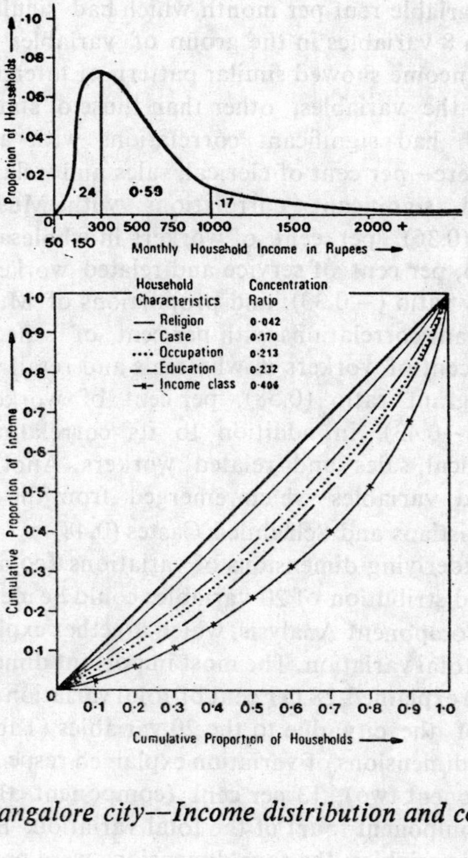

FIG. 5.1 : *Bangalore city—Income distribution and concentration*

Of the 20 variables, per capita income was significantly correlated (positively or negatively) with the maximum number (10) of variables viz., per cent Brahmins to total Hindu population (0.53), per cent professional, executive and related workers (0.74), per cent service, production and related workers (−0.63), income per household (0.87), per cent dwellings (0.83), household size (−0.55), fertility ratio (−0.47), persons per acre (−0.36), and houses per acre (−0.37). This showed that in areas where per capita income was high, proportions of Brahmins, professional, executing and related workers, income per household, and rent per dwelling were also high, but proportions of service, production and related workers, household size, fertility ratio, and population and house densities were low. The variable rent per month which had significant correlations with 8 variables in the group of variables related with per capita income showed similar pattern of interrelationships.

Among the variables, other than those of status, the variables which had significant correlations with at least five variables were—per cent of clerical, sales and related workers which had significant correlations with Muslims (0.34), Brahmins (0.36), per cent of workers in wholesale and retail trade (0.55), per cent of service and related workers (−0.77), and fertility ratio (−0.33); and proportions of Muslims which had significant correlations with per cent of scheduled castes (0.34), per cent of workers in wholesale and retail trade (0.34), resident-migrant ratio (0.58), per cent of workers in manufacturing (−0.43), in addition to its correlation with per cent of clerical, sales and related workers. Another pair of inter-related variables which emerged from the analysis was that of Christians and Scheduled Castes (0.48).

Four underlying dimensions of variations (components) in the spatial distribution of 20 variables could be identified using Principal Component Analysis, which together explained 63 per cent of the total variation. The most important dimension (component one) explained 28 per cent of total variation in the census divisions of the city, due to the 20 variables (Table 5.3). The other three dimensions of variation explained respectively 14 per cent (component two), 13 per cent (component three), and 8 per cent (component four) of the total variation. Based on the grouping of variables, the four dimensions were named as:

1. Socio-economic status.
2. Religion-based segregation.
3. Congestion.
4. Household character.

TABLE 5.3 : **Component loading of significant variables in the four components.**

Variables	Component loading
Component 1 : Variation explained 28%	
Per capita income	0.916
Income per household	0.863
Per cent professional etc., workers	0.823
Rent per dwelling	0.803
Per cent Brahmins	0.706
Per cent workers in services etc.	—0.787
Fertility ratio	—0.556
Houses per acre	—0.498
Persons per acre	—0.472
Per cent workers in manufacturing	—0.408
Component 2 : Variation explained 14%	
Per cent workers in wholesale, retail etc.	0.762
Per cent Muslims	0.749
Per cent clerical and sales workers	0.708
Resident per hundred migrants	0.562
Per cent workers in manufacturing	—0.496
Component 3 : Variation explained 13%	
Persons per acre	0.673
Houses per acre	0.628
Per cent rented houses	0.473
Per cent Scheduled Castes and Tribes	—0.599
Per cent Christians	—0.569
Component 4 : Variation explained 2%	
Females per thousand males	0.621
Persons per household	0.528
Resident per hundred migrants	0.428
Per cent women workers	0.398

Component 1—Socio-economic status

This component represented the group of variables reflecting the socio-economic status (Table 5.3). All the census divisions with high and high medium scores on the socio-economic component were in the central, north and south sections of the intermediate and periphery zones. The divisions with high scores had 43 per cent to 67 per cent households with per capita income of Rs. 200 and above, and the divisions in the high medium group had 26 per cent to 57 per cent of such households.

The divisions in the group of low socio-economic status were concentrated mainly around the two nuclei in the core, while the divisions in the low medium group were mainly in the east and west part of the periphery.

Component 2—Religion based segregation

Muslim segregation arises from an apparent need for proximity to co-religionists. The socio-economic status which forces

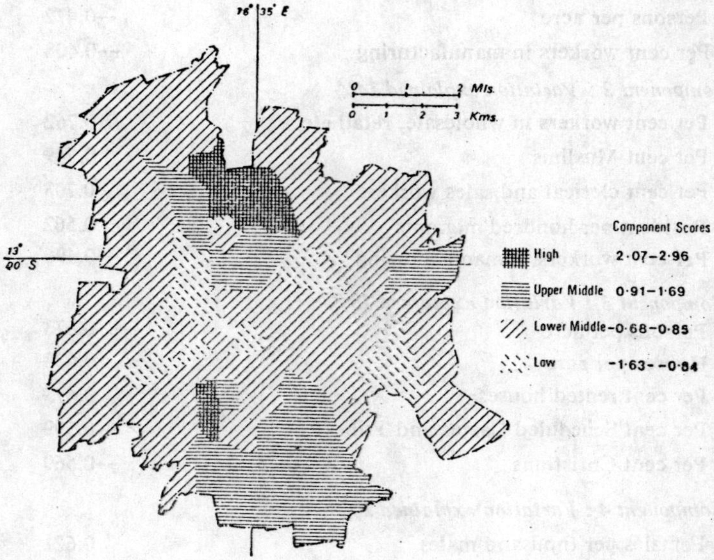

FIG. 5.2 : *Bangalore city—Socio-economic status*

Hindu households of differing status to live in separate areas has no relationship with the distribution of Muslim households.

Component 3—Congestion
The divisions with high scores on this component had high density of persons and houses and high proportion of rented houses. The divisions with low scores showed less congestion and larger proportions of Christians or scheduled castes or both.

Component 4—Household character
This component positively associated with females per thousand males, household size, resident-migrant ratio, and per cent women workers, had high positive scores for divisions in the north-eastern part of the city core.

Patterns of the city structure (Fig. 5.3)
The foregoing analysis showed that the city's structure was

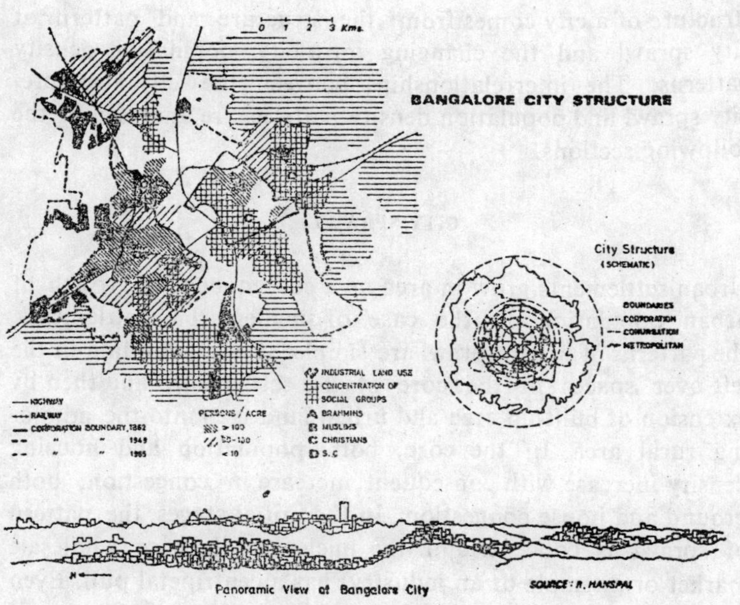

FIG. 5.3 : *Bangalore city—Structure*

found to be not simple "rich-centre and poor-periphery" but a complex one—middle class status city centre and both high status and low status periphery.

The outward moving periphery left behind older peripheries and constituted a distinct intermediate zone, not only by its intermediate geographical position between core and periphery but also by its intermediate and mixed position in the ecological scale. Regarding the tripartite city model mentioned earlier, the polarized socio-economic groups were multi-nuclear in distribution; concentric zonation was not mapable in simple geometrical forms, but the dominance of the city core and distance from the city core were found to be significant in socio-economic zonal patterns. Structural patterns did not emerge clearly, not because of their absence but because of the insensivity of the data. The distinct corridor pattern of mixed structure proved one strong evidence of this influence. The overall structure of the city revealed both east-west zonation, based more on religion and core-intermediate-periphery zonation based on socio-economic variables.

It needs no stress that the main thrust for the changing structure of a city comes from the structure and pattern of city sprawl and the changing intra-city population density patterns. The interrelationships between the city structure, city sprawl and population density patterns are analysed in the following sections.

CITY SPRAWL

Urban settlements grow in area as a consequence of growth of urban population. In the case of smaller urban settlements, the patterns of urban sprawl are simple—first by infilling in the left-over spaces in the core of the settlement, and then by extension of built-up area and urban land-uses into the adjoining rural area. In the core, both population and housing density increase with consequent increase in congestion, both ground and house congestion. In the initial stages, the pattern of sprawl is concentric if the nucleus of the core (wholesale market or a temple or an industry) has a centripetal pull. Even here the converging arterial transport routes or the transit main routes passing through the town promote growth and then the lateral or secondary routes pull the growth toward them. The pattern of growth is one of axial sprawl and then lateral (interstitial). Growth of factories, and residential colonization in the periphery of the town initiate extensive growth along with intensive infilling in the core. With the extensive and outward growth, the villages in the periphery get drawn into the town area by its extension, and get finally absorbed in the town, transforming both rural land-use and occupations into urban land-use and urban occupations. During this phase, the sprawl takes place in a haphazard manner along and across the road/or rail routes leaving out or thinly filling interstices. Infilling is intermittent and sprawl is haphazard. In the case of a smaller town, the sprawl is limited to the rural periphery of the town. In the case of cities, the sprawl takes on the scale of haphazard physical explosion. Residential colonies, industries, and public and semi-public institutions promote urban sprawl in the rural periphery. One of the consequences of urban sprawl into a rural periphery is the loss of cultivated land which cannot be avoided. It was found that during the period of 1920-1950, the loss of cultivated land in some of the Karnataka towns varied from 20 per cent of the town area in Chikballapur, a market town, to 63 per cent Nelamangala—a satellite to Bangalore (Prakasa Rao, 1964). A number of adjoining villages get incorporated for the extension of conservancy services or electricity or protected water supply. This enlarges the urban service zone. It is at this stage and scale, that the urban settlement starts developing its elemental regional or metropolitan function and develops a city-region. The pattern of growth is basically influenced by the character of its site and situation. It needs no mention that the physical constraints in the case of a port city, a city at the foot of lateritic plateau, and a city in a deltaic plain with its dense network of canals and distributary streams differ sharply, and hence the form and pattern of urban sprawl differ. The different physical landscape elements have the potential to add to the beauty of city landscape or can mar the landscape. The canals in a deltaic city can be lined with green avenues or slums polluting the canal water.

The characteristic patterns of sprawl also differ with different phases and scales of growth and specific development thrusts consequent upon developments in transport networks, or location of industries, or extension of residential layouts. In contrast to the simple patterns of infilling in the core and outward spill and incorporation of the adjoining village(s), characteristic of small and medium size towns, the pattern of sprawl of a large city, e.g. a metropolitan and million city, is more complex both in structure and scale. To demonstrate this, Bangalore is selected for study.

City sprawl of Bangalore*

During the period 1901-1971, the city area of Bangalore increased from 20.7 square miles with a population of 0.159 million to 60 square miles with a population of 1.422 million. Population growth was greater in proportion than increase in the city area, so there was an increase in population density from 12 persons per acre to 37 persons per acre (Table 5.4). Within this overall population density of 37 persons per acre, the intra-city density varied from 2 persons per acre to 357 persons per acre.

During the 70-year period of expansion in urban area, at least 100 villages would have been absorbed into the city structure. The City Development Plan (1981-2001) envisaged an overall density of 35 persons per acre in 1981, with an increase of nearly 40 per cent in population and 70 per cent in area over the 1971 area-population base. This would represent a reversal of the imbalance between area increase and population increase characteristies till 1971. By the year 2001, with the metropolitan area fixed at 124 square miles and with an estimated population of 3.8 million, the anticipated overall density will be less than 50 per acre. Table 5.4 and Fig. 5.4 clearly bring out that (i) a phase of conurbation-like contiguous growth which characterized the spread of the city up to 1961 was over, (ii) the imbalance between area expansion and population

*The two nuclei: the City Market area and the Russel Market area, railway lines (Bangalore-Madras, Bangalore-Mysore, Bangalore-Harihar, Bangalore-Guntakal, and Bangalore-Salem), the five national highways, and the north-east and north-west, and the south-east and south-west quadrats are taken as a framework to analyse the patterns of city-sprawl during the period 1901 to 1977. Based on the City Development Plan and the proposed city layouts, the anticipated pattern of growth during the period 1971-2001 is analysed.

TABLE 5.4 : Variation in area and population of Bangalore city, Bangalore metropolitan area—1901 to 2001.

Year	Urban area	Area in sq. miles	Population ('000)	Percentage change in population	Gross density per acre
1901	City+Cantonment	20.7	159	—	12.0
1941	City+Cantonment	24.4	407	156.0	26.1
1951	Corporation area	46.0	779	91.4	26.5
1961	Corporation	46.0	906	16.3	30.8
1971	Corporation area	60.0	1422	56.9	37.0
1981*	Metropolitan area	102.0	2300	61.7	35.2
2001*	Metropolitan area	124.0	3800	65.3	47.9

*Projected: Town Planning Department, Bangalore.

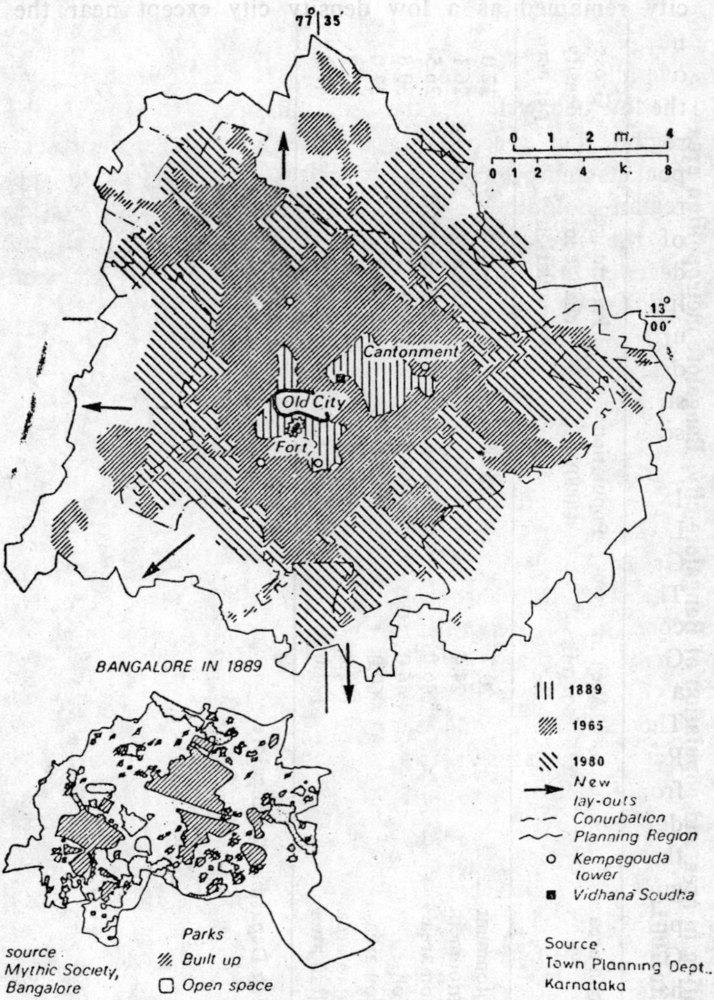

FIG. 5.4 : *Bangalore—City sprawl*

growth was reduced, and (iii) there are wide rural areas with as many as 218 villages located within the proposed metropolitan area, providing space for the future city and also a green setting. Thus, in spite of imbalances between area expansion and population growth during the 70-year period, the city remained as a low density city except near the city nuclei. The Development Plan also proposed to keep low the overall density of the city of the future. It is not only within the low urban density metropolitan area but also in the city region that green wedges should be planned to protect rural pockets and preserve open spaces. The villages in the city-region should be primarily oriented to the increasing demands of the city, instead of getting totally absorbed into the city, degenerating into pockets of high congestion and sub-standard living conditions, repeating the pre-1961 pattern of contiguous urban spread and haphazard sprawl. What is important for designing the zonal patterns is the process and the associated structure of urban growth, and this is discussed in the following section.

Bangalore Municipality had originally eight divisions in 1862—Palace, Balepet, Manovartepet, Halsurpet, Nagarthapet, Lalbagh, Fort, and High Ground. In 1894, Palace and High Ground divisions were grouped with the Palace division. This was the western section of the city. The cantonment consisted of six municipal divisions of Halsur, Southern, East General Bazaar, Cleveland town and High Ground. In 1889, a committee was formed for the development of extensions. The earliest to be added, in 1892, were—one northward from Race Course (Seshadripuram) and the other south-westward from the Fort (Chamarajpet). The next 25 years saw the rapid development of a number of new extensions to accommodate the growing population, both resident and migrant—Basavanagudi and Malleswaram in 1898, Frazer Town in 1906, Sankarapuram in 1908, and Richmond town in 1912, Sriramapuram and Gavipuram in 1915, Visveswarapuram in 1918, Gavipur Guttahalli, Taskar town, Cox town and Austin town in 1922-23, and Venkatarangapura in 1925. Then, Gandhinagar in 1930, and Kumar Park and Narasimharaja Colony in 1938 were added.

The city was spreading simultaneously north and south of the pre-urban nucleus (1537); in 1892, Chamarajpet to the south-west and Seshadripuram to the north; in 1898, Basavanagudi to the south and Malleswaram to the north-west; in 1915, Sriramapuram to the north-east and Gavipur to the south-west. In the Cantonment, the growth of built-up area was more contiguous. The Bangalore City Improvement Trust was formed in 1945, and further extensions were planned—Kumara Park West Extension 1947, Wilson Garden 1947, Vyalikaval Extension 1948, Sunkenahalli Extension 1948, Jayamahal 1949. In 1949, the Cantonment and the city were merged to become the City Corporation. The plans for new extensions continued and included Jayanagar, Indiranagar and Rajajinagar. In 1956, Mysore State was reorganized with Bangalore as the capital of the reorganized State. This further opened the gates of the city, as it were, for the migrants both to the city and to its adjoining areas. One major consequence of the urban-growth from the beginning was the invasion into the green setting and open spaces, except into the defence areas. The earliest green setting of parks and open spaces extended from the Indian Institute of Science in the north-west up to the Mental Hospital in the south-east connecting Palace Orchards, High Ground, Cubbon Park, Wilson Garden and Lalbagh. In 1889, the built-up area of the city was about 3.9 square miles out of a total city area of 18.1 square miles. Thus, the area under parks and open spaces was more than four times the built-up area. In the year 1971, the area under open spaces got drastically reduced to 4 square miles, with the city area as more than eight times the area under open spaces.

The Bangalore Development Authority (formerly, the City Improvement Trust Board) proposed to develop 25 layouts in a phased programme during the decade 1974-84, located adjacent to the corporation boundary, but well within the metropolitan area. Except to the north-east, these are also well within the conurbation boundary. These layouts, over an area of about 11,724 acres, could accommodate a population of about 586 thousand persons, with a gross density of 50 persons per acre. The main thrust of urban-growth is to the north-east in the interstitial areas between Bellary road and Madras road, where three main layouts would extend about two miles, beyond the present corporation boundary. A number of layouts (about six) were also planned to the south-east. These would fill in the interstitial area between the Madras highway and the road to Salem, where there are already pockets of urban development. To the south and south-west, the layouts (Sarakki and Banashankari) extend only about one or two miles beyond the corporation boundary. To the north-west, the built-up area extends a considerable distance along the Tumkur road, and infilling (industrial and institutional) has already taken place in the interstitial area between Tumkur road and Bellary road.

Thus, tracing the pattern and structure of urban-growth from the initial pre-urban nucleus (the fort) three types of sprawl with associated processes and structure could be identified. The earliest was mainly residential leapfrogging and residential infilling along with "ribbon shopping and commercial land-uses". The distance range involved was 2 to 4 miles from the Fort; leapfrogging of the Indian Institute of Science was an exception. The second type was characterized by leapfrogging of large-scale industrial complexes such as HAL, ITI, HMT and BEL, 8 miles from the nucleus, followed by residential infilling along major transport routes, and in the interstitial area, along with the growth of residential areas in the vicinity of the industries, and near the then edge of the city's built-up area. The third type was characterized by the leapfrogging of institutional complexes such as Bangalore University, and the new extensions to industrial complexes, and the infilling of residential layouts by the CITB, circumferentially to the city's built-up area to gain benefits of proximity to the city (Table 5.5). The result is that the city shape is tending to become oval and more compact. Only the residential corridors distort the shape.

In the process of leapfrogging and infilling of urban-growth of residential, industrial, and institutional land-uses the main determinants were, and will be, axial transport routes, particularly for industries, proximity to the city core, preference for location near the outward moving edge of the city to avoid congestion, and the very availability of space at the city's edge. The one common denominator in the spread of the city was the haphazard growth of the land use in spite of the City Master Plan. This is attributed to the multiplicity of jurisdictions involved in the city development, and the uncoordinated and individual decisions of the private developers. Nearer the outward-moving city boundary within a distance of 8 miles from the city centre, the steep slopes of the distance decay curves, the inter-lacing boundaries, the urban-industrial growth in isolated clusters and along the corridors, all indicate

TABLE 5.5 : City sprawl 1537 to 1976 (process of leapfrogging and infilling)*

Phase	Year	Pattern of city sprawl	Distance range	Example			
1	1537-1939	Residential leapfrogging Residential infilling	2 to 4 miles	to the north	Seshadripuram Malleswaram Gandhinagar Kumarapark	1892 1898 1930 1938	Leapfrogging infilling
				to the south	Basavanagudi Shankarapuram Visveswarapuram	1898 1908 1918	Leapfrogging infilling
2	1940-1959	Industrial leapfrogging (along axial routes)	6 to 8 miles	Hindustan Aeronautics Bharat Electronics Hindustan Machine Tools		1940 1948 1949	Leapfrogging
		Residential infilling (interstitial areas)		Sadashivanagar Indiranagar Rajajinagar			Infilling
3	1960 onwards	Institutional leapfrogging (along axial routes)	8 to 12 miles	University of Agricultural Sciences at Hebbal Bangalore University Campus at Kengeri			Leapfrogging
		CITB Layout infilling (interstitial areas)		CITB Layouts			Infilling

*Ranjana Hanspal (1977).

the irregular and leapfrogging urban-industrial and institutional growth. Residential and retail shopping centres contributed their shares to the haphazard and ribbon growth. The Bangalore Development Plan made a pointed reference to the chaotic and haphazard growth of the city into its adjoining countryside, a repetition of the earlier pattern of growth. The city corporation area, the conurbation area using the term conurbation loosely, and the metropolitan area are the three areas officially designated to accommodate the expanding metropolis. The Corporation had to shift its boundary in 1965 from the one in 1949, following the sprawl of the city. The conurbation boundary includes most of the built-up area. The rapid growth of the city fringe in non-agricultural population during 1961-71 and industrial development, induced urban spread and rural to urban transformation. Urban growth in the adjoining villages outside the Corporation boundary, as expected, tended to be haphazard. This situation forced the State Government to take decision to extend the Corporation boundary and consequently include about 110 villages within its limits, thus adding 210 sq. km. of area and population about 2,00,000. The urbanizable area of the city is estimated at 320 sq. km.

The newly constituted Bangalore Development Authority holds a promise for a better pattern and structure of urban growth, balancing between the rural and urbanizing and industrializing areas and between different land-uses, primarily through zoning and land acquisition, where necessary. Consequently, what will be the emerging density patterns, both within the city and taking the city as a whole ? Construction of any model of population density for a city requires an understanding of the theoretical base and density correlates and problems involved in generating data required for calibrating the models. An attempt is made to discuss some of these aspects in the following section.

URBAN POPULATION DENSITIES

Models and correlates, density profiles and their significance

Urban population density is much more than just a ratio of people per acre, gross or net. Density as a variable, has both policy aspects and structural ones (in terms of ground and house congestion) particularly when there is shortage in the available urban land within a given range of accessibility to the city centre. Density has also amenity and liveability aspects. The very neighbourhood attitude and tolerance of the residents are more important than just the ratio. The same density provokes different reactions with differences in individual and community preferences, tolerance and acceptability. Planners recognize more in theory than in application that "local living habits, standards and customs as well as the services available, have a considerable bearing on this problem" (Jansen, 1966). High densities and low densities are not necessarily related to negative and positive living conditions respectively. The urban population density is one basic element of urban form, and the city size, age and structure are expressed in this element. The changing density profiles in relation to land-use, employment structure and socio-economic status provide an analogue for the ongoing process of concentration and consequent congestion, infilling and dispersal within the city. The gradient form of the density profile emphasises the importance of centrality or maximum accessibility, and the humps, peaks and troughs in the profile indicate differences in land-use structure and patterns. The very shape and form of the city, which are changing, also influence the density profiles.

The theoretical rationale for the universality of the manner in which the population densities decline from the city centre, regardless of time and place, can be stated as follows, quoting extensively from Berry *et al.* (1963): "The competition for urban sites by different land-users and differences in their abilities to pay, result in bid-rent functions of varying gradients with highest value at the location of maximum accessibility. Thus, larger spaces at prime locations of higher accessibility are occupied by those with higher paying abilities. The residential users, therefore, occupy smaller proportion of land near the centre and larger proportions away from it. Here again, more people want to live near the centre due to its higher accessibility, however, as the land near the centre is more expensive, they consume little of it. Since land availability and extensive use increase with distance from city centre, population densities also decline with the distance. The factors influencing density in the city core and density gradients are many and changing—the age, size of residential lots, land-use, centrality and central functions and transportation technology".

The density gradient models are mathematical formulation of the theory of density decline with distance from city centre, in a generalized form. It has been proved in various studies that the most generalised form of the density gradients conforms to the first degree negative exponential function. The model was first proposed by Bleicher (1892), who proved its validity for Frankfurt. Later Clark (1951, 1958) demonstrated the validity of negative exponential model for density decline based on examples from thirty-six cities. Berry, Simmons and Tennant (1963) further examined the structure of urban population densities for about hundred available examples from various studies drawn from various parts of the world and concluded that "regardless of time or place, the model provides a statistically significant fit to the distribution of population densities within cities". As the model only provides a statistically significant fit and not the best fit, there were attempts, to try variations of exponential models and other models, like second degree and density crater functions, to find out the best fitting models e.g. by Sherratt (1960), Ajo (1965), Newling (1967, 1968), Casetti (1967, 1969).

In the case of Indian cities, the negative exponential model was first used by Tennant (1961) for Hyderabad and Calcutta. Kar (1962), applied the model to Calcutta and later Brush (1968), applied the model for a number of other Indian cities. These studies were related to intra-urban patterns. However, in a few studies, the distance zones are extended even beyond the municipal limits of the cities, e.g. Alam and Khan (1972), Nangia (1976), Bradnock (1974), Bogue (1949) have shown that the negative exponential model can be applied upto a distance of 300 miles from the city centre.

In the present study an attempt is made to examine—(1) the forms of the curves represented by selected density gradient functions, (2) problems of data generation and application of the models in the context of Indian cities, (3) some correlates of population density based on the density structure of Bangalore city.

Models of density gradients

The most widely used density gradient model is the negative exponential model, also referred to as the Bleicher-Clark model, which states that the density y at a distance x from the city centre can be expressed by the following equation:

$$y = \exp(a - bx) \tag{1}$$

where $\exp(a)$ is the density at distance $x=0$ from the city centre, or, in other words, the central density, and b is a constant indicating the constant rate of decline in natural logarithms of density with distance (Fig 5.5).

From equation (1),

$$\frac{dy}{dx} = \exp(a - bx)(-b) = -b \exp(a) \exp(-bx)$$

Thus the density gradient, rate of change in density with increase in distance, declines exponentially. In other words, the density is highest at the city centre, it decreases at a greater rate nearer the centre and at a gradually lower rate as the distance increases. The rate of change tends to be very small for large values of distance from the centre. The magnitude of rate of decline indicates the spatial pattern of the density structure. A sharp decline indicates high concentration of population while a moderate decline indicates a sprawling city.

Variations in the negative exponential functions were suggested by Tanner (1961), Sherrat (1960) and Ajo (1965). Tanner and Sherrat used the second degree negative exponential given in (2) for Sydney.

$$y = \exp(a - bx^2) \tag{2}$$

suggesting a rather slow decline of densities for the values of distance $x \leq 1$ and then an accelerated decline. Ajo used the square-root negative exponential

$$y = e\,(a - b\,V^{x}) \tag{3}$$

for the rural periphery of London.

The functions represented by equations (1), (2) and (3) all show a monotonic decline of population densities with increase in distance from city centre.

Casetti (1967) argued that the declining pattern emerges owing to the fact that residential locations are a function of distance from work-places and preference for uncongested

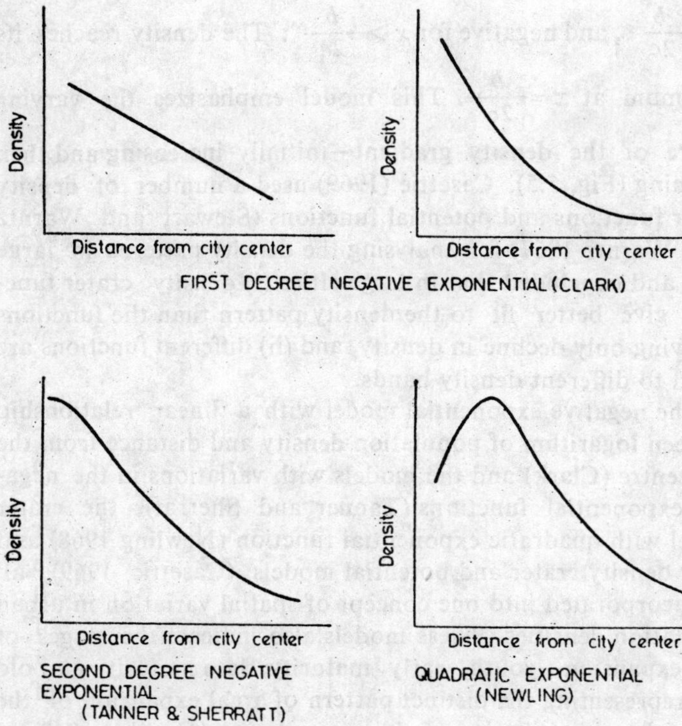

FIG. 5.5 : *Population distance patterns*

sites. In the case of large Western cities, it has now been shown that residential population is displaced from the central area by commercial and other land-uses giving rise to a density "crater" in the density profile. Therefore, Newling (1969) suggested the use of quadratic exponential function and tested it for most of the cities for which Clark used the negative exponential function. The quadratic exponential function is given by the following equation:

$$y = \exp(a + bx - cx^2) \qquad (4)$$

From equation (4)

$$\frac{dy}{dx} = \exp(a + bx - cx^2)(+b - 2cx)$$

Thus the density gradient is positive for values of

$x < \frac{b}{2c}$, and negative for $x > \frac{b}{2c}$. The density reaches its maximum at $x = \frac{b}{2c}$. This model emphasizes the varying nature of the density gradient—initially increasing and then declining (Fig. 5.5). Casettie (1969) used a number of density crater functions and potential functions (Stewart and Warntz 1958, Warntz 1967) for analysing the density patterns in large cities and concluded that in large cities (i) density crater functions give better fit to the density pattern than the functions involving only decline in density, and (ii) different functions are suited to different density bands.

The negative exponential model with a linear relationship between logarithm of population density and distance from the city centre (Clark) and the models with variations in the negative exponential functions (Tanner and Sherrat), the crater model with quadratic exponential function (Newling 1968) and other density crater and potential models (Casettie 1969), all are incorporated into one concept of spatial variation in urban population densities. These models also indicate the stages of city expansion—youth, early maturity, late maturity and old age, representing the distinct pattern of areal expansion of the city and a redistribution of city's population (Newling 1968).

Problems of data generation and applications of the models for Indian cities

Data used in the analysis of density structure are generally computed for circular rings of increasing distance from the city centre. This involves two important steps—identification of city centre and determining the width of the circular rings. The identification of the city centre is straightforward where the structure is dominated by a single centre of workplaces and commercial activities like the central business district in most American cities. But in cities where the structure is polynucleated or where there is no clear-cut city centre, the emphasis on the city centre poses problems.

In selecting the city centres in his study of Indian cities, Brush writes, "so far as possible, I have accepted as the nodal point in each city under examination that so identified by the authors of planning studies or monographs on that city, or I have relied on the advice of well-informed local officials and resident scholars, supplemented by field reconnaissance. In some cities, more than one nodal point must be recognized because of the pronounced dualism of the geographical pattern." Thus no uniform criterion was used in the selection, and it involved a subjective element. Moreover, using two nodal points is also subject to methodological criticism. For example, in Bangalore there are two major centres of high population density and trading activities, located more than three kilometres apart. In addition to these two, there is another centre of workplace dominance in the city core. Therefore, in analysing the density structure of Bangalore city, if the city market (Fig. 5.6) is taken as the city centre, the other centre, Russel market will lie at the same distance at which some peripheral areas of low density will also get included, and this violates the basic assumption of aggregating data. In Brush's study, the analysis for Bangalore and Hyderabad is subject to this criticism.

The most important consideration in the selection of the centre should be the one of maintaining near-homogeneous densities in the areal units used for data aggregation. Here the problem is often one of scale of observation which needs to be examined critically. In the cities with polynucleated structure, the centre could be based on either work or trading activities near the geometrical centre of the city, because centrality plays an important role due to the least aggregate transport costs in almost all types of city structures. Even if there is no important node near the geometric centre, it is likely that by selecting the geometric centre as the city centre, the other centres would fall in one ring and thus the homogeneity for data aggregation would be maintained. The significance of the geometric centre is related to homogeneity and compactness of city structure. A circular or near-circular city is an exception. "Asymmetry and lopsidedness are common, elongations and crenulations many" (Berry *et al.*).

The other problem in generating data for density gradient analysis is the selection of width of rings. The width has been of varying size in different studies. This loses its significance with the varying size and shape of unit areas. While in intra-city analysis, generally it varies from half-a-mile to one mile, in the city-region analysis, it varies from one to five miles. If the hypothesis of a declining trend is established through the models, it should yield similar results irrespective of the differences in the size of rings. But in order to have large number of observations, the width should be as small as possible, with the limitations of data measurements and size and shape of basic units. The principle is that rings should not cut across the basic units of data aggregation. In the Delhi Study (Nangia 1976) the values of density show large variation when the data were aggregated in one mile ring, but a general declining trend was observed when grouped in 5-mile distance zones. In such a situation, an analysis with different models for different distance bands could be useful.

Another problem relates to the computation of unit values for the different rings. To compute values of selected variables for each ring as the average value of the variable per settlement, is not correct. It must be mentioned here that a simple mean of relative measures (density, percentages, etc.) is not meaningful. The values of selected variables, should be computed for the whole ring taken as one unit by aggregating the component variables involved in the derived relative variables. For example, while computing density in a ring, the population and areas of all the basic units must be added to derive the value for the ring. The boundaries of the unit areas and their size and shape very rarely conform to the rings. Data aggregation at village level minimizes the problem of boundary adjustment in the city regions.*

Brush examined the gradient pattern of 21 Indian cities of population sizes (1961) varying from 57 thousand to 6 million. He fitted a model similar to Bleicher-Clark model, but not exactly the same, as reported in his paper, to all the cities.** The coefficient of determination varies from 0.07 to 0.81, and only in eight cases does distance explain more than 50 per cent of the variation in the density values. This shows that the

*For a summary of the analytical techniques to measure population distribution and the associated unresolved problems refer to Duncan (1957).

**The model used by Brush is $y=ab^x$ and is expressed in logarithmic form as $\log y=\log a + x \log b$ (p. 371).

model does not give a good fit to the density patterns in all Indian cities. This was also inferred by Brush in his paper (p. 374) but he did not try different models to fit to different cities. However, he identified four groups of cities based on their graphs of decrease in logarithms of densities with distance from the city centre. The first group included those cities where the highest density of population is found in a compact central area (e.g. Ahmedabad and Poona). The second group had a density pattern resembling that of western cities where the density in central areas is relatively low (e.g., Calcutta, Bombay and Madras). The third group represented cities with dual city centres of high densities (e.g., Bangalore, Hyderabad) and the fourth group included planned cities where the density is low throughout the urban area with little concentration in the central areas (e.g. Jamshedpur and Chandigarh). These patterns emerge from a generalized graph (p. 373) in the study, although the data presented in Table 11 (p. 370) do not appear to conform to the patterns.

Owing to the above mentioned problems and gaps in the studies on the density structure of Indian cities, there is a case for adopting a uniform method of data generation, and re-examining the density structure patterns of the cities.

Density patterns in Bangalore city (Fig. 5.6)

The gross population density of Bangalore city (1971 population : 1.54 million) was 37 persons per acre and was as low as 12 per acre in 1901 and 31 per acre in 1961. The city maintained it's over-all low gross density level over decades (Table 5.4), but could not escape from intra-city sharp variations in gross density, varying from less than 30 per acre in the periphery to 357 per acre near the city market, in the year 1971*. The spatial pattern of population distribution in 1971 revealed binodality which was also the characteristic in 1951 and 1961. The two population foci, one near the city market (density 357 per acre: Cubbonpet) and the other near Russel Market (density 322 per acre : Central Bazaar) were

*The highest locality density reported was 700 per acre near Cottonpet. This gets concealed by the size, shape and area of the division for which aggregate density was calculated.

separated by low-density areas of less than 50 per acre (Vidhana Soudha and Tasker Town). Thus, within the over-all distance decay pattern, the density profile was binodal, with a crater form.

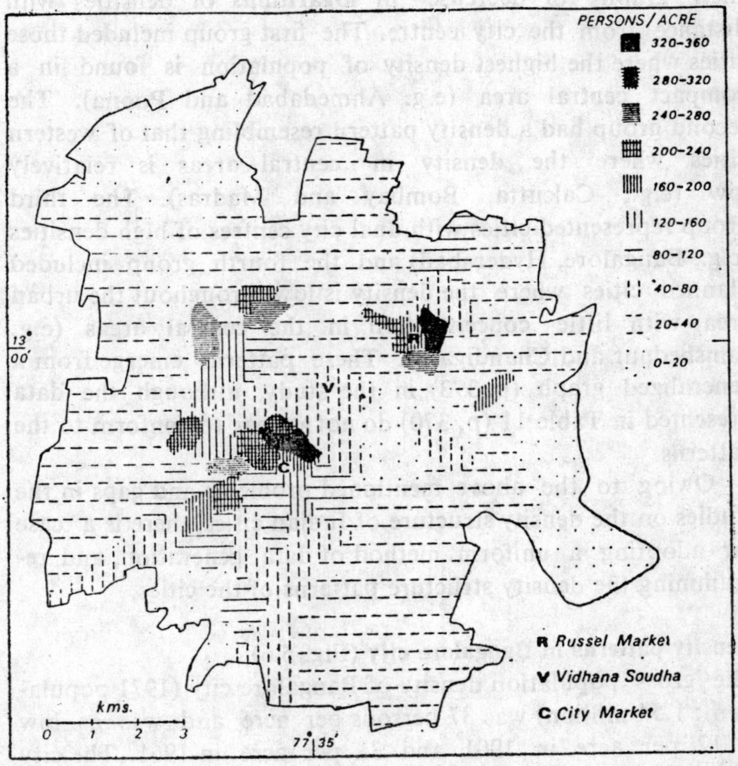

FIG. 5.6 : *Bangalore gross population density, 1971*

The crater form which broke the contiguity of most congested areas of the city, had open spaces like Cubbon Park, Brigade Ground and institutions like Vidhana Soudha (the State Legislature and Secretariat), the High Court, Public Works Department buildings, the Reserve Bank of India, All India Radio and the General Post Office and Telegraph Office. The formation of a density "crater" at the centre in western cities has often been explained as a result of displacement of residential population by non-residential activities, and is related to the stage of urban development. Absence of a density "crater" is supposed to mark an earlier stage of urban development. The low density crater form in Bangalore city was the result of the amalgamation of the city and cantonment areas, and the growth of administrative and educational institutions with extensive open spaces in between. Therefore, the crater form of the density structure in Bangalore city is the result of a phenomenon different from that in the case of Western cities.

In terms of change in area and population in different density classes 1951-1971, the most congested area (over 300 per acre) showed increase both in its share in area and population. In the highly congested areas, located both near the city market and Russel Market, the two kernels of the city, both the processes of concentration and deconcentration were operating. Some of the areas (like Kemmanagundi and Swami Setty Garden) showed a decline in density due to the invasion of commercial land-uses and functions and shifting of residences to the peripheral areas.* In some others (like Maharaja Mills and Central Bazaar) there was an increase in concentration of residential population. Some of these areas (like city market and Cubbonpet) were static, indicating saturation level. But the overall pattern of change in the core was one of increase in density.

The older residential areas with high concentration of trade, transport, commerce and household industry promoted densities ranging from 300 to 360 per acre. High concentration of industries and slums, with differential mix of commercial, including trade and transport, and residential areas get grouped in the density class 100—300. The density class of less than 100 was characterized by a large proportion of residential and institutional areas. The high status and prestige residential localities of Palace Orchards (27 per acre), High ground (33 per acre), Kodandarampuram (39 per acre) and the high middle class locality like Jayanagar (22 per acre) are

*A higher proportion of households moved out of the core than moved in. The households which have shifted their residences from core to periphery were mostly in the high income classes (Prakasa Rao and Tewari, 1979).

allocated in the density class of less than 50 per acre. The density zone 50—100 had the most balanced distribution in its share of area and population and was also characterized by low ground congestion (Table 5.6).

TABLE 5.6 : **Percentage of area and population density classes 1971.**

Gross Density per acre	Percentage area to total area	Percentage population to total population	Total population ('000)	Density of houses per acre
50	72.48	42.03	613	4.49
50—99	17.40	17.03	241	11.49
100—249	8.33	29.06	377	24.80
250—299	0.60	3.65	74	46.23
>300	1.19	8.23	117	45.39
Total	100.00	100.00	1422	7.38

An analysis of land-use and the residential density by fourteen sub-areas in Bangalore urban agglomeration (city and peripheral townships) showed that the density varied from 2,932 per acre in the sub-area around city market to less than 65 per acre in the sub-areas around peripheral townships (Table 5.7). The correlation of residential density with proportion of land under commercial uses was as high as 0.96 (Table 5.8) Thus higher residential densities were characterised by higher concentration of commercial uses in the neighbourhood. In the core areas, the proportion of area under commercial uses was 21 per cent and decreased with distance from city centre to less than one per cent in the outer periphery. Correspondingly, the residential density declined from 1,259 per acre in the core to 53 per acre in the outer periphery (Table 5.9.) In one of the sub-areas in the core with residential density, 2,932 per acre the proportion of area under commercial uses was 41 per cent.

TABLE 5.7 : Proportion of area under different land-uses and residential density by 14 sub-areas in Bangalore Urban Agglomeration.

Zone	Residential density per acre*	Proportion of area under land-uses to total area of a zone				Total area in sq. km.
		Residential	Commercial	Industrial	Others**	
1	162	11.51	3.19	8.18	77.12	8.9
2	178	22.22	8.43	2.21	67.14	18.0
3	132	20.51	3.41	0	76.08	6.9
4	131	31.73	3.16	14.77	50.34	11.5
5	430	8.13	2.30	0.74	88.83	16.8
6	261	22.88	10.47	1.13	65.53	13 1
7	227	21.54	3.97	7.44	67.05	13.0
8	350	15.85	6.42	11.47	66.26	11.7
9	270	27.41	8.77	19.84	43.98	13.6
10	2,932	7.49	40.67	1.15	50.69	5.9
11	680	10.28	11.20	0	78.52	12.4
12	44	10.77	0.23	44.71	44.29	30.0
13	51	12.76	2.46	20.45	64.33	7.4
14	62	24.40	0.73	22.94	51.93	15.6
Total	242	17.58	5.83	13.60	62.99	184.8

*Based on estimated population for 1974 and area under residential uses.

**Includes area under public/semi-public uses, roads, parks, open spaces and unclassified land.

TABLE 5.8 : Some correlates of residential density in Bangalore

Residential density	Correlation coefficient (14 observations)
Proportion of Residential area	−0.46*
Proportion of Commercial area	0 96**
Proportion of Industrial area	−0.34
Total employment	0.84**

*Significant at 1 per cent level.

**Significant at 0.1 per cent level.

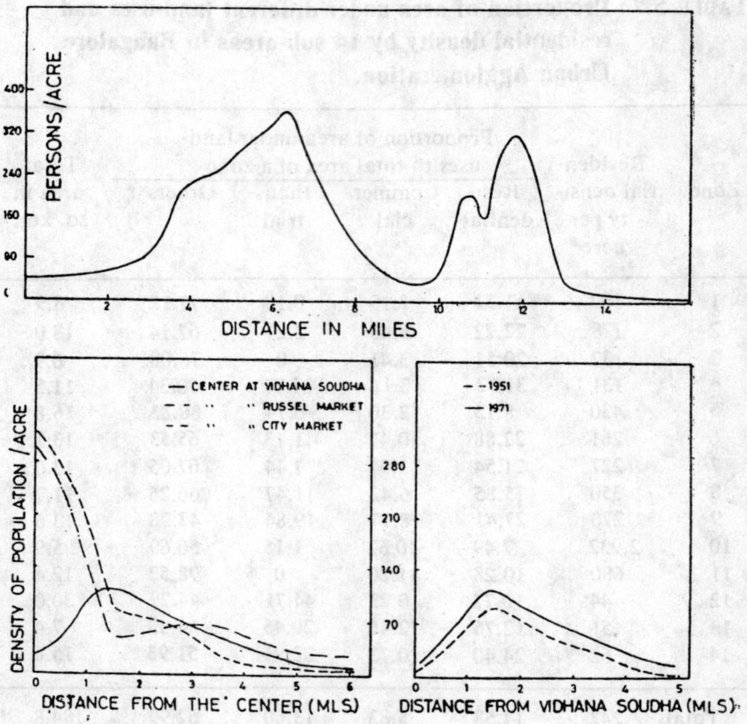

FIG. 5.7 : *Bangalore—Population density profiles, 1971*

The residential density was negatively correlated with proportion of area under residential uses implying that the larger the residential area in a zone the lower the density. The correlation of residential density with proportion of area under industrial use did not come out to be significant but at the aggregate level of core and periphery, low densities were associated with higher proportion of industrial land-use. The correlation of the density with total employment by place of work was also very high and positive, indicating high densities in the neighbourhoods of concentration of work places, a function of accessibility.

The gross density and the index of socio-economic status in the 63 census divisions of the city were negatively correlated

(0.47, significant at 0.1 per cent level).* While low status areas had both high and low densities, the high status areas had low densities (Appendix Table)

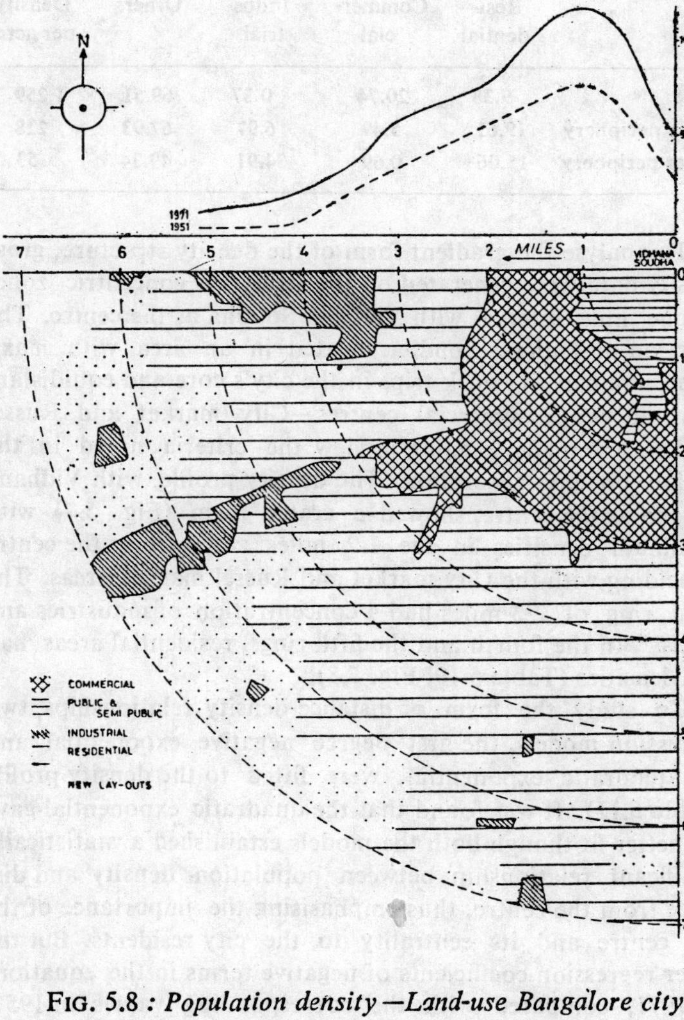

FIG. 5.8 : *Population density—Land-use Bangalore city*

*The index was computed based on selected socio-economic characteristics using principal component analysis, as a part of the 'ecological structure' analysis of Bangalore city (Prakasa Rao and Tewari, 1979).

TABLE 5.9 : **Proportion of area under different land-uses and residential population density in core and periphery—Bangalore urban agglomeration.**

	Residential	Commercial	Industrial	Others	Density per acre
Core	9.38	20.74	0.37	69.51	1,259
Inner periphery	19.61	5.49	6.97	67.93	228
Outer periphery	15.06	0.69	34.91	49.34	53

To analyse the gradient form of the density structure, gross density data were generated on the basis of concentric zones of one mile interval with Vidhana Soudha as the centre. The selection of Vidhana Soudha, located in an area with maximum number of work trips in the city's core and equidistant from the two commercial centres—City market and Russel market, was made, keeping in view the criteria noted in the section on data generation. The density profile, with Vidhana Soudha as the centre, showed a crater form (Fig. 5.7) with maximum densities in the 1-2 miles zone from the centre coinciding with the City market and Russel market areas. The third ring of 2-3 miles had a concentration of industries and slums.* In the fourth and the fifth rings, residential areas had low densities (Table 5.10, Fig. 5.8).

To study the form of distance-density relationships, two regression models, the first degree negative exponential and the quadratic exponential, were fitted to the density profile (Table 5.11). It was found that the quadratic exponential gave the better fit though both the models established a statistically significant relationship between population density and distance from the centre, thus emphasising the importance of the city centre and its centrality to the city residents. But the lower regression coefficients of negative terms in the equations in 1971, compared with the corresponding values in 1951, indicated a slight decline in the dominance of the city centre

*Industries generate slums but all slums are not generated by industries. Industries can also generate open spaces and residential areas under a green canopy, e.g. Binny Mill area.

TABLE 5.10 : **Gross population density in distance zones with Vidhana Soudha as centre.**

Year	Distance zone in miles				
	0-1	1-2	2-3	3-4	4+
1951	28.26	73.69	55.02	31.05	7.38
1971	46.92	101.97	72.35	51.56	22.63

TABLE 5.11 : **Estimate equations for the density profile**

Type of equation	Estimated equation	R^2
Negative exponential.	$\text{Log } D_{71}=2.303-0.214\text{ d}$	0.362
	$\text{Log } D_{51}=2.153-0.342\text{ d}$	0.394
Second degree negative exponential.	$\text{Log } D_{71}=0.705+1.155\text{ d} -0.228\text{ d}^2$	0.939
	$\text{Log } D_{51}=0.317-1.775\text{ d} -0.353\text{ d}^2$	0.982

d — distance
D_{71}— Population density 1971
D_{51}— Population density 1951

during the period 1951—71. Both during this period and after, the city had the benefit of the growth of a number of commercial, administrative and educational institutions away from the city centre, e.g., Yeshwantpur, Rajajinagar and Jayanagar, due to the outward spread of the city.

The studies on the spatial patterns of density structure, though not strictly comparable, owing to lack of uniformity in the methods of data generation, show that no single model gives the best fit to the pattern in all the Indian cities. There is a case for re-examining the density pattern in Indian cities based on an analysis with a uniform method of data generation. If the data permit, it would also be useful to fit different models in different distance bands in the case of metropolitan cities. In the analysis of distribution in space, the size of area has great significance. The smaller the area, the greater the homogeneity but there is no answer to the question, how small should be the unit area? Conceptually, a lower limit to the size of area may exist but to assess the effect of different areal units, empirical tests are necessary (Craig 1972). Both for analytical research and drawing meaningful conclusions from statistics for the formulation of urban development strategies, there is a case for standard and consistent unit areas. For comparative analysis, time series data for unit areas are needed. The unit area needs to be small enough to bring out inter-tract differences, and yet large enough for manipulation without increasing the cost of data analysis.*

The best fitting gradient models, and correlates of density with different types of land-uses, could be meaningfully used in monitoring the future density structure and pattern of a city. Any future plan for density patterns of a city should take into account the trends in the mix of land-use, changing socio-economic status with community group preferences, and density gradients within the envisaged city structure form and land-use design. If a city core tends to be overcrowded, it is essentially because of the land-use and occupational mix. What is a rational occupational and land-use mix which could enable a city, even within its existing structure, to develop a low density profile which would be in equilibrium, is a question to which adequate thought does not seem to have been given either by planners or by academic workers. The gradient models could also be used to predict density surfaces of different types to provide a rational basis for the future development plans of cities.

Green Belting the city

While gradient models could be used to monitor a city's density pattern and structure, the utility of the green belt model in monitoring the city sprawl cannot be underestimated. That the basic notion of a green belt has changed, is often not recognised; and in many Indian cities, a Green Belt exists, and it only needs to be protected. This is well illustrated by Bangalore.

*This was recognised by researchers as early as 30 years ago (Olds 1949) and yet the problem of unit areas varying in size and shape persists.

The concept of the Green Belt

The concept of the Green Belt developed out of social reform to provide the invisible benefits of attractive and open air countryside as a solace for the city resident from his highly congested environment. The basic notion as developed in the 19th century, and as applied to urban-industrializing countries like England, was that the functionally interdependent town and country should be kept physically distinct. Thus the concept was a product of "Garden City" philosophy, but with a distinct territorial dimension. To this function of providing recreation to "Urban man", two more functions have been added, to (i) introduce order in the haphazard urban sprawl and interrupt contiguous urban sprawl, and (ii) protect agricultural land and agricultural communities from total extinction as a consequence of the rapidly growing city, both in numbers and acres. Thus the green belt acquired the status of a multiple function planning instrument to monitor the sprawling and 'leapfrogging' city.

The classical structure of the green belt with no non-conformal uses and form, and as a constricting and frozen girdle with a barrier function, had to be modified due to increasing scale of urban pressures. As a consequence of this, the green belt of today is adapted to green wedges and a green setting with a permissible margin of urban development particularly in the inner zone. A critical assessment of the nature and success of Britain's green belts led to the conclusion that "while they have caused more problems than they have solved, they should be directed more specifically to the projection of particular and more carefully defined facets of landscape (David Thomas 1976). This deviation from the classical concept prompted statements like the green belt need not necessarily be "Green" and led to an emphasis on open spaces. Open space planning is *not* what to do with left-overs or provide space for recreation only. Rather, it is how to make the most of the open space character of areas within the built-up areas. Open spaces should (1) give structure, shape and form to the separating clusters, preserving wedges, and giving identity to urban communities and yet unite them through parks and playgrounds, (2) draw a "limit of development line" both within the city and around the city to prevent sporadic sprawl, and (3) open spaces are needed not only to provide recreation and to preserve scenic and historic sites but also to protect watersheds of even minor streams and provide natural drainage. Open and green spaces prevent the formation of extensive urban heat islands. What is often not recognised by the advocates of the green belt is the fact that even cultivated land, water, bare rocky outcrops, scrub and grazing lands and the like, constitute components of green belt. What is important in making the green belt zonation an effective instrument is the fact that it has to be integrated with the instruments of development like industrial licensing, land acquisition and zoning of Class I and also Class II agricultural lands. Here the land classification may become a tool in zoning land-uses, both for conforming and non-conforming land-uses in the green belt.

Delimitation of the Green Belt (Fig. 5.9)

The green belt for the city of Bangalore is delimited based on a series of overlays on quarter inch maps with the village as the unit of mapping. In the 1st stage of analysis, areas with 80 per cent and above as forest and cultivation are taken into consideration. In view of the highly scattered nature of this category, all land with 60 per cent and above under cultivation, and 60 per cent and above under forests and permanent pastures are identified. This land category along with water bodies and existing parks form a more or less contiguous ring lying at a distance of about 6 miles from the city centre, and beyond. The interruptions in the contiguity occur mostly in the north (parts of Hoskote and Devanahalli talukas). All land adjoining the Corporation boundary (Ring 1) is left as it is at present. A two-mile zone immediately adjoining the City Corporation boundary is delimited for industrial and residential spread. Another two-mile outer zone is delimited for the existing industrial and commercial land-uses and some extension of residential area. If, on the other hand, it becomes necessary to locate industries and their associated built-up area here, then it is desirable to leave open spaces between industrial land-uses.

Based on field reconnaissances, detailed land capability maps of the soil and land-use survey (IARI Hebbal—Bangalore)

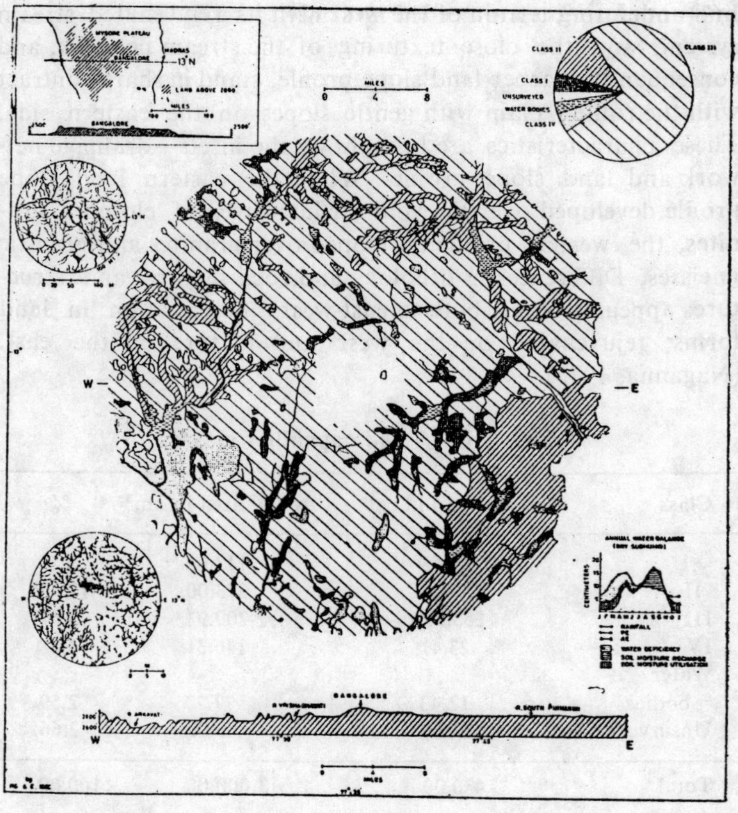

FIG.5.9 : *Land types—Bangalore and environs*

a generalized land capability map (quarter inch scale) is prepared based on irrigability, slope, erosion, soil thickness and availability of water. Rocky outcrops and water bodies are excluded from regrouping.

Of the four classified land types Class III is most extensive with 74 per cent of the area under this type. Land types Class I and Class II which need to be zoned for cultivation occupy 16 per cent (Table 5.12). The size, shape and contiguity or fragmented distribution of the four land types are brought out by Fig. 5.6. The relief profile along the 13° latitude passing through Bangalore brings out clearly the profile of Mysore plateau and the ridge on which Bangalore is situated. The hilly and undulating terrain of the west with its rejuvenated stream system, and the close texturing of the stream network, and consequently sharper land slope profile, stand in sharp contrast with the rolling plain with gentle slopes on the eastern side. These characteristics are brought by the insets—drainage network and land slope profile. While the eastern land slope profile developed over the younger intrusives of closepet granites, the western profile developed over granites and granitic gneisses. Differences in lithology and rock textures and structures appear to contribute to east-west differentiation in land forms; rejuvenated on the west and mature on the east. (Naganna, 1975).

TABLE 5.12 : **Land capability classes**

Class	Area on map in cm²	Actual area in km²	%
1	18.09	113.06	3.77
II	59.68	373.00	12.43
III	353.59	2,209.93	73.67
IV	23.41	146.31	4.88
Water bodies	12.43	77.70	2.59
Unsurveyed	12.80	80.00	2.66
Total	480.00	3,000.00	100.00

Both in the eastern and western sections, the best agricultural lands (Class I) are in isolated patches located in the flat valley bottoms of the streams and streamlets and tank ayacuts. The dominant land-use is paddy and sugarcane. Class II type occupies mostly as gently sloping uplands, and mixed crops and ragi, fruits, vegetables and tree plantations are the main land-uses. Class III, the most dominant type and which adjoins the city, is used for grazing, forest, tree plantations and rainfed mixed crops.

The low land-capability of Class III and Class IV is reflected in the dissected and hence undulating terrain over a ridge (900 metres above msl) on which Bangalore is situated. This ridge developed as a consequence of headward erosion of two river basins of Akravati and south Pinakini under a semi-arid climate with its steppe type of vegetation—scrub forest and dry deciduous forest with thin alluvial and lateritic soils and red sandy and gravelly soils developed over granites and granitic gneisses.

The proposed zonal land-use plan for the Bangalore metropolitan area according to the Outline Development Plan, gave maximum weightage to industrial land-use in the rapidly growing city periphery. This resulted in further infilling in the Yelahanka-Jalahalli area in the north-west and the Madras highway-airport area in the north-east. While increasing the recreational area by nearly three times, there was a deliberate proposal to invade the extensive Defence areas, and reduce their relative share from 23 per cent to 10 per cent (Table 5.13). This could be justified only when the released Defence areas will be used to give structure, shape and form to the city's landscape, instead of liberally allowing residential infilling.

The City Development Plan proposes to keep the overall population density of the city's edge at a low level—50 persons per acre. This indicates that extensive residential land-use is preferred to intensive residential use with higher densities. The city edge is a moving edge, and should be treated as a part of the adjoining rural landscape which is characterized by dichotomy between corridor urban-industrial and interstitial rural land-use with high concentrations of non-agricultural population in all the villages adjoining the corporation boundary. While open spaces should be used to regulate and monitor city sprawl internally, the green belt with its wedges should be planned to regulate and monitor urban-industrial growth in the fringe of the city and preserve open spaces and protect rural pockets. A single village or a few villages in the city fringe get trampled down by the sprawling city and industries. The numerous perennial and non-perennial tanks that dot the rural fringe get beheaded from their local drainage and feeding channels. The transport network drags the city into the fringe invading the different land types irrespective of their land capability levels. A properly designed green belt supported by appropriate zoning, industrial licensing and appropriate transport network should prevent the repetition of the haphazard city sprawl which is frequently lamented. It is known that the consequence of haphazard city sprawl is a total absorption of

TABLE 5.13 : **Land-use—Bangalore metropolitan area**

	Urban Development Plan 1968		Urban Development Plan		Revised and Approved 1972	
	1961		1971		1981	
	Area in acres	%	Area in acres	%	Area in acres	%
Industrial	3,069	10.96	3,069	8.74	12,483	19.10
Public—semi-public buildings*	2,100	7.50	3,952	11.25	7,123	10.90
Commercial	,683	2.44	,958	2.73	2,219	3.40
Parks and playground	2,206	7.88	2,485	7.08	6,443	9.86
Residential	10,528	37.60	14,537	41.39	27,845	42.60
Defence land	6,474	23.12	7,179	20.44	6,641	10.16
Agricultural	2,940	10.50	2,940	8.37	2,604	3.98
Total	28,000	100.00	35,120	100.00	65,358	100.00

*Including transport.

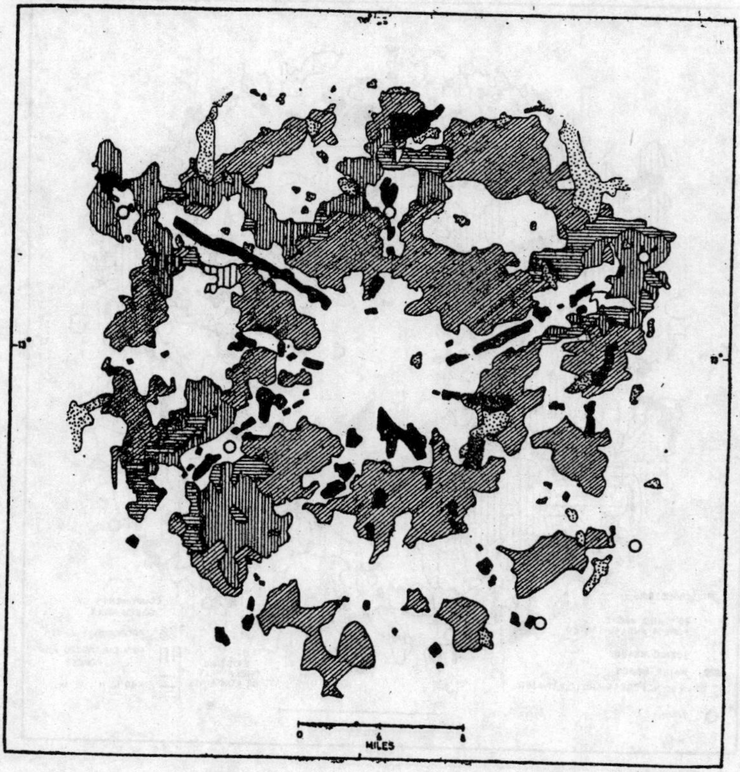

FIG. 5.10 : *Bangalore and environs*

the villages into the city degenerating into pockets of high congestion and sub-standard living conditions. Only the village well, or the temple or the village tree often stands out as a relict of the earlier village nucleus.

The green belt need not be contiguous and extensive in its areal extent. Balancing between industrial corridors, residential areas, rural strips and rural neighbourhoods, with central villages, as enclaves surrounded on all sides by a green setting give structure, shape and form to the city region (Fig. 5.10). A

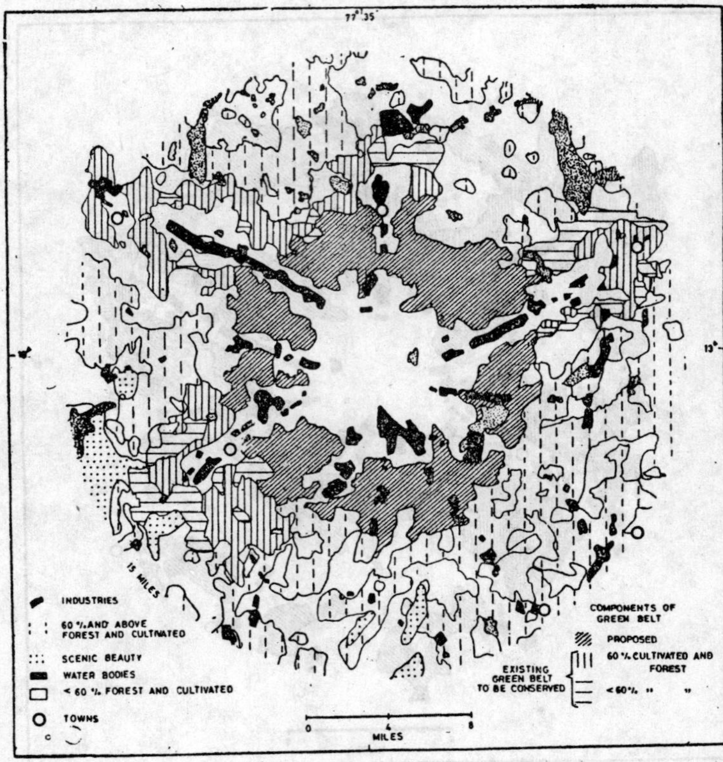

FIG. 5.11 : *Bangalore and environs*

green belt exists around Bangalore city. Only protection and intensification are needed within a regional framework (Fig. 5.11), and not new creation and development.

APPENDIX

Census Division Number	Name of the Census Division	Population density per acre	Socio-economic status index
1	2	3	4
3	Subramanyapura	2	−0.03
1	Yeswanthapura	7	−0.22
51	Joughapalyam	12	0.19
60	Maclever Town	16	0.80
31	Hanumanthanagar	20	0.59
35	Jayanagar	22	0.98
21	Binnypet	23	−0.18
46	Munireddypalyam	24	−0.40
59	Tasker Town	25	−1.38
2	Rajajinagar	25	0.22
45	Palace	27	2.49
50	Murphy Town	32	1.69
44	High Grounds	33	1.33
36	Wilson Gardens	33	1.12
63	Austin Town	35	−1.17
53	Swamy Shetty Garders	38	−0.09
62	Shanthinagar	39	0.44
5	Kothandaramapuram	39	2.07
49	Cox Town	40	0.21
4	Malleswaram	40	1.66
43	Vidhana Soudha	42	−0.48
34	Yediyur	43	0.91
24	Azadnagar	40	−0.42
61	Ashoknagar	52	0.26
37	Mavalli	56	0.67
29	Shankarapuram	65	2.96
47	St. John Hills	68	0.79
14	Gandhinagar	68	0.19
13	Subashnagar	74	−0.84
33	Basavanagudi	79	0.22
30	Kempegowdanagar	82	−0.37
48	Frazer Town	83	−0.21
27	Fort	92	−0.07
38	Town Hall	92	−0.36
28	Visveswarapuram	102	0.95
23	Padarayanapuram	110	−1.08
32	Basaveswara Temple	116	0.98
8	Seshadripuram	117	1.42
19	Kemmanagundi	134	−0.68

APPENDIX—contd.

1	2	3	4
39	Kalasipalyam	136	−0.01
9	Maharaja Mills	152	−1.63
12	Ramachandrapuram	157	−1.03
40	Dharmarajaswamy Temple	181	−1.10
52	Ulsoor	184	−1.12
25	Chamarajapet West	192	−0.47
57	Broadway	198	−1.12
6	Swimming Pool Extn.	202	−1.28
26	Chamarajapet East	209	−0.58
58	Shivajinagar	211	0.86
17	Kashi Visveswara Temple	222	−0.18
11	Bhashyamnagar	240	−1.03
20	Super Talkies	245	−1.60
7	Dattatreya Temple	249	−0.07
54	Commercial Street	253	0.03
10	Srirampuram	267	−1.34
22	Kempapura Agrahara	289	−1.16
18	K.R. Market	305	−0.65
15	Rangaswamy Temple	306	0.15
55	Bharathinagar	320	0.05
56	Central Bazar	322	−0.63
41	Anjaneyaswamy Temple	332	−1.29
16	Chickpet	338	N A
42	Cubbonpet	357	−0.95

6

CITY SLUMS

THE SLUM is a worldwide urban phenomenon, and is cast into a stereotype image with a heavily negative bias—a 'rash' on city landscape, 'a blot on civilization', over-crowding, filth, sub-standard housing, drinking, vice, violence, apathy and poverty. A positive attitude is to recognise the slum as a 'component' of city evolution, an 'element of urban complex', as a 'transitional settlement' at that low level of survival, and to appreciate the contribution of the slum dwellers to the city's low-wage labour force and its gross product. The slum represents both physical and human adjustment to poverty, and in developing countries, depicts 'subsistence' urbanization. It is necessary to recognise the slow change for the better that is taking place in the slums, the increasing community cohesiveness and the awareness of the social evils and at best sensitivity to them. This is being brought about by the cultural and even some of the political organizations as in some of the slums in India. It is known that no other community within a city has that vigour and community bond that can at best be manifest in the slum. What seems, however, to be a disintegrating force is the voting right of the slum dweller that is making him flexible to yield to the 'power politik'. He is now sandwiched between the 'political lord' and the 'slum lord'.

Origins and types

Origins of slums are varied—roots lie in the fisher communities in port cities, migrant labourers in industrial cities, construction workers drawn by the huge building construction programmes and canal and road construction works, and the refugee migrants flooding the cities as a consequence of political wars and natural disasters. Some politicians think that even civic polls cause growth of slums. This needs to be tested.

Definition of slums has its roots mainly in deteriorating and sub-standard housing and overcrowding, sanitation, poverty, and the character of the very site/area occupied by the slum, and its location in the ecological setting within the sprawling city. The Slum Act of 1956 defines slums mainly in terms of sub-standard structure of housing, overcrowding, lack of ventilation, zero or near zero sanitary facilities, all conspiring to promote slum life which defies health and morals. Some of the city master plans define a slum as an area with more than 20 huts.* The city municipality of Vijayawada identifies an area as a slum, if it has a majority of huts and has no proper civic amenities. Thus many factors combine in the definition of a slum, and definitions vary. There are also different categories of slums—immigrant slums, squatters, *in situ* slums (some of the villages which are drawn into the city as it expands, and acquire some of the physical characteristics of slums). This further compounds the problem of definition of slums, and makes it difficult to get at precise numbers of slums. Added to this, slums appear and disappear particularly the squatters, often consisting of 'marginal and floating population', and monitoring their location and shift becomes difficult.

Population size and growth of slums

Slum population, whether in regular and legalized slums or in illegal squatter hutments, accounts for a substantial share of city population, and in some of the countries, the share could be as high as 80 per cent (1964) as in Buenaventura in Columbia in South America. In Ankara and Izmir in Turkey, the percentages are 60 and 65 respectively (UN Report, 1970). In India, slums are to be found in cities of different sizes and types—a million city, an industrial city, a commercial city, a temple town and a district headquarters town. Even medium

***Master Plan, Visakhamahanagar, Town Planning Trust, 1968.**

and small towns have slums. Even a planned city like Chandigarh could not escape slums, a typical case of initially unplanned growth of slums and then a planned shift to the fringe sectors of the city. The newly industrializing cities have a higher proportion of their city population, living in slums (Visakhapatnam 35%). The percentages for the metropolitan cities of Calcutta, Bombay, Madras, Ahmedabad and Bangalore are 34, 25, 24, 22 and 10 respectively. In absolute numbers, the slum population in a city could be as high as one million people (Bombay).

There is large variation in the population size of slums within a city, e.g. from 50 to 9,958 in Hyderabad, 34 to 8,935 in Bangalore, 21 to 4,623 in Surat, 1,290 to 12,992 in Vijayawada. Considering the transient and shifting nature of slums, and in the absence of a continuing city register of slums, it becomes difficult to fix the age of slums.

The frequency distribution of slums by population size for Bangalore and Hyderabad is given in Table 6.1. Here, a number of questions crop up. What is a viable population size for investments in slum development at this sub-standard income levels of slum dwellers ? Should there be regrouping of slums into viable population sizes to justify a certain level of investment ? How will this regrouping disturb the existing work-place-residence distance relationships ? There are yet no ready answers to these questions.

TABLE 6.1 : **Distribution of slums by population size**

Population size	Number	
	Bangalore	Hyderabad
<100	12	14
100-300	36	55
300-600	44	61
600-1000	30	49
1000-2000	20	69
2000-4000	17	35
Total	159	283

Slums are growing in numbers in spite of city authorities' attempts to clear them and eliminate them. In Madras, the slums grew in number at an accelerating rate from 189 with 15,942 huts in 1933 to 548 with just over 4,12,000 people in 1961, and to 1,202 with 7,40,000 people in 1971. The number of slums in Hyderabad-Secunderabad increased from 106 in 1962 to 283 in 1972, and 357 in 1976. While the city population increased by 44 per cent during 1961-71, the slum population increased by 132 per cent during 1962-72. In Bangalore, the slums increased from 159 in 1971-72 to 290 in 1978.

With differences in the definition of a slum, with each city being open ended for the slum migrants, and with no effective agency to trace and monitor the sprouting of slums, any statistic on the growth of slums and their population size loses its precision. One can get only a feel of the magnitude.

Congestion and living conditions

Ground and room congestion associated with unhygienic conditions is one distinct characteristic of all slums. Slum houses are mostly huts and kacha houses. These are exposed to fire hazard. Their proportion to total houses varies—64 per cent (1972) in Hyderabad-Secunderabad, 79 per cent (1970) in Madras, 52 per cent (1970) in Chandigarh, 81 per cent (1973) in Surat. In Hyderabad-Secunderabad slum population density varies from 49 persons per acre to 3,571 persons per acre. The maximum density is to be found near the wholesale market (old Hyderabad). Room congestion varies from 2 persons per room to 21 per room. Ground congestion of houses varies from 10 houses per acre to 595 houses per acre.

Congestion is often a function of the size of the slum—number of people and number of shelters, its age, the site area and its locational setting. In the city centre, where there is concentration of employment, and where land is scarce, slums have the highest densities. In the peripheral areas, where the population pressure on site is not high, the newly mushrooming slums, which are small, have low ground densities. Within the overall density variations in the city, the slum densities stand out as 'ant-hills'.

In contrast to the large and extensively sprawling cities, in the compact and commercial cities located in a setting with physical constraints like river, flood plain, narrow and eroding beach, and hills, the city densities (excluding slum areas) and the slum densities do not differ much. In Vijayawada, a compact and a commercial centre located at the apex of the Krishna delta, with canals running through the city, the non-slum area density is 108 per acre while the slum density is 119 per acre. Some of the non-slum areas in the city core, with its wholesale market, have higher densities (just above 800 per acre) than the densities in some of the slum areas (400 per acre). Slums encapsulated in the city have relatively higher densities. The density factor needs to be interpreted within the physical and ecological setting of the slum. Some of the planned slums in the city fringes are being designed for very low densities (7 persons per acre Mutyalampadu Housing Colony in Vijayawada). But Such a low density by itself cannot sustain the slum even for minimal services. If it is far removed from its place of work, the transplanted workers do not have enough inducement to stay at the new site.

Generally, the physical conditions of the slum present a picture of total neglect; there is absolute lack of any order; there are minimum facilities like water and sanitation, and electricity are conspicuously absent or woefully inadequate. Cesspools stagnate in front of each house. While the exterior of a slum is, to say the least, ugly and unattractive, the inside of a slum-house in a number of cases presents a picture of order. Although all activity is mostly in one room, which is 'the house', each and everything is where it should be, the metal pots and pans are gleaming, the clothes are folded and hung on a line, and the floor is swept clean. The walls are adorned with colourful calendars, of National leaders, film stars, saints and gods and goddesses and with glass framed photographs of the 'near and dear ones' of the family. Where the residents can afford it, the floor is of cement, the walls are lime washed inside and outside. Regardless of where they live, the slum dwellers have little interest in the type of 'privacy' of the middle-class families; while they do want to be left alone, they are not averse to the aural or visual proximity of their neighbours.

In (Bangalore), more than 50 per cent of the 313 slum households surveyed, around 6 persons on an average live and sleep in one single room. Herein, again, the size of a room is to be seen to be able to comprehend the nature of congestion. A room, more often than not, is not larger than 10′ ×8′ and here adults (men and women) children and adolescents live and sleep together. While the average number of people living in one single room is 6, cases of 10—15 people living in one room are not infrequent. Interestingly enough Muslims, Catholics and Hindu Adidravidas were the 3 communities where cases of 10-15 people (adults and children) living in one room repeated themselves. More than one married son lives with his wife and children, in the same room as his parents. Of the total households, only 50 (15.97%) lived in rented houses; the rent varied from Re. 1 per month to Rs. 40 per month with an average rent of Rs. 10.66. Of the 50 households, 72 per cent paid less than Rs. 15 per month and except in one case where the rent was Rs. 40, all others paid less than Rs. 26.

If urban amenities are examined, 99 per cent were without water taps, 98 per cent without latrines, 92 per cent without bathrooms and 61 per cent without a kitchen. How can there be even a minimum standard of cleanliness and hygiene when there is no running water in every house? Rain or shine, there is a long queue of people with containers of all kinds, shapes and sizes waiting before a street tap. Often the containers alone form a queue and the owners come later when the water flows in the taps at particular hours of the day. Quite often, children and women make several trips a day to the water tap at the corner of the street, and quarrels over who took how much water are frequent, and these seemingly innocent and petty quarrels do turn into serious feuds.

Since the houses were not provided with latrines, and there were no common latrines for most slums (exceptions being those of the slums that have been chosen for redevelopment by the Bangalore Corporation or the City Improvement Trust Board) the entire open space, however large or small, surrounding a slum and the lanes and streets had become one continuing latrine. This poses a health hazard to the slum dwellers and to the wider community of urban citizens. The rural habit of going into the fields is continued, only the 'fields' are not there to absorb the human excreta. Even in the slums chosen for redevelopment (Baglur), where several rows of latrines and bathrooms had been constructed, but adults did not always use them, and as a rule children never did. They preferred to use the streets and sides of houses. A habit handed down from one generation to the next is very difficult to change (Rukmini Srinivas 1979).

Location of slums : Distributional pattern (Fig. 6.1)
The city of Bangalore had 159 slums (1971-72) with a population of 1,32,000 : 10 per cent of the city's population.

The distribution of slums within the city of Bangalore is uneven, and is inversely related to population densities (Table 6 2). The locational frequency brought out the concentration of slums in the divisions located mainly in the city's peripheral and intermediate zones. The core of the city with only 6 slums in 2 (54 and 56 out of 14 divisions) only pointed to the fact of non-availability of land, attracting slum dwellers.

TABLE 6.2 : **Distribution of slums by population density of the census division of their location—Bangalore.**

Density of population per acre	No. of slums
Less than 50	77
50—100	33
100—200	31
200—300	11
300+above	2
Total	154*

* 5 slums were outside corporation limits.

The older peripheries (intermediate zone) in the city had the maximum number, with 66 in periphery two, and 53 in periphery one, the latter adjoining the city-core with City Market, Vidhana Soudha and Russel Market as the three foci (Fig. 6.1). The present edge of the city, the outermost periphery, had only 11 slums. With this edge moving further

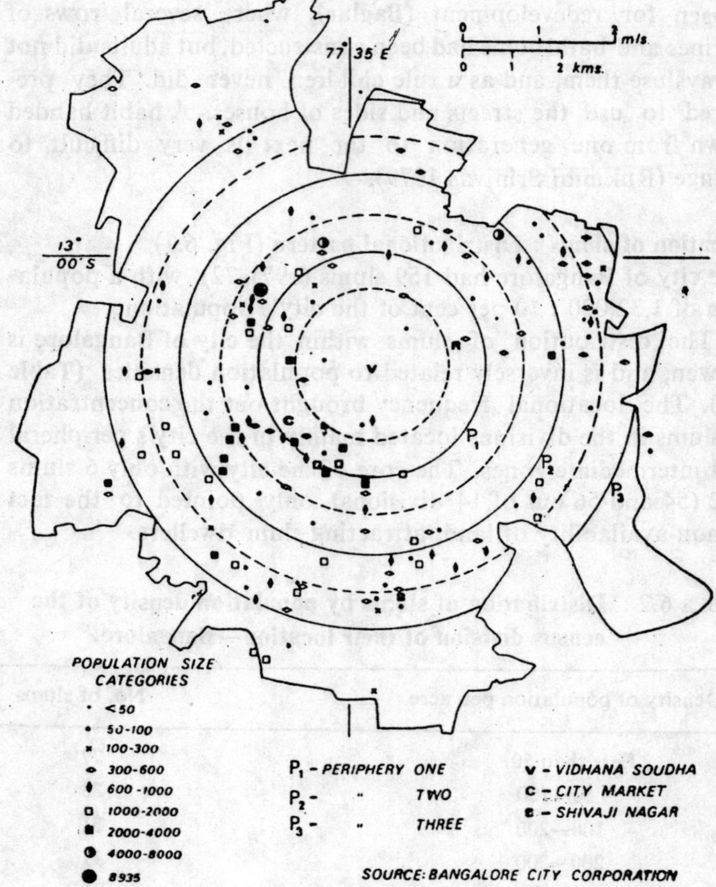

FIG. 6.1 : *Slums—Bangalore city corporation, 1971*

outwards, this outermost periphery, becomes the inner periphery, and will be the potential zone for the growth of future slums, both *in situ* and immigrant, if the locational history of slums is to repeat itself. In Census divisions the maximum number of slums (11) was in division No. 49 (Table 6.3).

Out of a total of 159 slums, only 14 were in the vicinity (within a distance of 1/4 km.) of major industries. Herein again 5 of the 14 slums were located near the Binny Group of Mills (Table 6.4). The Anandapur slum with a population of

TABLE 6.3 : Distribution of slums by census division and zone of location —Bangalore.

Core		Intermediate				Periphery	
Division Number	Number of Slums	Division Number	Number of Slums	Division Number	Number of Slums	Division Number	Number of Slums
15	—	13	—	11	2	1	9
16	—	14	3	12	3	5	2
17	—	38	5	22	1	45	3
18	—	39	4	52	—	46	6
41	—	27	2	61	—	48	7
40	—	20	5	60	—	49	11
42	—	19	1	23	5	50	5
54	1	53	2	25	3	51	1
55	—	47	1	26	1	63	4
56	2	3	—	30	2	62	4
57	—	4	1	29	1	35	9
58	—	6	—	28	1	34	6
43	2	7	1	37	2	31	1
59	1	8	4	33	1	24	1
		44	1	32	6	21	6
		9	4	36	8	2	3
		10	—				
Total	6		34		36		78

Note: Out of 159, 5 slums were outside the 63 divisions.

TABLE 6.4 : Slums in the vicinity of major industries—Bangalore

Industry		Number of slums within a radius of ½ km.
Around Govt. Soap Factory	—	1
Around Maharaja Mills	—	2
Around Mysore Spinning and Weaving Mills and Minerva Mills	—	1
Around Binny Mills	—	5
Around REMCO	—	2
Around Motor Industries Co.	—	2
Around Bangalore Woollen, Cotton and Silk Mills Ltd.	—	1
Total		14

2,700 was a typical example of a slum which had grown on the government waste land of Komena Agrahara. Thus, while industries may be one of the factors promoting growth of slums in their vicinity, whether on government or private land, the growth of all slums need not necessarily be associated with industrial development. Out of 14 slums, 9 were located in the contract zones between industrial and (a) commercial (5), (b) residential (2), (c) open space (1), and (d) public and semi-public land (1).

While extending this locational analysis of slums, within a framework of land-use zones, it was found that 88 out of 159 were located along the contact zones of the land-use categories like residential and commercial industrial and semi-public lands and open spaces. (Table 6.5).

TABLE 6.5 : **Distribution of slums by land-use, location and contact zone—Bangalore.**

Location	Contact Zone						
	Resi-dential	Public and semi-public	Indus-trial	Open space	Commer-cial	Tank	Total
Residential	45	9	4	11	32	1	102
Public and semi-public	7	9	—	—	3	1	20
Industrial	2	1	7	1	5	—	16
Open space	2	—	1	7	4	—	14
Commercial	1	2	—	1	1	—	5
Unclassified	—	—	—	—	—	—	2
Total	57	21	12	20	45	2	159

It must be mentioned here that as many as 44 out of 88 were located along the contact zones with commercial land-uses. Thus, the commercial sector appeared to play a greater role in promoting slums than did the industrial sector.

There is yet another characteristic, typical of the location of slums, and that is the character of the slum siting. Quarry pits, tank beds or other ill-drained hollows, railway siding, and near the cemeteries, slaughter houses and timber yards seem to be ideal sites for slum location, although slums are found elsewhere too. The location of cemeteries, slaughter houses, timber yards and the like, is peripheral to the City core. Some of the sites like tank beds and low lying areas, e.g., Munivenkatappa Thota-Ulsoor, and Dhoby Ghat Slum, get flooded during the rains, and the residents are forced to move temporarily to higher adjoining areas, only to find on their return, the partial or total destruction of their houses. Frequently in order to avoid these seasonal shifts to higher ground, they move to another site, adjoining a slum, by their decision or by the city authority. More often than not, wherever there is a nucleus of a slum, it grows by accretion—this is one spatial pattern of growth : here the settlement sprawls, occupied by squatters. Where slums grow by accretion, they are sometimes separated by roads, storm water drains and open nullahs, e.g., Christian Colony and Gautham Nagar slums. While most of the slums stand out conspicuously owing to their physical segregation from the adjoining areas, there are exceptions to this pattern as in the case of the slum at Kalasipalyam where the slum area has merged almost inconspicuously with its highly congested surroundings.

The slum households

In the following section, the migrant status and the socio-economic characteristics of 313 slum-households in Bangalore city are analysed in detail.* The total population covered in the sample was 1,852 which had a high proportion of population in the 0-14 age group constituting about 43 per cent (city population : 0-14 age group: 38%); female children constituted 44 per cent, and male children 42 per cent. The sex ratio (number of females per 1000 males) was quite high (943) in

*The slum study is a part of the Bangalore city study (Prakasa Rao and Tewari 1979). The 313 households were selected from 11 slums in the city, selected on the basis of location and type. V. K. Tewari, V. Samba Murthy, Mrs. Rukmini Srinivas and T. R. Shama Bhat contributed to field work, data processing, analysis and drafting of the report which provided the base for this chapter. I acknowledge their valuable contributions.

slums as compared to the ratio of 884 in the city population (1971). Married constituted 90 per cent, and widowed and single persons constituted 7 per cent and 2 per cent respectively.

*Migration**

Of the 313 households, migrants constituted 59.7 per cent. Migration to slums was mainly in search of employment—any employment or specific employment. The motive to migrate was dominantly economic. Those who migrated were mainly from the adjoining rural areas and belonged mainly to lower socio-economic status groups. Migration of individuals or families followed a pattern based on a spontaneous strategy along the social slope—caste, kinship, language and religion, through information flows channelled through social links. Kinship network played an important role in the recruitment of migrants to jobs and the choice of locality for residence. Caste and kinship loyalties are strong among all migrants. They are stronger among the lower castes. The majority of the migrants had an acquaintance in the city to which they migrate. The occupation of the acquaintance had a bearing on the occupation of the migrant—contract labour, salaried job, or casual labour.

Of the migrants, 94.5 per cent were males and only 5.5 per cent were females. More than 70 per cent of the migrants as well as non-migrants belonged to the age group 15-49. Most of the migrants (98.5%) belonged to the four Southern States i.e., Karnataka, Tamil Nadu, Andhra Pradesh and Kerala. Of the total number of migrants, 46.0 per cent belonged to Karnataka. Next in importance was Tamil Nadu which contributed 36.4 per cent of the total migrants, followed by Andhra Pradesh with 15.0 and Kerala with 1.1 per cent.

When analysed on a district basis, it was found that Bangalore district contributed the maximum i.e. 29 per cent of the total migrants. North Arcot district of Tamil Nadu contributed 18.2 per cent. Districts in Karnataka other than Bangalore district sent 17 per cent. It may be mentioned that all the migrants from Karnataka were from nine districts—Bangalore,

*A migrant, as defined in this study, was one who was not born in Bangalore city, but was residing in the city at the time of survey.

Chickmagalur, Chitradurga, Hassan, Kolar, Mandya, Mysore, Shimoga and Tumkur. Of the total migrants, 53 per cent were rural born and the remaining were urban born. Karnataka born migrants were more rural, while those born outside Karnataka, in particular from Tamil Nadu were more urban. As distance from Bangalore city increased, rural to urban migration declined and urban to urban migration increased.

Duration of residence

Before 1954, 44.5 per cent of the migrants arrived in Bangalore city; 36.8 per cent arrived between 1954 and 1964, and only 14.3 per cent between 1964 and 1974. Maximum migration of rural born migrants was in the decade 1954-64, that of urban born migrants was prior to 1954. Of the two migration streams, the one originating in the rural areas showed over time a fluctuating trend, and the one originating in the urban areas showed a steady decline over time.

Karnataka born migrants came to Bangalore city more recently than those born outside Karnataka. Of the Karnataka born migrants, 66.3 per cent came to Bangalore city after 1954, whereas in case of those born in other states 59.0 per cent came to Bangalore city before 1954. In the case of Tamil Nadu born migrants 63 per cent came to Bangalore city before 1954 of which 79 per cent were from North Arcot district. Half of the Andhra born migrants came to Bangalore city before 1954 and the other half after 1954.

Step migration

A substantial proportion of migrants, i.e., about 83 per cent came from their place of birth, straight to Bangalore city. The role played by step migration was small. Step migrants here are those who had at least one place of residence, other than the place of birth, before coming to Bangalore city. Migrants who have moved only once and those who have moved at least twice can be thus identified.

Among migrants born in Bangalore district, only 2 per cent moved to some other district of Karnataka before coming to Bangalore city. Approximately 6 per cent of the migrants born in Karnataka but outside Bangalore district had lived in Bangalore district before moving to Bangalore city.

More migrants had come to Bangalore city straight from a rural place of birth than from an urban place of birth. Only 9 per cent male migrants went through step migration. Among the female step migrants all of them had an urban locality as their place of birth as well as place of last residence. Only 2 per cent male step migrants had a similar movement.

Reasons for migration

A good proportion of migrants, 76 per cent, came to Bangalore city in search of employment. This cause was predominant and accounted for 77 per cent male and 70 per cent female migration (Table 6.6). Others migrated along with parents or on account of marriage, studies, transfer etc. Migration on account of marriage and moving with parents was more among females than males.

More migrants born outside came in search of employment than migrants born in Karnataka. Marriage or family quarrels as reasons for migration were more important for Karnataka born migrants than for migrants born outside Karnataka. Transfer or studies as reasons for migration existed only for migrants originating in Karnataka. Before migrating, 25 per cent migrants were unemployed, while after migration only

TABLE 6.6 : **Percentage distribution of migrants by reasons for migration and rural/urban characteristics of place of birth—Bangalore.**

Reason for migration	Migrants		
	Total	Rural	Urban
Came with parents	9.34	10.42	7.06
Marriage	3.30	3.12	3.53
Family quarrel	2.19	1.04	3.53
Employment	76.37	78.13	75.29
Studies	0.55	—	1.18
Transfer	0.55	—	1.18
Others	3.85	2.08	5.88
Unspecified	3.85	5.21	2.35
Total	100.00	100.00	100.00

3 per cent were unemployed. On arrival in Bangalore city, 65 per cent of migrants had to wait for less than one month in order to secure employment.

Social composition

Not all slums in the sample could be classified as a type; some were heterogeneous in composition—people hailing from different States, speaking different languages, following different faiths and earning a livelihood from different occupations lived in one physical unit. And yet, there were other slums that go by particular names like 'Sweepers Colony', 'Christian Colony' 'Harijan Colony'—so obviously indicating the composition of the people. There was yet another category which goes by the names of important landmarks, public buildings or original villages. Some may be homogeneous in the sense that the majority of the population was Muslim and Urdu speaking, or it may be homogeneous in that the majority of the people migrated from Andhra Pradesh and spoke Telugu or they migrated from Tamil Nadu and spoke Tamil. Of the three religious groups represented in the slums, 205 of the 313 households were Hindu (65.50%), 62 Muslim (19.80%) and 46 Christian (14.70%). Of the 46 Christian households, two reported the existence of other members in the household who were Hindus. Of the 1,852 persons in the 313 households, 1,147 were Hindus (61.93%), 411 Muslims (22.19%) and 294 Christians (15.88%).

The 30 Hindu castes reported were grouped into seven categories on the basis of the broad traditional occupations pursued by them (Table 6.7). As many as 33 respondents did not reveal their caste identity, but stated merely that they are scheduled castes or Harijans.

Of all the caste categories, the scheduled caste category was the most dominant numerically. This category accounted for 54.14 per cent of the Hindus (Table 6.8). The agricultural caste category came next with 22.59 per cent. The Okkaligas in this category were numerically dominant. The artisan and servicing caste category was the next with 10.73 per cent. The Kumbara and Acharis together accounted for more than half the number under this category. The trading castes accounted for 9.27 per cent. The Mudaliyars and Balija Naidus together

TABLE 6.7 : **Castes of the Hindu household heads in slums**

Caste Category	Castes
Brahmin	Mulkinadu (Smartha)
Lingayat	Lingayat
Trading Caste	Banajiga, Chettiar, Mudaliyar, Nagartha, Vyshya Setty, Baliga Naidu
Agricultural Castes	Gounders, Kunchitiga, Nair, Reddy, Okkaliga and Thigla or Vannekula Kshathriya
Warrior/Soldier	Rajput, Naiker, Pallegar and Marati
Artisans/Servicing	Kurubas, Vishwakarma Achari, Agasa, Kumbara and Idiga
Scheduled Caste	Adi-dravida, Adi-Karnataka, Korma Setty, Wodda or Bovi, Adi-Andhra, Arundhathia and Mochi.

TABLE 6.8 : **Percentage distribution of households by caste and language of household head.**

Caste	Language				Total
	Tamil	Kannada	Telugu	Others	
Brahmin	—	—	2.08	—	0.49
Lingayat	—	1.52	—	—	0.49
Trading Caste	10.34	4.54	14.58	—	9.27
Agricultural caste	13.79	43.94	8.33	33.33	22.93
Warrior/ Soldier	1.15	1.52	—	66.67	1.95
Artisan and service	5.75	22.73	4.17	—	10.73
Scheduled caste	68.97	25.75	70.84	—	54.14
Total	100.00	100.00	100.00	100.00	100.00
Number of households	88	66	48	3	205

constituted nearly 1/3 of the total respondents in this category. The proportion of migrants in artisan and servicing castes was 95.45 per cent followed by that among the agricultural castes (78.72%), trading castes (63.16%), and scheduled castes (57.7%). Tamil was the preponderant language spoken in the slums, accounting for 35.46 per cent of the households. This preponderance of Tamils among slum-dwellers was observed in the earlier studies also (Woodruff 1959). Kannada came next (22.05%) followed by Telugu (21.73%), Urdu (19.81%) and others (Hindi, Marathi and Malayalam) (0.95%). The Urdu and Kannada speaking groups were homogeneous groups in both religion and language (entirely Muslim and almost completely Hindu respectively). Persons speaking Tamil and Telugu were found among Hindus and Christians. Thus the slum population consisted of both homogeneous and heterogeneous groups in language and religion (Table 6.9.)

TABLE 6.9 : **Percentage distribution of households by religion and language of household Head.**

Religion	Language					Total
	Tamil	Kannada	Telugu	Urdu	Others	
Hindu	79.28	95.65	70.59	—	100.00	65.50
Muslim	—	—	—	100.00	—	19.80
Christian	20.72	4.35	29.41	—	—	14.70
Total	100.00	100.00	100.00	100.00	100.00	100.00
Number of households	111	69	68	62	3	100
Percentage to total	35.46	22.05	21.73	19.81	0.95	100.00

The caste composition of the Hindu-language groups provided yet another evidence in support of the prevalent contrast between the Kannada group on the one hand, and the Tamil and Telugu groups on the other. While the agricultural castes dominated the Kannada group, the scheduled castes dominated the Tamil and Telugu groups (Table 6.8). The distinct character of the Kannada group was borne out by another piece of evidence. It was among them that the highest proportion of migrants were found (76.81%). It was very clear that the Hindus as a religious group were different from the other two minority religions. Two-thirds of the Hindus were migrants. Among the Muslims and Christians on the other hand non-migrant and migrant proportions were almost equal.

Social composition and education

The majority (52.40%) of the slum respondents were without any formal education (Table 6.10). The educational level ranged from primary level to graduation. The Christians were most educated, while the Muslims were least educated. Caste-wise, the trading castes were the least educated and of the seven educated, 3 had studied up to the middle school level which was the highest educational level among this caste group. Among members of the agricultural castes, there was one who was a graduate and 4 who had completed secondary level education. Of the 111 scheduled caste persons, one was a graduate and 53 were not educated (Table 6.11). Of the educated persons, the maximum proportion was Telugu speaking and least was that of Urdu speakers.

TABLE 6.10 : Percentage distribution of households by education and religion of household head.

Education	Religion			Total
	Hindu	Muslim	Christian	
No Education	54.14	69.35	23.91	52.71
Primary	20.97	14.32	30.44	21.09
Middle	16.59	12.90	30.44	17.90
Secondary	7.32	3.23	13.04	7.35
Graduate	0.98	—	2.17	0.95
Total	100.00	100.00	100.00	100.00
Number of households	205	62	46	313

TABLE 6.11 : **Percentage distribution of households by education and caste of household Head**

Education	Caste							Total
	Brahmin	Lingayat	Trading caste	Agricultural caste	Warrior/ Soldier	Artisan/ Service	Scheduled Caste	
No Education	—	—	63.16	51.05	100.00	54.54	53.15	54.15
Primary	—	100.00	21.05	19.15	—	18.18	22.52	20.98
Middle	—	—	15.79	19.15	—	13.64	17.12	16.58
Secondary	100.00	—	—	8.51	—	13.64	6.31	7.32
Graduate	—	—	—	2.14	—	—	0.90	0.97
Total	100.00	100.00	100.00	100.00	100.00	100.00	100.00	100.00
Number of households	1	1	19	47	4	22	111	205

Social composition and size of household

The size of the Muslim and the Christian households was mainly medium and large while that of the Hindu households was mainly medium. In the very large family category the proportions of the Muslims was the highest (Table 6.12). In contrast to the size variation among religious groups, there was no marked variation in size amongst the caste groups; medium size was the most dominant in all groups (Table 6.13).

TABLE 6.12 : Percentage distribution of households by religion of household head and household size.

Household size	Religion			
	Hindu	Muslim	Christian	Total
2-3	18.59	8.06	10.87	15.34
4-6	53.17	41.94	39.13	48.88
7-9	21.46	40.32	41.30	28.11
10+	6.83	9.68	8.70	7.67
Total	100.00	100.00	100.00	100.00
Number of Households	205	62	46	313

Social composition and household type

All the slum households were kinship units and 55 per cent of the units were nuclear, and 45 per cent were non-nuclear. Based on religion, the Muslim (60%) and Christian (63%) communities were more nuclear than Hindus (51%) while based on caste, the warrior/soldier (75%) and scheduled castes (56%) were more non-nuclear.

Religion, occupation and income

Among Christians, 8.14 per cent earners were in the highest occupational status category of professional workers which included occupations like inspectors, supervisors, school teachers and contractors; the corresponding proportions among Hindus and Muslims were less than one per cent (Table 6.14). While Hindus and Christians were engaged more as construction

TABLE 6.13 : **Percentage distribution of household by caste of household Head and household size**

Household size	Caste							Total
	Brahmin	Lingayat	Trading caste	Agricultural caste	Warrior/ Soldier	Artisan and Servant	Scheduled Caste	
2-3	—	100.00	31.58	12.77	25.00	13.64	18.92	18.54
4-6	100.00	—	52.63	61.70	50.00	63.64	47.75	53.17
7-9	—	—	10.53	21.27	25.00	18.18	24.32	21.46
10+	—	—	5.26	4.26	—	4.54	9.01	6.83
Total	100.00	100.00	100.00	100.00	100.00	100.00	100.00	100.00
Number of households	1	1	19	47	4	22	111	205

workers, Muslims were more in the categories of mechanics, carters, drivers and cleaners.

TABLE 6.14 : Percentage distribution of earners of religion and occupations.

Occupation	Hindu	Muslim	Christian	Total
Professional workers and contractors	0.78	0.79	8.14	1.85
Clerical and sales workers	14.51	12.70	4.65	12.71
Service workers	22.28	9.52	13.95	18.39
Farmers and loggers	1.55	0.79	4.65	1.84
Construction	21.50	5.56	25.58	18.73
Cooly labour	13.99	16.67	6.98	13.54
Basket and Agarbathi making	5.18	6.35	1.16	4.85
Mechanics	3.89	7.94	9.30	5.52
Cartmen, drivers, cleaners	2.33	13.49	5.82	5.18
Other production workers	13.99	26.19	19.77	17.39
All occupationers	100.00	100.00	100.00	100.00
Number of earners	386	126	86	598

The monthly income per household was higher among Christians (Rs. 248.63) than among Hindus (Rs. 203.61) and Muslims (Rs. 183.85). The pattern was similar for monthly income per capita (Table 6.15).

Earners, occupations and income

Of the 598 earners 79.43 per cent were males and 20.57 per cent were females; 6.02 per cent below 14 years and 5.85 per cent were aged 60 years or more; 51.00 per cent were in the age group of 20-39 years. Earners (598) constituted 32.29 per cent of the total sample population (1,852). Male and female earners constituted 49.84 per cent and 13.68 per cent of the total sample male and female population respectively. The percentage was highest (99) for males in the age group 30—39 and for females (34) in the age group 50-59; it was found that the children and the very old were also earners, sharing 6 per cent each. It was very significant to note that it was almost 100 per cent (99%) employment for the male middle age group (30-39 years) among the males.

TABLE 6.15 : Percentage distribution of households by income and religion of the Head.

Household income per month in Rupees	Religion			
	Hindu	Muslim	Christian	Total
0-100	14.14	12.90	15.22	14.06
100-200	40.49	51.61	23.91	40.26
200-300	26.34	27.42	21.74	25.88
300-400	12.68	3.23	26.09	12.78
400-500	3.41	3.23	6.52	3.83
500 and above	2.93	1.61	6.52	3.19
Total	100.00	100.00	100.00	100.00
Monthly income per household in Rs.	203.61	183.85	248.63	206.32
Monthly income per person in Rs.	36.47	27.73	38.90	34.91

The 598 earners in the sample were engaged in 41 occupational groups, but 73 per cent were employed in 10 occupations (Tables 6.16 and 6.17).

While the majority of the earners in all the selected slums except Goripalya were production and related workers, there was occupational diversification within the slums. The tendency for concentration of one class of workers in any particular slum was found in only one case (Goripalya—the Corporation Sweepers' Colony). Construction, cooly labour and services (such as those of peons, watchmen, maid servants) were the occupations of 51 per cent of earners (Table 6.18).

Males were mostly employed in construction (21%), as coolies (16%), as watchmen and other service workers

TABLE 6.16 : List of occupations of sample household Heads in slums.

1. Accountant (1)
2. Working proprietor (2)
3. Rubber and plasters product makers (1)
4. Electrical fitters and related (7)
5. Transport equipment operators (24)
6. Printing and related (4)
7. Clerical and related (21)
8. Building care-takers, sweepers, cleaners and related (54)
9. Protective service (11)
10. Glass foremen, potters and related (3)
11. Teachers (5)
12. Spinners, Weavers, Knitters, buyers and related (11)
13. Cooks, waiters, bartenders and related (4)
14. Machinery fitters, machine assemblies and precision instruments makers (33)
15. Physician (1)
16. Miners, quarrymen, well drillers and related (3)
17. Food and beverage processors (4)
18. Forestry workers (4)
19. Blacksmiths, tool makers and machine tool operators (12)
20. Labourers, NEC (15)
21. Carpenters, cabinet makers and related wood workers (15)
22. Stone-cutters and conversers (1)
23. Jewellery and precious metal workers and metal engravers (1)
24. Service workers NEC (1)
25. Plumbers, welders, sheet metal and structural metal-preparers and erectors (5)
26. Other farm workers (6)
27. Tailors, dress makers, upholsterers and related (11)
28. Metal processors (9)
29. Engine and related equipment operators (7)
30. Bricklayers and other construction workers (112)
31. Merchants and shopkeepers (24)
32. Material handling and related equipment operators (66)
33. Shoe makers and leather goods makers (1)
34. Cultivators (1)
35. Painters (4)
36. Salesmen, shop assistants (31)
37. Nursing and related (1)
38. Professional workers NEC (1)
39. Production and related NEC (29)
40. Tobacco preparers and tobacco product makers (3)
41. Maids and other housekeeping service workers (40)

Note : Figures in parentheses denote number of workers in the occupation. Occupations are arranged in descending order of the average earnings.

TABLE 6.17 : **Distribution of earners by selected occupations**

Occupation	No. of earners	Percentage of total earners
Construction—brick layer etc.	112	18.73
Cooly—material handling	66	11.03
Sweepers—building caretakers	54	9.03
Maid servants	40	6.68
Fitters assemblers etc.	33	5.52
Salesman, shop assistance, production workers not elsewhere classified.	31	5.19
(basket weaving, agarbathi making etc.)	29	4.85
Transport equipment operators	24	4.01
Merchants and shopkeepers	24	4.01
Clerical and related workers	21	3.51
Total	434	72.56

TABLE 6.18 : **Percentage distribution of earners by occupation and sex.**

Occupation	Earners		
	Male	Female	Total
Professional workers and contractors	1.47	1.47	1.84
Clerical and sales	13.05	11.38	12.71
Service	9.89	51.22	18.39
Farmers	2.32	—	1.84
Construction	20.84	10.57	18.73
Cooly labour	16.00	4.07	13.55
Basket and Agarbathi makers	2.53	13.82	4.85
Mechanics	6.53	1.62	5.52
Craftsmen, drivers, cleaners	6.53	—	5.18
Other production workers	20.84	4.07	17.39
Total	100.00	100.00	100.00
Number of earners	598	475	123

(10%). Females were mostly employed in service as maid-servants and sweepers (51%) or in basket weaving and agarbathi (incense sticks) making (14%) and construction (11%).

If the 23 females employed as sweepers in the City Corporation living in the Goripalya slum are excluded, a clear pattern is revealed. Females were mostly employed in activities in which they could be employed at or very near their residence. This may be because females had household duties as a main activity and yet tried to supplement the household income.

Nature of employment

Employment of 37 per cent of the earners in the sample was casual. It was only in the Goripalya slum that 96 per cent of the earners were in regular employment. Certain occupations seemed to offer only casual employment. For instance 110 of the 112 construction workers, all the 10 stone cutters and 4 painters in the sample reported that their employment was casual. So did the majority of earners working as carpenters (11 out of 15) and coolies (59 out of 71) among others.

The distribution of earners in casual employment by number of days worked in the previous month showed that nearly 35 per cent of them worked 26-30 days a month, while 25 per cent worked between 21-25 days; 7 per cent of them remained unemployed on 30 days. While 25 per cent remained unemployed on 10 days. By occupations, 49 per cent of the construction workers and 18 per cent of the coolies had worked 20 days or less.

Earnings

Of the earners, 49 per cent had incomes less than Rs. 100 per month and 37 per cent earned between Rs. 100 to Rs. 200. Only 14 (2%) earned more than Rs. 300 per month (Table 6.19). High income group with earnings of Rs. 300 or more per month—Eight of them earned Rs. 300 and 3 earned Rs. 400 or more per month. All were males and were between 20-59 years; 50.00 per cent were in the age group of 30-39 years; 57.15 per cent were Christians and 28.57 per cent were Hindus (of whom 75 per cent were of scheduled castes). Of the six migrants in the group, 4 migrated from Andhra Pradesh and 2 from Karnataka. Only 2 of the 14 had no education while 42.85 per cent had secondary education or more. All were in regular employment mostly in factories and government service; 10 of them (71.43%) were skilled workers. Further only 3 of these had fathers who were unskilled workers. It seems only those with some skills or education and in regular employment can reach an income level of Rs. 300 per month. The occupation of the father and religion also appear to influence one's occupation and earnings.

The earner with maximum earnings in the sample was a Christian living in Christian Colony slum, Srirampuram. For three generations his family has been living in Srirampuram. He studied up to SSLC. His grand-father was an agricultural labourer and father was a mason; and his mother had secondary education and was working as nurse. He became a contractor.

Distribution of earners by monthly earnings and occupation showed that except among professional workers, in all other occupations, more than 75 per cent of the earners earned less than Rs. 200. per month. Thus within the range of occupations described, whatever was the occupation pursued, earnings tended to be low for the majority of earners. It was because many of the occupations in which these earners were engaged (e.g. construction, cooly labour, maid-servant, milkman, quarryman, agarbatti maker, etc.) were by nature low-income yielding.

Further the earning capacities of these earners were also limited as they lacked the required skills and their educational levels were low. Only 26.92 per cent of the earners could be classified as skilled and semi-skilled workers working as blacksmiths, tailors, carpenters, electricians, welders etc. That the skills possessed by even these were quite low can be seen from the fact that only 21. 43 per cent of the skilled workers earned Rs. 200 or more per month. It was only among these that 6 per cent earned Rs. 300 or more as against less than 2 per cent of the earners in other groups excluding the professional workers.

Of the 598 earners in the sample 355 had no education, and only 8 per cent had completed at least secondary level.

TABLE 6.19: **Percentage distribution of households by earnings and occupations**

Earnings in Rs.	Occupation										Total
	Professional and contractors	Clerical and sales	Service	Farmers	Construction	Cooly	Basket, agarbatti making	Mechanics	Craftsman, driver, cleaner	Other production	
100	36.36	50.67	45.45	63.64	55.86	55.56	86.21	42.43	19.35	42.31	49.50
100-199	18.18	37.33	30.91	27.27	39.64	40.74	13.79	33.33	58.07	42.31	37.08
200-299	27.27	10.67	22.73	9.09	3.60	3.70	—	15.15	9.68	13.46	11.07
300 +	18.18	1.33	0.91	—	0.90	—	—	9.09	12.90	1.92	2.35
Total	100.00	100.00	100.00	100.00	100.00	100.00	100.00	100.00	100.00	100.00	100.00
Number of earners	11	75	110	11	111	81	29	33	31	104	596
Mean earning in Rs.	203.18	105.99	114.83	102.73	91.66	94.23	48.21	127.88	159.84	115.88	108.01

While 58 per cent of those with no education earned less than Rs. 100 per month, 27 per cent of those with secondary education or more were in that income group (Table 6.20). This concentration of earners in the low income group was also due to the nature of employment and wage differences between males and females.

TABLE 6.20 : **Percentage distribution of earners by earning and education.**

Earnings	Education						Total
	No education	Primary	Middle	Secondary	Graduates	Others	
50	25.99	21.43	6.02	11.36	—	—	21.14
50-99′	21.49	22.32	25.30	15.91	—	100.00	28.36
100-149	15.82	24.11	26.52	20.45	50.00	—	19.13
150-199	17.80	16.07	22.89	13.64	—	—	17.95
200-299	7.34	13.39	15.66	27.27	—	—	11.07
300+	0.56	2.68	3.61	11.37	50.00	—	2.35
Total	100.00	100.00	100.00	100.00	100.00	100.00	100.00
Number of households	354	112	83	44	2	1	596

As noted earlier, the more important occupations of these earners (e.g. construction etc.) offered only casual employment. The earnings of the casual workers depend upon the number of days worked and 39 per cent of the 222 casual earners in the sample worked 20 days or less in a month. More than 75 per cent of the casual workers earned less than Rs. 100 per month. Only 5.0 per cent of them earned Rs. 300 or more as against 19 per cent of those in regular employment. The average monthly earnings of earners in casual employment (Rs. 94) were less than those of earners in regular employment (Rs. 116). Thus for a significant number of earners, earnings were not only low but were uncertain as well.

While the earnings of both males and females were low, those of females were even lower. The average monthly earnings of female earners were Rs. 72 as against Rs. 117 of male earners. More conclusive was the fact that of the 123 female earners, only 30 earned Rs. 100 or more per month; of whom 21 were in Goripalya slum working as sweepers in the City Corporation.

Earnings also varied with the age. All earners in the age group 5-14 and 84 per cent of these in the age group 15-19 earned less than Rs. 100 as against 27 per cent and 51 per cent of the earners in the age groups 20-59 and 60 years or above respectively.

The 36 earners in the age group 5-14 constituted 14 per cent of the sample population in the age group and the average age of the working child was 13 years; 75 per cent of these were boys and 75 per cent had no education. The average earnings of a child were Rs. 33.83 per month. Of these 36 children, 42 per cent belonged to the households with per capita income between Rs. 30-40 and per capita income of Rs. 50. It seems children from households with a per capita income of Rs. 50 are not usually sent to work.

Of the children 13 (36%) were working as construction workers and coolies. An examination of the occupations of their parents showed that children of unskilled workers tend to become unskilled workers. Thus it was found that in the low income households, children start working early without obtaining any education and take up largely unskilled occupations. It implies that the child would grow into an adult worker and continue to be a slum-dweller.

It was thus obvious that any attempt at improving their earnings should begin with the provision of skills; should assure continuity or regularity in employment; should provide opportunities of employment to the female workers near their residence. While the earnings of majority of earners were low, the average earnings of earners differed between occupations. They ranged from Rs. 203.18 among professional workers to Rs. 48.91 among basket-agarbatti makers. Ranking of all occupations by the average earnings of persons engaged showed that 'maid servants' had the lowest average earnings (Rs. 25.35) per month and 60 per cent of earners were engaged in occupations with average earnings between Rs. 90 and Rs. 140 per month.

Household income

The average monthly income of the sample household was Rs. 206.32. The distribution of households by income showed that only 10 (3%) had an income of Rs. 500 or more while 43 (14%) had an income of less than Rs. 100 per month. Majority of the households in the sample (66%) were in the income range of Rs. 100 to Rs. 300 per month (Table 6.21). The average household income increased with the size of the household; that of a 2-member household was 146 as against that of Rs. 247 of a household with seven members or more.

TABLE 6.21 : **Percentage distribution of households by household income and household size.**

Monthly income in Rs.	Household Size						Total
	2	3	4	5	6	7+	
100	15.39	22.86	22.50	6.67	22.64	7.21	13.78
100-199	69.23	31.43	37.50	61.67	32.08	33.33	40.38
200-299	7.69	25.71	32.50	16.67	18.87	34.23	25.96
300-399	7.69	17.14	5.00	10.00	18.87	13.51	12.82
400-499	—	2.86	—	3.33	7.54	4.50	3.85
500+	—	—	2.50	1.66	—	7.22	3.21
Total	100.00	100.00	100.00	100.00	100.00	100.00	100.00
Number of households	13	35	40	60	53	111	312
Mean income per household	146.15	182.66	176.65	183.58	199.98	246.85	206.32
Mean income per person	73.08	60.89	44.16	36.72	33.73	27.90	34.91

Per capita income

The per capita income per month was Rs. 34.91. The largest percentage in the sample (29%) was in the per capita income range Rs. 20-30 per month; 72 per cent of the sample population had per capita income of less than Rs. 40 and 79 per cent less than Rs. 50 per month (Table 6.22).

The per capita income varied inversely with the size of the household. The average income per person in a 2-member household was Rs. 73.08 which declined to Rs. 27.90 in a household with 7 or more members.

TABLE 6.22 : **Cumulative percentage distribution of households and population by per capita income.**

Per capita Income per month	Cumulative percentage of		
	Households	Persons	Income
Lesss than Rupees			
10	2.56	3.15	0.67
20	16.35	19.52	7.56
30	42.63	48.21	27.14
40	65.06	72.02	50 18
50	72.76	79.34	59.37
60	82.37	87.47	71.53
70	89.10	92.35	80.45
80	93.27	95.39	86.76
105	98.08	98.75	95.38
165	100.00	100.00	100.00

Income distribution

The Lorenz ratio obtained was 0.3070. At the bottom, below the per capita income level of Rs. 10, 3 per cent of the sample population shared 0.67 per cent of the total income while at the top, above the per capita income level of Rs. 105, 1 per cent of the sample population shared 5 per cent of the income.

The households, when classified into fractiles showed that the per capita income in the lowest fractile was Rs. 11.32 as against Rs. 92.60 in the highest fractile (Table 6.23).

Household expenditure

Details of household expenditure on 10 broad groups of items were collected from 311 households. While details of expenditure on food, fuel, rent, entertainment and liquor related to the calendar month prior to the date of interview, those on

TABLE 6.23 : **Percentage distribution of average income by fractile groups of sample population.**

Fractile	Upper limit of fractile	Average income of the household	Average income per person
0-10	15.00	83.16	11.32
10-20	20.00	111.03	18.51
20-30	24.00	154.34	22.38
30-40	26.67	173.09	25.81
40-50	31.43	182.59	30.25
50-60	36.00	210.58	34.00
60-70	44.32	241.77	39.85
70-80	54.50	250.45	49.13
80-90	70.00	286.29	62.39
90-100	162.50	383.21	92.60
All groups		206.32	34.90

education, health, clothes and 'others' related to the previous year. They were all reduced to monthly expenditure on seven broad groups.

The average household monthly expenditure was Rs. 203.34. The per capita monthly expenditure was Rs. 34.33, of which 87 per cent was spent: on food (70%), fuel (10%) and clothes (7%). Of the per capita monthly expenditure on various items, that on food (Rs. 23.90) was the highest and that on rent (Rs. 0.29) was the least (Table 6.24).

Movement for work of slum-dwellers

The distribution of 598 workers by the distance classes of their work places and places of residences (i.e. slums) showed that 14.32 per cent of the male workers and 26.83 per cent of the female workers worked either in the slum of their residence or within a very short distance (1/4 km.) from their residences. An examination of the occupations of these workers, who did not go beyond 1/4th of a kilometre for work, showed that they were engaged in the occupations, like priest, carpenter, blacksmith, agarbatti (incense sticks) and basket making.

The percentages of male and female workers who had not reported one specific place for their work were respectively

TABLE 6.24 : Percentage distribution of items of expenditure and monthly per capita expenditure

Item	Monthly per capita expenditure in Rs.						Total
	<15	15-27	28-42	43-54	55-74	75+	
Food	70.72 (8.89)	71.30 (15.31)	71.97 (24.51)	70.42 (33.42)	66.85 (40.61)	58.98 (55.09)	69.62 (23.90)
Fuel	16.94 (2.13)	11.80 (2.61)	10.12 (3.45)	10.47 (4.97)	9.40 (5.71)	8.67 (8.10)	10.48 (3.60)
Rent	— —	0.67 (0.15)	0.82 (0.28)	1.27 (0.61)	0.89 (0.54)	0.61 (0.57)	0.84 (0.29)
Education	0.88 (0.11)	1.44 (0.32)	1.14 (0.39)	1.60 (0.76)	1.60 (0.97)	1.43 (1.34)	1.40 (0.48)
Health	0.88 (0.11)	2.75 (0.61)	2.76 (0.94)	1.90 (0.90)	3.01 (2.05)	10.60 (9.90)	3.28 (1.13)
Clothing	5.09 (0.64)	7.67 (1.68)	6.08 (2.07)	6.48 (3.08)	8.18 (4.97)	7.77 (7.26)	6.96 (2.39)
Others	5.49 (0.69)	4.37 (0.97)	7.11 (2.42)	7.86 (3.73)	10.07 (6.12)	11.94 (11.14)	7.43 (2.55)
Total	100.00 (12.57)	100.00 (22.10)	100.00 (34.05)	100.00 (47.46)	100.00 (60.12)	100.00 (93.40)	100.00 (34.33)
Number of households	14	99	100	46	37	15	311
Number of persons	100	682	606	241	155	58	1842

Note : Figures in parenthesis are average per capita expenditure.

20 per cent and 7 per cent. This category included the responses like anywhere in the city; broad areas like Jayanagar, 'Cantonment' and 'all over the city'. These workers included drivers, construction workers, street vendors.

In between these two extreme categories, were the other 66 per cent male workers whose work places were between 0.25 to 12.0 km. and 66 per cent female workers whose work places were between 0.25 to 6 km. of their residences. Thus female workers did not go beyond 6 km. from their residences for work. In fact, about 83 per cent of the female workers worked within 4 km. This distance pattern also conformed to the occupations of these female workers, a majority of whom were maid servants and sweepers and these occupations did not involve long distance movement for work. The average distance of work place for male workers was 2.8 km. and for female workers 1.6 km.

About 70 per cent of the male workers had their work places within 6 km. of their residences. The male workers from Baglur, Christian Colony and Jayanagar VIII Block travelled more than those from other slums. The average distances for work for these slums were 4.6, 4.2 and 3.7 respectively. The workers whose work places were in the distance class 6 to 12 km. were mostly workers in factories, shopkeepers, waiters in restaurants, teachers, mechanics etc.

An examination of places of work (110) showed that the maximum number of workers (54) worked in city market, a majority of whom were engaged in material handling and in shops as shop assistants. The other places where more than 10 workers worked were Banashankari second stage, Railway Station, Kalasipalyam, Srirampuram, Corporation Office, Gandhi Bazar, Mavalli, Basavanagudi, Armugam Circle, Jayanagar, Yediyur village and Tannery road. These workers were mostly construction workers, coolies, production and related workers, sweepers, labourers and shop assistants. The other places were scattered upto a distance of 12 km. from the selected slums and the workers going to these places for work were involved in various occupations, like factory workers, clerks, teachers, shopkeepers, blacksmiths, tailors, watchman, carpenters and stone cutters.

There was no relationship between distance and mode of

travel for slum dwellers movement for work. Some of the workers whose places of work were even at a distance of 6 to 12 km. walked and some of the others used buses for smaller distances. The percentage of workers who walked for work was 86 per cent; 6 per cent used cycle and 8 per cent buses for the movement.

The above analysis brings out that the majority of slum dwellers are migrants from the adjoining rural areas to a city, and are of low skilled with low occupation status and low incomes, and are drawn mainly from the weaker sections of communities. Consequently, slum dwellers have no option but to live in houses of sub-standard quality. Then slums should be equated first with the poverty of people then to sub-standard housing. The policy maker should recognise that just providing a house and even a better environment to live in cannot solve the problem of growth of slums which has its roots in the very demand for low level occupations.

7

CITY CLIMATE*

WITH the increasing emphasis on planning for healthier and comfortable physical environments in cities, the need to recognise the role of cities in creating climatic change and especially climatically inhospitable environments has become greater. This chapter on city climate demonstrates that some of the city landscape elements (e.g. concrete structures, slums, and pollutant industries) can modify or create climates which add to the city residents' discomfort and even ill-health. Drawing the climatic factor into urban planning explicitly increases the complexity of urban planning, and adds one more challenge to the urban planner who has to widen his vision, if he wishes to use the city climate, both natural and modified, in designing and structuring the future city.

The climate of the city and the countryside

It is recognized that the climates of cities generally tend to be warmer than those of the surrounding countryside. Cities differ from the countryside not only in respect of their temperature but also in respect of other climatic elements. By climate is meant the net meteorological result of the various interacting physical variables, like temperature, the amount of water

*This chapter draws heavily from the project reports on "urban meteorology of Visakhapatnam" (1974-1978) and "city climates" (1979-80) prepared by Prof. V. P. Subrahmanyam, S. Sachidevi and P. Viswanadham, with the assistance of B. Hemamalini, M. V. Kamaraju, M. M. Ali, N.S.N. Murthy and Kesava Rao of the departments of Meteorology and Oceanography and Geography, Andhra University, Visakhapatnam. The valuable contribution of Prof. Subrahmanyam and his team of workers, in field survey, data analysis, mapping and drafting the report is hereby acknowledged.

vapour in the air, the speed of the wind, the amount of solar radiation and the amount of precipitation.

Very often, the city itself is the cause of climatic differences. Its compact mass of buildings and pavements, the very activities of its inhabitants, and the natural landscape elements are a considerable source of heat. Together, these account for five basic influences that set a city's climate as differentiated from that of the surrounding area.

The first influence is the difference between surface materials in the city and in the countryside. The predominantly rock-like materials of the city's buildings and streets can conduct heat about three times as fast as heat conducted by wet, sandy soil. Second, the city's structures have a far greater variety of shapes and orientations than the features of the natural landscape. The walls, roofs and streets of a city function like a maze of reflectors, absorbing some of the energy they receive and directing much of the rest to other absorbing surfaces. Third, the city is a prodigious generator of heat, particularly in winter when the heating systems are in operation. Even in summer, however, the city has many sources of heat; among them are factories, vehicles and even air-conditioners, which of course must pump out hot air in order to produce their cooling effect. Fourth, the city has distinctive ways of disposal of precipitation. In the cities, precipitation water is quickly removed from the surface through the well-engineered drainage systems whereas in the country much rain water remains on the surface. Thus, in the countryside, either free water on the surface or that which has infiltrated into the soil is available for evaporation, which is of course a cooling process powered by heat energy. Because there is less opportunity for evaporation in the city, the heat energy that would have gone into the process is utilized for heating the air. Finally, the air in the city is different in that it carries a heavy load of solid, liquid and gaseous contaminants.

Each city has its own landscape profile and thereby has its own climate, hence it is difficult to infer the climate of all cities by generalizing from observations within one or a few cities. Yet, it is clear that cities are warmer, cloudier, dirtier, rainier, less sunny and less humid than the surrounding countryside. There is evidence that cities of middle latitudes receive 15 per cent less sunshine on horizontal surfaces than is received in the nearby rural areas, 5 per cent less ultraviolet radiation during summer months and 30 per cent less during winter. The average maximum temperature difference between the city and the countryside is about 3°C but differences of the order of 15°C do occur (Table 7.1). In Bombay, it was found that the temperature excess of the city area over the rural surroundings was of the order of 6°C in the early mornings (cold weather season). The excess gets reduced to 3-4°C in the hot season, and to 1-2°C during the monsoon season (Phillip *et al.*, 1973).

TABLE 7.1 : Climatic changes produced by cities (after Landsberg) 1962.

Elements	Comparison with rural environs
Temperature	
Annual mean	1.0 to 1.5°F higher
Winter mean	2.0 to 3.0°F higher
Relative humidity	
Annual mean	6% lower
Winter	2% lower
Summer	8% lower
Dust particles	10 times more
Cloudiness	
Clouds	5 to 10% more
Fog, winter	100% more
Fog, summer	30% more
Radiation	
Total on horizontal surface	15% to 20% less
Ultraviolet, winter	30% less
Ultraviolet, summer	5% less
Wind speed	
Annual mean	20 to 30% lower
Calms	5 to 20% more
Precipitation	5 to 10% more

The city atmosphere is liable to pollution, particularly as the result of combustion, by smoke, dust, sulphur dioxide and other gases. These have the effect of changing the thermal properties of the atmosphere, cutting down the passage of sunlight and providing abundant condensation nuclei. The increase of particulate matter in the atmosphere is bound to affect the climate since particles not only scatter and absorb solar radiation but also have an effect on the outgoing infra-red radiation from the surface of the earth. Consequently, cities receive less solar radiation than rural areas. And there is yet another fact, that cities have 10 per cent more clouds which also affect the incoming solar radiation. City wind speeds are lower than those in the surrounding open country, owing to the sheltering effect of the buildings and blocks. The thermal characteristics of urban areas are in marked contrast to those of the surrounding countryside. The factors responsible for this contrast are the direct production of heat by combustion, the gradual release of solar heat, stored during the day by the concrete structures and other heavy materials, and the downward reflection from the atmospheric pollution layer of outgoing radiation back to surface.

The rapid growth of industries changes city climates to large extent, by injecting materials and heat into the atmosphere. The by-products of combustion are water vapour, carbon dioxide, carbon monoxide, oxides of sulphur and other undesirable minor constituents, all of which are released into the atmosphere and constitute what is called "air pollution". The automobile is another important source of air pollution. The transport system contributes oxides of sulphur, nitrogen, carbon and several other irritating organic compounds (due to photochemical reactions in the atmosphere). Surface transportation of people and goods may contribute to the modification of city climate in two ways—first by the emission of particulate and gaseous exhaust products into the atmosphere (that can impact on radiation fields and precipitation); and second by the modification of the reflective and thermal properties of the land surface by highways.

Another important distinguishing element between the urban and rural settings having a strong climatic impact is the vegetation cover. The natural or agricultural vegetation in the countryside contributes to moderate air temperatures, higher humidity and cooler climate though the diurnal temperatures, may be small. On the other hand, the city climates are likely to be more continental due to lack of or sparseness of vegetation and, therefore, have higher temperature ranges and lower humidities. The resulting temperature and humidity profiles sometimes produce peculiarities in local rainfall distributions in a city quite different from the country where rainfalls are of longer duration.

Case studies

Three cities are selected to study their city climates—Visakhapatnam—an industrializing port city; Vijayawada—a city of intense commercial activity and Bangalore, now an industrial city and naturally air-conditioned as it were, by virtue of its altitude.

Visakhapatnam is a rapidly growing industrial city situated on the Bay of Bengal coast of South India between two east-west hill ranges of the Eastern Ghats—The Kailsa range on the north and the Yarada range on the south. These two hill ranges with a height of about 600 ft. from the ground level, run at right angles to the coast and produce a channelling effect in trapping and directing the winds across the city. The Bay of Bengal forms the eastern boundary of the city. The western side is an extensive tidal basin, a major portion of which is being slowly reclaimed for industrial and city expansion.

Vijayawada is a commercial city with a high degree of nodality, located at the apex of a river delta on the northern bank of the river Krishna at about 50 miles from the sea coast. There are small hill ranges and isolated hillocks, bare and denuded, around Vijayawada city, which contribute their shares to the extremes of the city's summer climate.

Bangalore which is an air-conditioned city by the gift of nature, is located in the heart of the southern Deccan plateau. Physically, its location on the top of a ridge running through the middle of the plateau from north to south, at an average elevation of just above 3000 feet (900 metres), is of climatic significance in terms of human comfort.

The climatological data used in the present study of the city climates of Visakhapatnam, Vijayawada and Bangalore are taken from the climatological tables of India Meteorological Department (Climatological tables of observatories in India 1931-1960). For Vijayawada, the recorded data of Gannavaram meteorological station, situated at about 8 miles from Vijayawada are used.

Climatic elements and comfort indices (Fig. 7.1)

(a) Air temperature,
(b) Air humidity,
(c) Rainfall,
(d) Winds,
(e) Water balance, and
(f) Comfort indices.

At Visakhapatnam, May is the hottest month and January is the coldest month of the year with average temperatures of 30.9°C and 22.5°C respectively. The mean annual range of temperature (defined as mean temperature of the warmest month minus the mean temperature of the coldest month) is 8.4°C which is what may be expected for a coastal station. The curves of mean monthly maximum and mean monthly minimum temperatures shown in the diagram indicate that the mean maximum temperature is the highest in May (34.0°C) and the mean minimum temperature is the lowest in January (17.3°C). At Vijayawada too while May is the hottest month with a mean maximum temperature of 39.7°C and an average temperature of 33.7°C. December is the coldest month with an average temperature of 24.4°C and a mean minimum temperature of 19.1°C. Annual temperature range here is 9.4°C, slightly higher than that of Visakhapatnam because of the interior location of Vijayawada. Bangalore on account of its higher altitude of 3,021 feet naturally records lower temperatures when compared to Visakhapatnam and Vijayawada. It can be seen from the figure that April is the hottest month with a mean maximum temperature of 34.0°C and an average temperature of 27.6°C while December is the coldest month with a mean minimum temperature of 15.4°C and an average temperature of 21.1°C. Mean annual temperature range is only 6.5°C which is much lower than the range at Visakhapatnam. This is due to the effect of elevation and the variation of maximum and minimum temperatures (Table 7.2).

At Vijayawada the minimum relative humidity is in the month of May (43% 1730 hrs.) and the maximum is in September and October (81% 0830 hrs.), the range being 38 per cent. Bangalore has a still higher range of 62 per cent with the maximum of 86 per cent in July-August (morning reading)

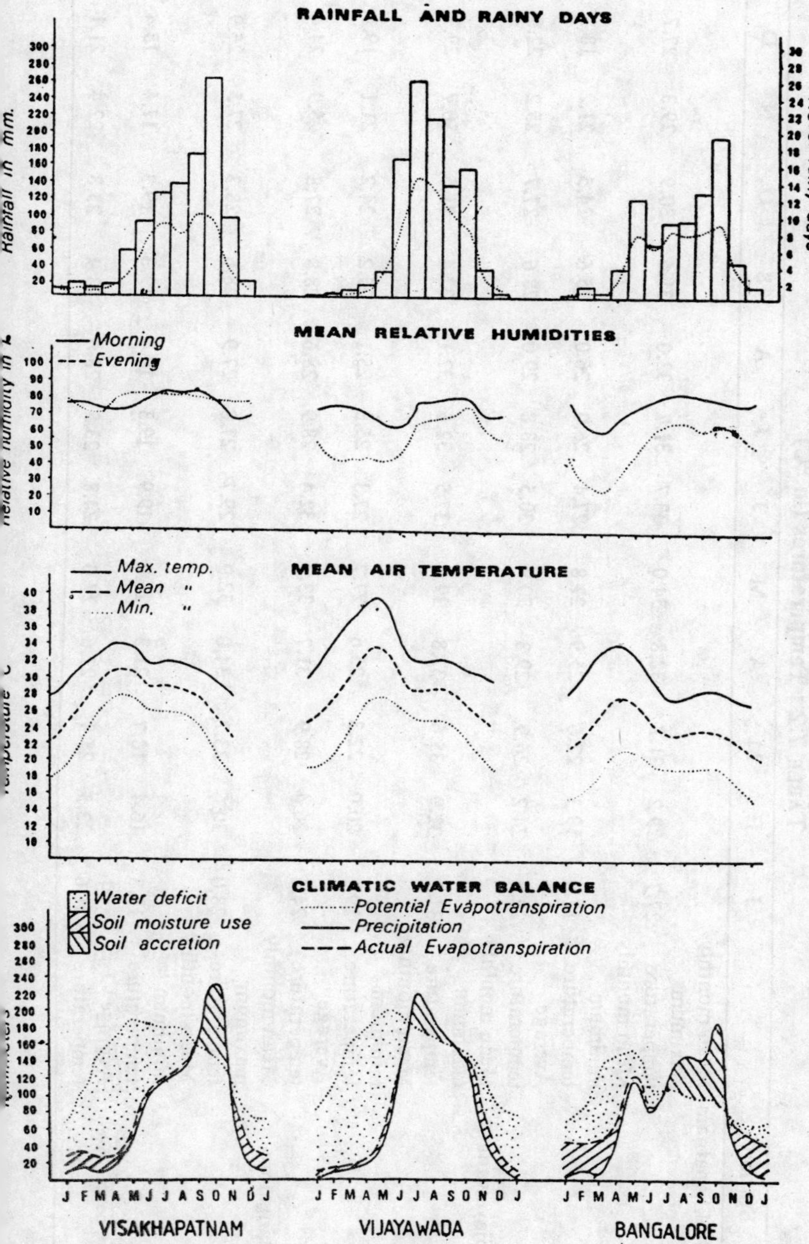

FIG. 7.1 : *Rainfall, Relative humidity, air temperature and climatic water balance*

TABLE 7.2 : Temperatures (in °C)

Station		J	F	M	A	M	J	J	A	S	O	N	D
Visakhapatnam	Mean monthly maximum temperature	27.7	29.2	31.2	32.8	34.0	33.7	31.7	32.0	31.6	30.9	29.3	27.7
	Mean monthly minimum temperature	17.3	19.3	22.6	25.9	27.8	27.4	26.0	26.0	25.6	24.5	21.2	18.3
	Average temperature	22.5	24.2	26.9	29.3	30.9	30.5	28.8	29.0	28.6	27.7	25.2	22.5
Vijayawada	Mean monthly maximum temperature	31.1	32.9	35.6	37.8	39.7	37.5	32.6	32.1	32.4	31.5	30.7	29.7
	Mean monthly minimum temperature	19.1	20.0	22.3	25.6	27.7	27.3	25.3	25.1	25.2	24.2	21.1	19.1
	Average temperature	24.6	26.4	28.9	31.7	33.7	32.4	28.9	28.6	28.8	27.8	25.9	24.4
Bangalore	Mean monthly maximum temperature	28.0	30.6	33.2	34.0	32.9	29.7	27.8	27.9	28.6	28.3	27.5	26.9
	Mean monthly minimum temperature	15.3	16.4	18.7	21.3	21.2	19.9	19.3	19.4	19.3	19.3	17.4	15.4
	Average temperature	21.6	23.5	25.9	27.6	27.0	24.8	23.5	23.6	23.9	23.8	22.4	21.1

and minimum of 24 per cent in the month of March. Bangalore's comfortable summer is due to lower humidities and lower minimum temperatures during summer months.

The coastal station of Visakhapatnam on the other hand has the highest relative humidities (83-84%) in the evenings right from May to September. The morning relative humidities are not too different in these months varying from 80 to 84 per cent from June to September. This is due to the sea breeze circulation which raises the water vapour content of the air and maintains its steady through the day. On account of the highest air temperatures during these months, the climate is very oppressive and uncomfortable. Though there is not much variation in relative humidity in other months, even between morning and evening observations, still the rapid lowering of temperatures from November to February makes the climate more comfortable during this period (Table 7.3).

At Visakhapatnam, October is the wettest month with maximum rainfall of 259.3 mm and January is the driest month with minimum rainfall of 7.2 mm. Maximum amount of rainfall in the month of October is on account of the cyclonic activity during the transition season producing heavy falls in a short time. The cyclonic effect may be observed at the other two stations too, though with varying magnitudes (Vijayawada 155.2 mm and Bangalore 184.9 mm).

Both the amount of rainfall (1031.6 mm) and number of rainy days (62.1) are higher at Vijayawada than at Visakhapatnam. The slight rise in October rainfall compared to that in September is clearly the result of cyclonic activity though not so pronounced as at Visakhapatnam. Bangalore has a different regime of rainfall since the maximum of 184.9 mm occurs in October, being the result of the cyclonic storms from the bay during the transition season. Next higher values are during the southwest monsoon period from July to September. The maximum rainfall in May is due to the pre-monsoon thunderstorm activity. The maximum number of rainy days is in August, the secondary maximum being in October. The amount of rainfall and the corresponding number of rainy days for individual months at each station are a useful guide since their ratio gives the climatic intensity of

TABLE 7.3 : Relative humidity (in %)

Station	Hours of observation	J	F	M	A	M	J	J	A	S	O	N	D
Visakhapatnam	0830 Hrs.	77	77	74	73	75	80	84	82	81	78	68	70
	1730 Hrs.	78	73	71	80	83	83	82	83	84	79	73	74
Vijayawada	0830 Hrs.	74	77	76	72	65	64	79	79	81	81	70	71
	1730 Hrs.	54	44	44	45	43	48	65	69	71	76	62	56
Bangalore	0830 Hrs.	77	67	63	70	75	82	86	86	85	83	78	78
	1730 Hrs.	40	29	24	34	46	62	68	66	62	64	59	51

rainfall per rainy day which is useful in water use planning (Table 7.4).

For many phases of industrial and urban planning, wind speeds and directions are a useful guide. The two main wind directions are westerly during the summer and the southwest monsoon seasons, and easterly during the northeast monsoon and the winter seasons. When the southwest monsoon breaks in early June, the wind velocity reaches its peak intensity during June and July. Occasions with wind speed varying from 20 to 61 km. per hour are rare, occurring as gales perhaps during severe cyclonic storms and for brief periods of time. The maximum percentage of calms occurs as expected during the northeast monsoon and winter periods. The information about windroses is of immense importance in several phases of planning like location of industries, residential colonies, runway orientations as well as wind breaks and shelterbelts.

Water balance (Fig. 7.1)

Climatic water balance represents the extent to which water supply by rainfall at any station matches the various water demands like evapotranspiration, soil storage, stream flow etc. A detailed knowledge of water budget is essential not only for agricultural and hydrological planning but also for assessing the water potentialities for purposes of municipal and industrial use. The water balances for the three cities under study are worked out using the book-keeping procedure of Thornthwaite and Mather (1955). The water need (potential evapotranspiration) is computed using the formula and procedures proposed by Thornthwaite (1955). The data on a monthly basis including the derived water budget parameters i.e. actual evapotranspiration, water surplus and water deficit, are shown in Table 7.5, and are graphically represented. The charts show that all the three cities experience large amounts of water deficiency during a major period in the year and there is no water surplus at all in any month of the year. The slight excess of rainfall at the stations during the southwest monsoon season is hardly sufficient even to replenish the soil reservoir which has a capacity to hold about 200 to 300 mm of water. The result is that the soil is never saturated climatically, and therefore, there is no surplus moisture for contribution to

TABLE 7.4 : Rainfall

Station		J	F	M	A	M	J	J	A	S	O	N	D
Visakhapatnam	Rainfall in mm	7.2	14.9	8.7	12.7	53.5	87.8	121.9	132.2	167.3	259.3	90.6	17.5
	Number of rainy days	0.6	0.9	0.6	1.0	2.5	6.1	8.5	7.2	9.6	9.0	3.2	0.9
Vijayawada	Rainfall in mm	0.9	2.8	9.4	16.3	32.9	165.9	259.1	214.4	134.1	155.2	35.0	5.6
	Number of rainy days	0.1	0.4	0.4	0.9	3.1	8.8	14.2	12.8	9.9	8.3	2.3	0.9
Bangalore	Rainfall in mm	3.3	10.2	6.1	45.7	116.5	80.1	116.6	147.1	142.7	184.9	54.3	16.2
	Number of rainy days	0.4	0.5	0.6	3.0	7.2	6.5	9.0	10.2	8.4	9.0	3.9	1.4

TABLE 7.5 : Climatic : water balance

Station	Elements (in mm)	J	F	M	A	M	J	J	A	S	O	N	D	Total
Visakhapatnam	PE	72	101	148	167	188	182	176	172	156	147	109	74	1692
(1901 to 1978)	P	10	17	10	21	52	101	119	128	169	227	98	14	966
Lat. 17°41′ N	AE	28	33	26	29	56	102	120	128	156	147	103	38	966
Long 83°18′ E	WD	44	68	122	138	132	80	56	44	0	0	6	36	726
	WS	0	0	0	0	0	0	0	0	0	0	0	0	0
Vijayawada	PE	80	117	163	177	198	190	176	167	157	148	113	83	1769
(1951-1977)	P	1	5	11	16	51	129	218	186	162	141	51	13	984
Lat. 16°32′ N	AE	11	14	15	18	51	129	176	167	157	144	73	29	984
Long. 81°47′ E	WD	69	103	148	159	147	61	0	0	0	4	40	54	785
	WS	0	0	0	0	0	0	0	0	0	0	0	0	0
Bangalore	PE	68	82	130	145	152	109	103	101	95	95	72	65	1217
(1931-1960)	P	3	10	6	46	117	80	117	147	143	185	54	16	924
Lat. 12°58′ N	AE	43	44	46	66	123	83	103	101	95	95	71	54	924
Long. 77°35′ E	WD	25	33	84	79	29	26	0	0	0	0	1	11	293
	WS	0	0	0	0	0	0	0	0	0	0	0	0	0

PE=Potential Evapotranspiration
P=Precipitation
AE=Actual evapotranspiration
WD=Water deficit
WS=Water surplus.

sustained stream flow. The moisture recharge of the soil does not take place uniformly during the same period in the three cities. While Visakhapatnam experiences maximum precipitation during the retreating southwest monsoon season of October mainly due to the Bay cyclonic activity. Vijayawada has its heaviest rainfall during the southwest monsoon season itself i.e. July-September. On the other hand, the interior highland station Bangalore in the far south, experiences a large amount of precipitation both during the southwest monsoon season as well as in the post-monsoon season, the magnitude being somewhat higher in the latter period.

While the soil has a capacity to hold as much as 200 to 300 mm of water at any time, it receives around only 93 mm of water during September and October at Visakhapatnam, 66 mm of water in July and August at Vijayawada, and 198 mm of water from August to October at Bangalore. Consequently there are annual water deficiencies of 726 mm, 785 mm and 293 mm respectively. This is mainly on account of the annual water need of Bangalore being the lowest (1217 mm) though its precipitation is lower than the other two. Though Vijayawada receives higher amount of rainfall than Visakhapatnam, its water deficiency too is higher as a result of its higher water need. Thus the water potentialities of a station cannot be assessed purely on the basis of rainfall or water need but by a systematic comparison of the two as done in water balance computations.

According to 1955 water balance procedure and the revised scheme of climatic classification, the moisture indices of the three stations work out to be —42.9 per cent, —44.4 per cent and —24.1 per cent. Hence Visakhapatnam and Vijayawada belong to the semi-arid type while Bangalore belongs to the dry sub-humid type.

Comfort indices (Fig. 7.2)

The main climatic factors that determine human comfort or discomfort are temperature and humidity. High temperatures and high humidities cause maximum discomfort. All the three cities under study being situated in the tropical belt have high temperatures and high humidities throughout the year and especially during summer. Compared to Visakhapatnam and

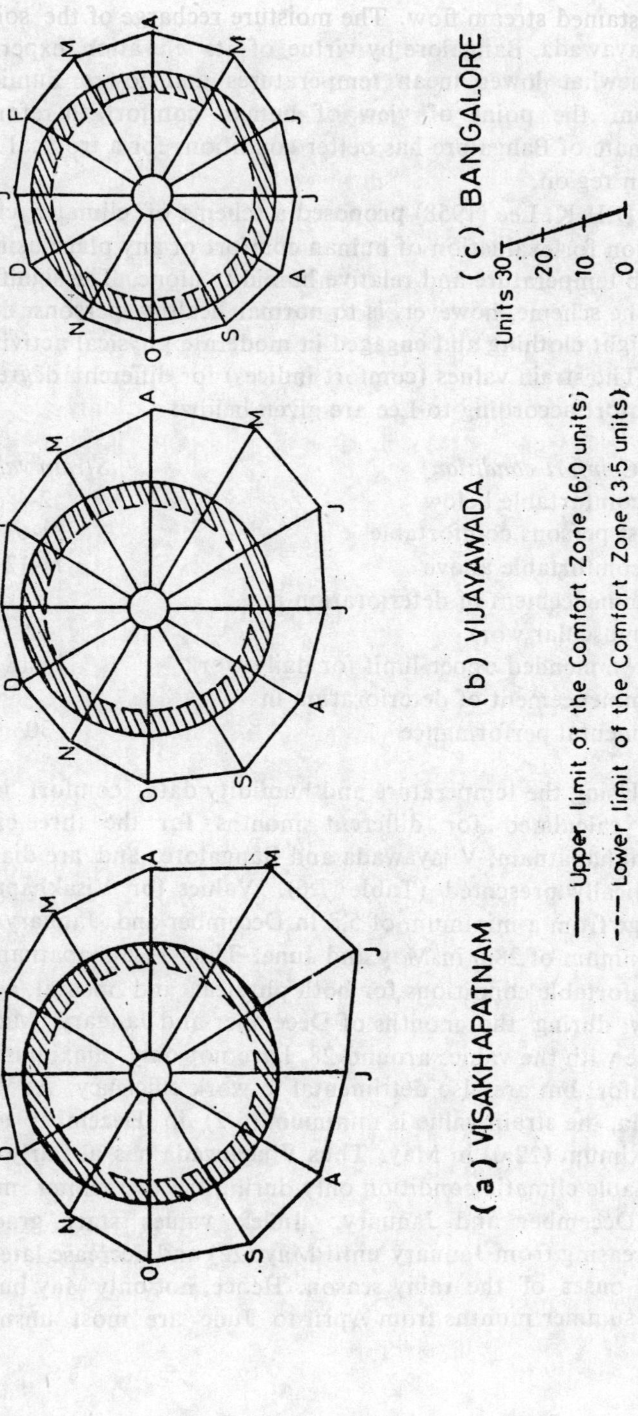

FIG. 7.2 : *Comfort indices*

Vijayawada, Bangalore by virtue of its elevation experiences somewhat lower mean temperatures and lower humidities. From the point of view of human comfort, therefore, the climate of Bangalore has better conditions for a tropical monsoon region.

D.H.K. Lee (1958) proposed a scheme of climatic classification for evaluation of human comfort of any place using dry bulb temperature and relative humidity alone. The significance of the scheme, however, is to normal healthy persons dressed in light clothing and engaged in moderate physical activity.

The strain values (comfort indices) for different degrees of comfort according to Lee are given below:

Comfort condition	*Strain value*
Uncomfortable below	2-4
Most persons comfortable	3½-6
Uncomfortable above	7½-12
Commencement of deterioration in muscular work	12
Recommended upper limit for daily work	14-18
Commencement of deterioration in mental performance	30

Using the temperature and humidity data, comfort indices are calculated for different months for the three cities—Visakhapatnam, Vijayawada and Bangalore, and are diagrammatically presented (Table 7.6). Values for Visakhapatnam range from a minimum of 5.8 in December and January to a maximum of 28.0 in May and June. Thus Visakhapatnam has comfortable conditions for both physical and mental activity only during the months of December and January. May and June with the values around 28, have not only maximum discomfort but are also detrimental to work efficiency. At Vijayawada, the strain value is minimum (6.2) in December and is maximum (22.0) in May. Thus Vijayawada has a fairly comfortable climatic condition only during the two winter months of December and January. Index values start gradually increasing from January until May (22) and decrease later with the onset of the rainy season. Hence, not only May but also the summer months from April to June are most unsuitable

TABLE 7.6 : Comfort indices

Station		J	F	M	A	M	J	J	A	S	O	N	D
Visakhapatnam	1. Dry bulb temperature in °C	24.0	26.0	28.3	30.5	31.8	31.0	29.3	29.5	29.1	28.3	26.2	24.3
	2. Relative humidity in %	77.5	75.0	72.5	76.5	79.0	81.5	83.0	82.5	82.5	78.5	70.5	72.0
	3. Strain values	5.8	8.6	13.0	19.0	28.0	28.0	17.0	18.0	18.0	14.0	8.2	5.8
Vijayawada	1. Dry bulb temperature in °C	25.3	27.3	29.8	32.1	34.0	32.6	29.2	28.7	28.9	27.9	26.3	25.1
	2. Relative humidity in %	64.0	60.5	60.0	58.5	54.0	56.0	72.0	74.0	76.0	78.5	66.0	63.5
	3. Strain values	6.2	9.2	13.0	18.0	22.0	18.5	14.0	13.5	16.0	13.0	7.8	6.2
Bangalore	1. Dry bulb temperature in °C	22.4	24.7	27.3	28.2	27.2	24.7	23.3	23.5	23.9	23.8	22.7	21.4
	2. Relative humidity in %	61.5	47.0	43.0	52.0	62.0	70.5	75.0	75.5	72.5	73.5	68.5	66.5
	3. Strain values	4.0	5.0	6.8	9.0	9.0	6.2	5.4	5.8	6.0	5.8	4.4	3.5

for outdoor physical work; persistence, however may lead to physiological ailments both short term and sudden (like sunstroke and heat exhaustion) as well as slow and prolonged mental inefficiency and paralysis. The higher strain value of 28 at Visakhapatnam in May is on account of higher humidity compared with that at Vijayawada.

Fig. 7.2 shows that the comfort indices at Bangalore range from a minimum of 3.5 in December to a maximum of 9.0 in April and May. Thus Bangalore with its equable climate never becomes uncomfortable in any part of the year. It is most comfortable from February to October. Slightly less comfortable conditions prevail from November to January due to lower temperatures and lower humidities. Owing to its fine and healthy climate, Bangalore attracts many people especially during summer.

Urban heat islands

The urban heat island is a city area with excessive warmth compared with its surrounding area, and develops progressively after sunset. The size, shape, strength and location of heat islands are generally controlled by the size and shape of the built-up area and the meso-scale weather patterns. The heat island is characterized by a temperature gradient, and is influenced by the direction and strength of wind. The formation of heat islands is due to higher thermal capacity of city structures and pavements, power generation, transportation, high density of housing units, and reduced wind-speed due to city structures. The heat islands add to the development and self-sustenance of a 'dust-dome' and a 'haze-hood' of contaminating particles. The size and intensity of heat islands vary from city to city, and from season to season in the same city.

Urban heat islands in Visakhapatnam

Different environments in the city were selected for the study of the formation of urban heat islands. Surface temperature surveys were carried out employing whirling psychrometers in the different environments during the winter months from November 1979 to February 1980. The survey period chosen was near the minimum temperature epoch, with lowest temperatures and flat temperature curve. During the surveys as required, the skies were clear and winds were calm, at least during observation periods. As a matter of routine, the surveys were always started from a suitable point in each of the selective areas, and values of dry bulb and wet bulb temperatures at a number of predetermined points were measured using Assman Psychrometer by two or three teams of field workers simultaneously on each occasion. The survey was always terminated with repetition of an observation at the first point thus completing the observational circuit.

The observational points which vary from 30 to 50 on each of these surveys were so chosen as to ensure adequate coverage and representativeness of the area. In order to obtain actual temperatures during the period of survey, bimetallic thermographs were installed in the previous evening at representative locations, and observations at each point were reduced to a common time-base by applying a correction for the time-trend of temperature during the period of observations. The temperatures were then plotted on maps and isotherms were drawn taking topography into account.

The six areas selected and their characteristic environmental types are given below:

Area	*Representative environment*
Pithandibba	Urban slum
Jalaripet	Beach
National Highway 5	Foothill
Chinna Waltair	Urban village
Jagadamba area (Yellammathota)	City core (New Town)
Reading room	City core (Old Town)

The surveys in different areas of the city on six dates viz. 11.11.1979; 19.12.1979; 27.12.1979; 5.1.1980; 26.1.1980 and 6.2.1980 represent mainly the cold weather period when heat islands are usually prominent. Figs. 7.3, 7.4 and 7.5 show the patterns of isotherms for selected slums during the days of the survey.

Pithandibba—Urban slum (Fig 7.3)

The Pithandibba urban slum is located between the two main roads of the city—the Waltair Main Road and the Jail Road. It is a 'L' shaped slum with two clusters of houses—Ganjipeta

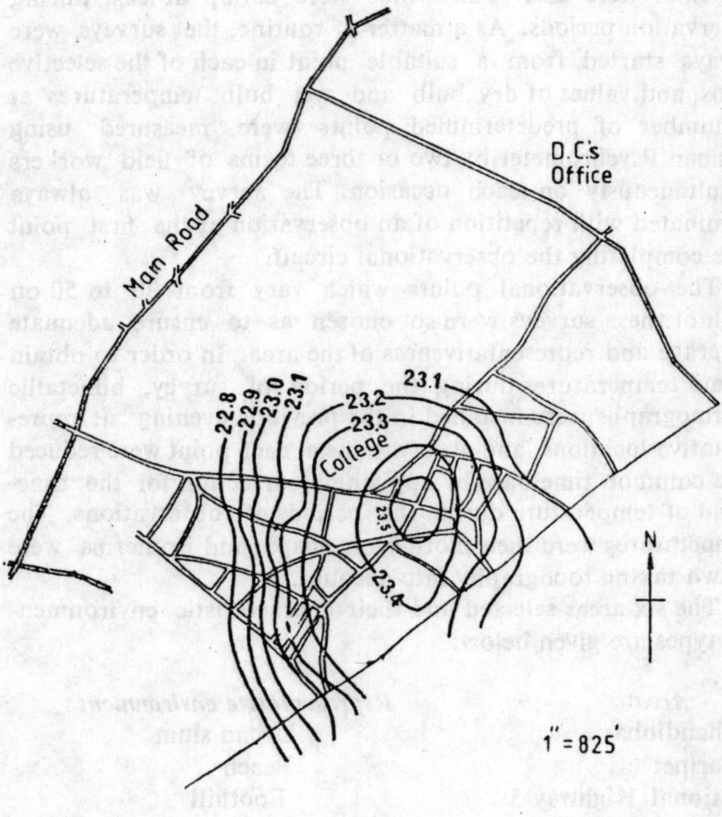

FIG. 7.3 : *Surface isotherms—Urban slum*

and Pithandibba, one on each arm of the L. The two slums are separated by a sewage drain which runs almost midway between them. Pithandibba and Ganjipeta are considered as a single unit for this study as they are adjacent to each other. According to the latest survey, about 596 families are estimated to be residing in both the slums, together covering an area of 14 acres. The majority of them are industrial labourers. The surface temperature distribution over this area is shown in Fig. 7.4. The isothermal pattern in the Pithandibba area appears to bear close resemblance to the pattern of dwelling concentration in the slum. Two intensive heat islands stand out conspicuously with their central cores over the central parts of the slum dwellings one over the Pithandibba slum and the other over the Ganjipeta slum. The highest temperature in the central areas of both the slums was around 24.8°C whereas the temperature at the outer area was 23.8°C. Though temperature difference between the outer area and the core was only about 1°C, the temperature gradient ranged from 0.4°C to 0.8°C per 100 feet. While the Pithandibba heat island was almost circular in shape, the Ganjipeta heat island was more elongated, and this has perhaps relevance to the areal spread of the slum. The southeast of this urban slum is surrounded by a compact built-up area at a higher altitude known as Ramnagar. On the northwestern side is a marshy low land area called Gollapalem with a low vegetation cover. The temperature distribution shows clearly that concentration of houses and people contributes to high temperatures.

Jalaripet—Beach environment (Fig. 7.4)

The second area 'Jalaripet' is a slum of fisherfolk situated right on the beach. The population and housing density are higher than that of the Pithandibba slum. But the occupation of the slum dwellers is different. Fishing with its typical equipment, is the main occupation of the slum-dwellers. To the southeast, the slum is bordered by the beach road and the coast line; and to the northwest by a ridge with the city main road. To the northeast of the slum, lies the Naval-Coastal Battery, and to the southwest, there is a well developed and high -density residential colony. Thus the slum area merges with the residential colony only on one side, and opens out abruptly into the open areas on the other three sides.

Examination of the surface temperature profiles reveals that the core of the slum, despite its openness on three sides, still maintains a heat island though of a lesser intensity. In spite of the larger slum size and higher population density, the heat island intensity is lower than that at Pithandibba. This is on account of the proximity of the slum to the sea, and therefore, prevalence of higher humidity which exercises a moderating influence on the temperature extremes normally generated in the slum. The shape of the heat island is again circular presumably due to haphazard nature of the slum disposition, and

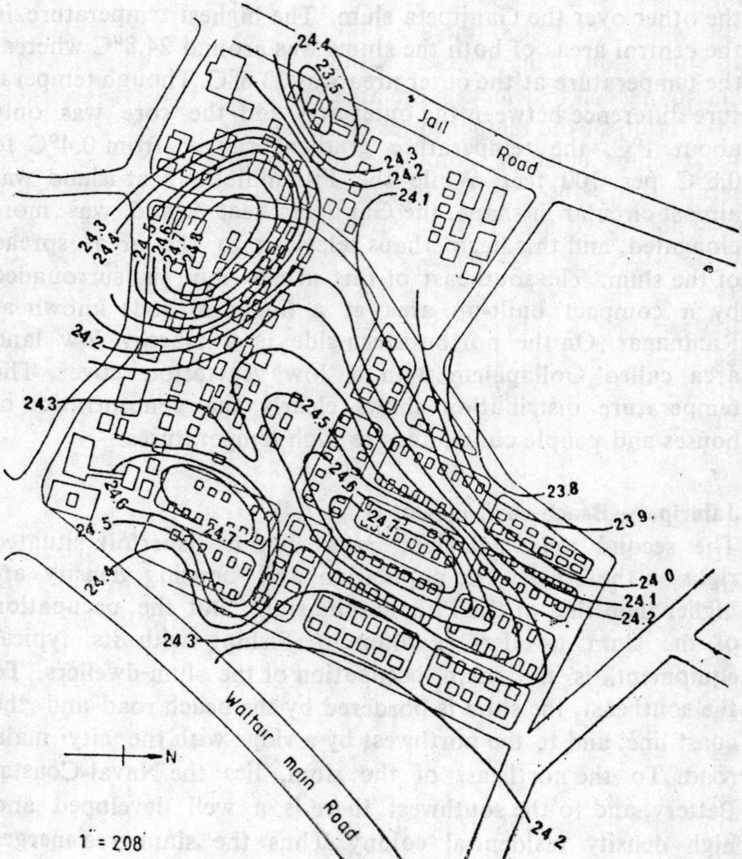

FIG. 7.4 : *Surface isotherms—Beach*

the temperature gradient is steep only on the side on which the slum spreads into the residential colony. The minimum temperature recorded during the survey was 22.8°C which is a good illustration of the influence of the sea on the thermal behaviour of the slum, other factors remaining the same.

National Highway 5 : Foothill environment

This is a stretch of National Highway (No. 5) from Maddilapalem cross road to Gopalapatnam cross road which has a total length of 6 miles. Strictly speaking, this is not a single concentrated slum but has a number of small clusters of hutments (Sanjevayyanagar, Leprosy colony etc.) scattered on either side of the highway without any slum-core as such. The main idea in selecting the area was to study the level of interaction of the temperatures between the foothills and the linear slum clusters along the highway. The highway runs parallel to the south of the Kailasa range of hills. The peak heights of this range vary from 1000 feet to 1550 feet MSL. The gap between the road and the hill range varies from a few yards to about half a mile. To the south of the highway, are a number of residential buildings and blocks interspersed with open area. The natural vegetation cover on either side of the road is relatively thicker than that at the Pithandibba and Jalaripet slums.

Surface temperature distribution in this area is represented in Fig. 7.1. The hillward side temperatures were relatively lower than those on the other side—22.8°C being the temperature on the hillward side, and 23.4°C on the other side with a variation of 0.6°C across the highway. No strong heat island as such is noticed here for the reason that the area does not have dense clusters of slum dwellings. Further, the slums are interspersed with some vegetation and open areas. Lower temperatures, along the hillward side may be due to the draining of cool air from the altitudes to the foothills, and also due to the vegetation around. The temperatures away from the hill slopes were, therefore, relatively higher, due to a higher density of residential houses.

Chinna Waltair : urban village

Chinna Waltair was originally a village. During the phase of urban sprawl of Visakhapatnam, this village was absorbed by the city, but still retains most of its inherent rural characteristics like narrow and winding road layouts, a number of thatched houses, and poor and open sewage disposal system. With an increase in the demand for housing from higher income groups, the Visakhapatnam Urban Development Authority constructed wide roads in the vacant lands surrounding the village, and developed residential colonies. As a result, the high density Chinna Waltair urban village stands out as an island in the midst of well-developed and relatively low density colonies.

This area, can be conveniently divided into two slums which face each other diagonally on either side of the Chinna Waltair main road. Excepting the sea coast to the east, at a distance of about half a kilometre, no other physical feature appears to influence the surface temperature distribution. Two conspicuous and well developed heat islands are found. The size, shape and intensity of the heat islands coincide with the size and shape of the slums. Since the village is enclosed by, and at the same time quite insulated from the low density colonies all around, the generation of higher temperatures is restricted only to the thickly populated slum area. The variation between the highest and the lowest temperatures was 0.8°C with a gradient of 0.3°C rise per 100 feet of distance into the interior. This village can be regarded as a typical example of how a thickly populated slum standing out as an island of high density, influences the surface temperature distribution.

Old town area and Jagadamba Area : City core (Fig. 7.5)

While the old town area is the old core of the city which has not much changed in its land-use and density, in spite of rapid developments all round, the Jagadamba area is the new and emerging core. Both represent the city core and have similar characteristics in structure and function, and hence are grouped together.

Both the core areas have well developed structures on either side of the roads with well-laid out roads. There are traffic nodes where many routes converge, and have both commercial and residential functions. The "Old town" area is the most congested area in the city and has higher temperatures. The zones of high temperatures coincide with built-up and congested areas near the town hall and the Reading Room. The temperatures from the core to the outer area varied from 23.7°C to 23.1°C. In the core of the new town area, the heat island envelops Suryabagh market area and the college-down area. The temperatures here varied from 22.6°C in the core to 21.5°C in the outskirts, registering a difference of 1.1°C. Both the

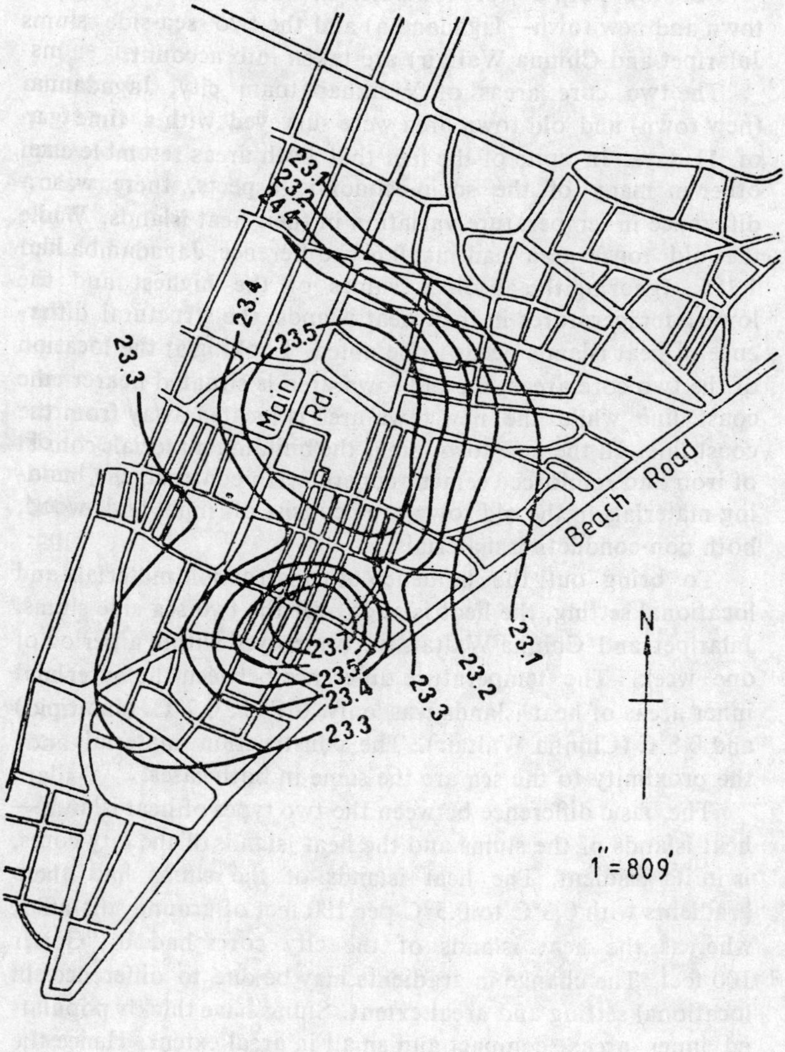

FIG. 7.5 : *Surface isotherms—Old city*

city cores exhibit heat islands of a well-developed nature due to the fact that the building complexes are massive, and also because, most of the surface is covered with heavy concrete and asphalted materials which absorb heat during day time, and emit out during nights.

For the purpose of comparison, the two core areas (old town and new town—Jagadamba) and the two sea-side slums Jalaripet and Chinna Waltair) are taken into account.

The two core areas of Visakhapatnam city, Jagadamba (new town) and old town area were surveyed with a time gap of 11 days. In spite of the fact that both areas resemble each other in many of the socio-economic aspects, there was a difference in temperature variation in their heat islands. While the old town area had just 0.6°C difference, Jagadamba had 1.1°C. Ignoring the absolute values of the highest and the lowest temperatures in their heat islands, the structural difference of heat islands needs to be noted. Looking at the location of the two core areas, the old town area is situated nearer the coast line while the new town area is located away from the coast line. In the new town area, the building materials consist of iron and reinforced cement concrete. In contrast, the building materials in the old town area consist of lime and wood, both non-conducting materials.

To bring out the influence of construction materials and locational setting, the heat islands over the two sea side slums, Jalaripet and Chinna Waltair were surveyed within a period of one week. The temperature difference between the outer and inner areas of heat islands was only 0.1°C : 0.7°C (Jalaripet) and 0.8°C (Chinna Waltair). The construction materials and the proximity to the sea are the same in both cases.

The basic difference between the two types of heat islands—heat islands of the slums and the heat islands of the city cores, is in its gradient. The heat islands of the slums had steep gradients with 0.3°C to 0.5°C per 100 feet of ground distance, whereas the heat islands of the city cores had 0.1°C per 100 feet. The change in gradients may be due to differences in locational setting and areal extent. Slums have thickly populated inner areas, compact and small in areal extent. Hence the heat islands have closely spaced isotherms.

From the study of heat islands it becomes evident that their formation is influenced by both natural and cultural landscape elements. They have multiple locations with seasonal incidence, and their intensification is not abrupt but is continuous. They play a significant role in modifying the natural climate of a city and contribute to intra-city climatic variations. How to insulate the city residents from the heat island effect is a challenging question to the city planner, and this adds a new dimension in city planning.

Temperature inversions and air pollution hazards*

When an increase of air temperature with height prevails at lower levels of atmosphere, temperature inversion occurs and air tends to stagnate, and hence becomes 'stable'. This is an ideal situation for air pollution as pollutants do not get dispersed under stable atmospheric conditions. The heat islands contribute their due share as pseudo-convective sources, and bring about some mixing of the pollutants within the boundary layer. It is the vertical thermal structure of heat islands that leads to accumulation or concentration of gaseous or particulate pollutants. It is the cool weather season which has maximum human comfort scale that experiences low level temperature inversions and intense air pollution incidents. Based on radiosonde data at Visakhapatnam for the 17 years period (1957-1974), it was found that the 'ground inversions' which spread pollutants occurred in the layer of 900 mb. from the surface. December experienced the highest number of inversions (61% of the days), closely followed by February and January and November, in that order. In the year 1970, inversions were found on 27 out of 31 days in December. The most frequent thickness of inversions was found to be in the range of 201 m to 500 m throughout the season. Lapse rates of the order of 1 to 10°C/km. were observed on about 73 per cent occasions during November, December and January and on 60 per cent occasions in February. The most frequent lapse rates (86 to 92%) throughout the season, however, were in the range of 1° to 20° C/km.

Both the heat island configuration and the vertical thermal structure of the atmosphere over Visakhapatnam would not have drawn the attention of the scientists, the planner and the city residents but for the negative impact of industrialization of the city on the city climate. The air pollution episode on the 2nd April 1975, with its consequential discomfort to the residents of the city for about an hour, woke up all the

***Satyanarayana and Subramanyam 1975 and Vittal Murthy, *et al.* 1977.**

authorities concerned, the local press and the scientist. Everyone traced the root cause to the pollutant industries located near the city. The oil refinery stink provided all the needed evidence. The air pollution episodes of the 30th and 31st October, 1974 were still fresh in the minds of Visakhapatnam residents.

Attention is now being drawn to the blind manner in which the city's new extensions are being planned, and intra-city open spaces are being filled by residential growth. The industrial location is such that southwest prevailing winds carry the pollutants of the Coromandel and Caltex industries, and spread them over the residential areas in the north and northeast. "Near isothermal and sub-adiabatic conditions in the lower layers of the atmosphere topped by strong inversions above, it is inferred, produced the fanning and looping of the pollution plume" (Fig. 7.6).

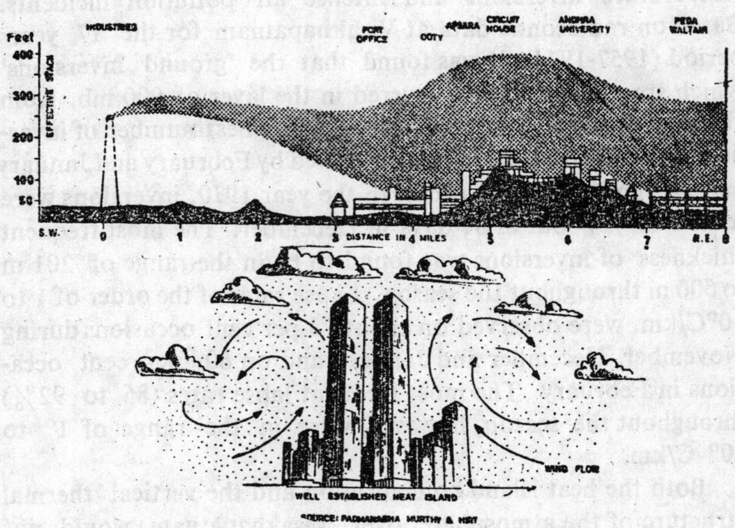

FIG. 7.6 : *Plume dispersion (Visakhapatnam)*

A model constructed based on ground concentration of air pollution as a function of source of emission and prevailing meteorological conditions, indicates that the northeast sector of Visakhapatnam and the foothills zone of the Erada hill are the pollution-prone areas. The northwest and the southwestern areas are the best for residential spread, and the northeastern area is best suited for locating all the future industries as the pollution spread will be into the ocean.

While there could be alternative models, this study of the climate of the city clearly brought out the influence of natural landscape elements and locational setting of the city on the city structure, and the role of city structure in the modification of the natural climate, more to the disadvantage of the city residents.

IN SEARCH OF URBAN DEVELOPMENT POLICY

IN SEARCH OF URBAN DEVELOPMENT POLICY

FRAMEWORK FOR THE POLICY

URBANIZATION needs to be equated not only with increasing employment in non-agricultural sector and the associated higher technology and income levels but also with urban infra-structure, both economic and social, to promote dispersal of development and the quality of life of the people. In this context, urban development policy is concerned with ensuring that urban centres play a positive role in national and regional development, and also provide healthy living environments. Here the policy goal is to develop an urban-rural continuum replacing the existing urban-rural dichotomy, and an articulated settlement and regional hierarchy system.

Urbanization has national and regional (inter-city and city-regional) and intra-city dimensions, and the hierarchical framework gives a useful working basis (see next page and also refer to Table 2. 27).

The basic principle underlying the settlement hierarchy, along the hamlet-megalopolis settlement spectrum is that in the lower orders of regional and urban hierarchic system (V order and below), city-regional reciprocal relationships are more dominant, as in resource towns and market towns and their hinterlands, while in the higher orders (above V order), inter-urban and inter-regional relationships are more dominant. The level of the hierarchic rank of an urban centre is related to the level of its functional specialization. The problem of the Indian urban system is its truncated character, particularly at the metropolitan level, and the associated functional and spatial gaps, and the city-regional parasitic relationships. Urban regional functions are more 'generative' in the urban-commercial sector with market towns and medium size industrial cities in contrast to the 'parasitic' metropolitan—industrial cities. Urban India is still polarized structurally and spatially though the degree of polarization is getting reduced. (Ref. Chapters 2 and 3).

Hierarchical framework

Regional	Administrative	Settlement	Hierarchical order
Country	Nation	National capital: Metropolis.	I order
Macro-Region	Group of States	Regional metropolitan city.	II order
Meso-Region	State	State capital: Metropolis.	III order
Sub-Region	Group of districts	Rigional city Metropolis.	IV order
Micro-Region	District	District capital city.	V order
Tract	Taluk	Rural Service Centre Medium town or small town	VI order
Sub-tract	Sub Taluk	Rural service centre (large village)	VII order
Village*	Village*	Village/Hamlet*.	

*While non-agricultural activities are spreading in the rural areas, the rural component still persists even in the metropolitan cities. It is the telescoping of functions due to the changing patterns of development that makes the hierarchic system dynamic.

What is important to the policy maker is knowledge about the ongoing changes in the urban and regional hierarchic system, and the deviations from the 'nesting' of functions due to (1) changes in the level of production and transport technology, (2) diversification in resource use, (3) increased incomes, (4) the changing consumer and producer travel behaviour leading to bypassing of a number of intervening opportunities (Ref. Chapters 2 and 3), and (5) policy intervention itself. Unless there is a feedback through appropriate and sensitive data base and information system, the policy maker's decisions to select locations for investment often turn out to be ill-founded, at most a complete failure. In operational terms there are different policy makers—industrial, commercial, housing, and transport, to mention a few. Here, any effort to co-ordinate sectoral policies has so far not led to functional integration.

In any settlement hierarchic system, the new towns, single industry towns, project towns, railway towns, military towns, temple and tourist towns should be treated as independent centres, and should be excluded from the hierarchic system. The development plans for these centres should be town specific, oriented to the specific function. These centres get drawn into the system as they grow and their economic base gets diversified. The national, regional and local economies are organised through the settlements of different sizes and functions (Ref. Chapter 2). There is no need to repeat that development of settlements cannot be just equated with the construction of houses and development of infra-structure.

Urban development and the five year plans

In the first Five Year Plan, the problem of urbanization was equated with the problem of increasing housing shortage in urban areas as a consequence of heavy population shifts from rural to urban areas. The plan recommended that the tendency to inflate land prices and speculation should be controlled through legislation. The Second Five Year Plan endorsed the expansion of the housing programme, and emphasized slum clearance, slum improvement and land acquisition and development. The Third Five Year Plan recognized that housing policies need to be set in the larger context of economic development and industrialization. It was decided that master plans for capital cities and rapidly growing cities, and regional plans for selected resource regions should be prepared. The main ingredients of urban development policy were (a) to locate new industries away from the capital and metropolitan cities, (b) to integrate and strengthen the interdependence between the town and the surrounding rural area, and (c) to diversify the occupational base of the rural areas. The Fourth Five Year Plan, included the expansion of urban community development programmes which were started in the third plan. Exploring new dimension in urban planning, there was serious, not merely casual, awareness of the planners to spatial implications and problems of urbanization. The emphasis was on regional urban plans, though these were regional extensions of master plans. The need for a more balanced spatial distribution of economic activity was reiterated, and the regional approach to urban development with the restructuring of local areas and reorganization of local administrative set-up was recommended.

The Fourth Plan also stressed the need for decongestion and dispersal of population in the metropolitan cities like Calcutta and Bombay, urban dispersal through medium and smaller cities, creating a strong legal structure for plan implementation and rationalizing the urban administrative structure. To finance housing and urban development projects, the plan provided for the establishment of a Housing and Urban Development Finance Corporation.

The Fifth Plan recognized the need for a complex and multifaceted strategy, and stated the objectives in terms of a more comprehensive and regional basis for metropolitan problems and development of small towns and new towns on a relatively self-contained basis. The thrust of urbanization policy was to increase the rate of growth of small and medium towns. This rate of growth strategy should be adapted to the development of appropriate functional structure of small and medium towns giving weightage to their hierarchic levels. Here, it is the regional policy which becomes more important than national 'blanket policy'. Then we have to formulate different regional strategies. The Sixth Plan made a significant point that the articulation of national urbanization policy should, in the context of sharp inter-state and inter-regional variations in urbanization, involve explicit consideration of the region-specific urban development problems within the matrix of rural development which has its sharp structural variations, as in the irrigated, endemic drought prone and desert and hill-forest landscapes. Here the settlement framework cannot be dichotomised or divorced from the regional resource development framework. The main thrust of urbanization policy during the next decade would be to develop adequate infra-structural facilities in the small and medium towns. Here, the State Planning departments should not follow this thrust blindly. Blanket distance standards or a standard package of infra-structural facilities without taking into account the changing travel behaviour and preference patterns of the rural folk, partly because of increased incomes and partly because of changing transport network patterns, only adds to sharp imbalances in infra-structure. Then the dictum "a bad plan is worse than no plan" holds good.

The Sixth Plan places major emphasis on (1) environmental improvement of slums; (2) integrated development of small and medium towns with a population of less than 1,00,000; (3) urban development programmes; (4) development of National Capital Region to deconcentrate economic activity from the core of Delhi into regional towns and also (5) research and development to provide a scientific base for the formulation of urbanization and urban development policy. These are naturally much more specific than the highly generalized objectives of the National Urbanization Policy like optimum distribution of population between rural and urban settlements and to disperse economic activity into small and medium towns to achieve maximum economic growth for the future.

From the above review, it becomes evident that urban oriented development policy and urban planning followed a step by step formulation through the Six Five Year Plans. The States faithfully transferred the shifting policies to sub-regions and districts without the necessary modifications and consistency. Consequently, the role of urbanization at different hierarchic levels became confused leading to functional and spatial imbalances.

The policy of development of counter magnets, ring towns and satellites needs to be corrected where necessary, and population size and functional structure of the urban centres, their regional setting, and distance from the primate city, and between the proposed centres need to be taken into account. There cannot be a mixed pattern of these urban centres with sharp structural and regional differentials—one, a city ready to take off, and the other, an inaccessible and a stagnant town without a strong economic base, and a small agricultural and a household industry town. The Karnataka urban plan has proposed such a mixed pattern to counter the growth of Bangalore. In fact, in Karnataka, priority should have been given to the development of regional metropolises in the first stage. Regional dispersal of urbanization is brought in through the controversial "Growth Centre" strategy and regional planning which itself is shifting its roots and emphasis to area planning, district planning, integrated rural development and target group planning.

The policy areas

Urban development policies are concerned with a wide range of problems, and the spectrum of problems is wide. The major problems and the associated policies relate to urban size and growth; growth of slums—housing; urban land development; traffic and transportation; deterioration of urban environment, both physical and social; urban administration; and mobilization of financial resources for urban development. These policy areas are to a high degree, mutually interdependent, and have strong roots in geographic space. In the following section, only some of the above mentioned policy areas are discussed.

Urban size and growth

It is the increase in the absolute numbers of urban population and also rural population that is disturbing, and not so much the increase in the proportion of urban population to total population.

During the decade 1961-71, the urban population increased by 30.2 million from 78.9 million in 1961 to 109.1 million in 1971. The rural population during the same decade increased by 78.7 million from 360.3 million in 1961 to 439.0 million in 1971. The increase in the percentage of urban to total population was by 1.9 from 18 in 1961 to 19.9 in 1971. The two largest cities—Calcutta and Bombay increased by 1.1 million and 1.8 million respectively (1961-71). The population of the cities with more than 1,00,000 population increased by 21.3 million from 39.6 million in 1961 to 60.9 million in 1971.

It is recognized that optimal city size is a myth. Population threshold size has perhaps some operational significance, even accepting the problems involved in the calculation of threshold sizes and aggregation of sizes for different services, and the variations over time and between regions. Threshold sizes not only vary but the size spectrum is also large. The size-range of 1,30,000 to 3,00,000 has been found to be critical, and could be taken as a policy guideline for promoting industrial agglomeration. Here in again, certain types of industries are associated with certain city sizes (Chapter 1). Population threshold sizes for medical and engineering colleges vary from 75,000 to 1,00,000; for Arts and Science Colleges 24,000 to 25,000; for hospitals 5C00 to 13,000; and for banks 2600 to 8000 (Chapter 4). These are only indicative, and give some feel for the significance of the city-size in industrial and infra-structural locational planning. Population thresholds provide a rational base for restructuring settlement hierarchies.

It is known that the growth rate of urban population is higher than that of the rural population (U=37.8 per cent, R=21.8 per cent (1961-1971). Rapid urban population growth is specific to the type of the city and its position in the growth phase. While high growth rates (<4% per annum) are associated essentially with migration, and the share of the migrant population in the rapidly growing cities is high ranging from 40 per cent to 60 per cent and above (Chapter 1, urban population size, growth and type correlates), there is the need to recognise the importance of the share of natural growth in urban growth. During the sixties, natural increase accounted for 61.4 per cent of urban growth (Premi 1981). The family type of rural to urban migration has its major share in this natural growth rate. Then, urban growth policy should take both natural growth rate and migration rate into account in regulating the future urban growth. Both policy measures require long-term strategies—the first one through family planning and the second one through monitoring the location of employment, both industrial and tertiary.

Education has a positive effect on the attitude to family planning. Increase in wives' education level leads to an even more favourable attitude compared to increase in husbands' education. The proportion of ever-users is positively related to the educational level. Husbands' income is also positively related with the practice of family planning. In Bangalore city, among the currently married women, about 64 per cent approved family planning. This proportion was highest (70%) in the age group 25-34 followed by the age group 15-24 (60%). In general, the main reasons for the approval of family planning were that with fewer children, the health of the mother would improve, that given a small family, the mother could bestow greater attention on every child, and that the family's economic position did not permit a large family. On the other hand, the disapproval of family planning was mostly on religious grounds, and partly due to the apprehension that family planning was harmful to parents' health (Prakasa Rao and Tewari 1979). It becomes clear from this that education can be used as a tool to adopt family planning. This naturally requires a long-term strategy, both in urban and rural areas.

It is becoming evident that the tertiary sector, both high income and low income, with its multipliers, is tending to become more important than the industrial sector with its multipliers. In the metropolitan cities, the tertiary sector is more important, and in the smaller cities and medium and small towns, the industrial sectors is more important. Decentralization of both the sector requires a dispersal of infra-structure and transport and communication network.

Migration needs to be treated both as a policy issue, and also as a structural variable. The correlates to migration are known, and the characteristics of the migrant are known (Chapter 1). Some of the solutions to regulate migration are known e.g. development of counter magnets and land reforms. The failure lies in the non-implementation or partial implementation (land reforms) and wrong locational planning (counter magnets). Regional development policies in the migration catchment areas (refer Chapter 1, section on Migration) tapping fully the natural resource potential, and not promoting capital intensive urban-industrial projects, should change the direction of migration. In such areas, the policy should be to urbanize the countryside with appropriate vertical hierarchic links. Here, commercialization of agriculture and cosequent improvement in rural incomes becomes important. In such a situation, commuting to higher order urban centres takes the place of migration. Rural development in a region with subsistence urban infra-structure discourages townward migration of lower income groups, but it increases commuting to extra-regional urban centres, and would even encourage migration of higher income and high skilled groups to the nearby higher order urban centres. Then, there should be a regional plan to develop urban centres of appropriate hierarchic levels. Here, the settlement policy, there source development policy and the migration policy need to be integrated judiciously. In this context, the national policy guidelines cannot capture the regional realities.

The slum problem and development policies

The slum development policies should be both short-term (housing and sub-standard living conditions) and long-term (education and improvement of skills). Just by providing houses and cleaning the slum environment and legislating that the growth of slums is illegal, the slum problem cannot be solved. Slums are not just huts, but are occupied by people with complexities of social-networks, sharp socio-economic stratification, and dualistic group and segregated spatial structures. The slum structure and behavioural patterns are changing, though at a slow rate. In some of the industrializing cities, a working class and work solidarity are emerging cutting across caste, language and religion.

In contrast to the cosmopolitanizing slum population of an industrial city, the slum population of a commercial city (Vijayawada city) with its dominant trading and transport activity with manual labour attached to the wholesale merchants, transport companies and railways, is characterized by strong ethnicity. Here, the occupation-caste interrelationships are stronger. While these relationships are changing, the overall economic level of the new occupations remains low. Export trade in agricultural commodities, particularly fruits and vegetables, creates demand for containers (baskets), and the 'Medari' caste groups with traditional skill in basket weaving find their shelter in slums through kinship and rural links. Likewise the 'Vaddara' caste groups with their traditional occupation in earth work get employed as sand workers, transporting sand from the river bed to the cement factory located on the river bank (Vijayawada City).* The ethnicity

*Socio-economic Study of Vijayawada City (1973).

and the traditional living styles of slum population should be recognised in any slum development programmes. While slums are essentially people of equal importance are their ecological setting and the slum sites. Ownership of the land on which the slums are located poses problems in any programmes of rehabilitation and relocation. Most of the slums are located on private lands. But the percentage of slum population to total population in a city, staying in slums on private lands varies: 78 per cent in Ahmedabad, 66 per cent in Hyderabad, 36 per cent in Bangalore and 32 per cent in Madras. The question is whether or not the slums located on lands with different types of ownership will receive the same benefits of development. The profit motive of the private land owners is in conflict with the social motive of the government and institutional owners. There is no question of ownership of land as such, in the case of 'informal sector' with its 'street' and 'floating economy'. Here all norms of development strategy are defied. Should these be rehabilitated into organized and localized clusters taking into account their field of operation?

The short-term approach to relocating slums, or improving the slum environment and meeting the housing shortage, must be separated from a long-term approach to treating the slum problem as a part of the development problem. Development and decentralization strategies in the catchment areas of slums should conserve the potential immigrants in their home localities. The roots of the slum problem partly lie in the rural catchments of city slums. But as long as slum generating factors—demand for low occupation and low income status workers—availability of slum shelter with slum hospitality and persistence of kinship network, operate and persist, slums persist, grow and multiply. Both social investment on better education and better skills to slum children and the younger generation should be given a high priority. The future of slums lies particularly in slum children, who should be prepared for better opportunities and a better life.

The 'functional role' and the self-generating capacity of slums need to be explicitly recognized in any policy framework. It is also becoming evident that some of the slum dwellers are there not just to earn their bread. There are 'slum lords' and some others are there to escape the city authority's 'tax-net'. These tendencies cannot be curbed at least in the short run. While slums present a cohesive front to meet external intervention, internally the social and economic structure is heterogeneous. A blanket development strategy to clear or rehabilitate or even to construct stereotyped low income 'box-houses or multi-storeyed structures' will only lead to a failure or a partial success. In contrast to the complex, and real world situation regarding slums, the views expressed about slums by those in power though perhaps exaggerated reveal the confusion: "slums must be cleared, not merely improved"; "slum clearance is mirage"; "slum clearance, all plans and no follow-up". Amidst this confusion, a blanket approach to providing taps, toilets, baths, living rooms, street lights and multi-storey buildings seems to be the accepted rule.

Urban administration

Effective urban planning requires effective urban administration. The problems are many and only some of the problems are mentioned below.

Jurisdictional fragmentation with unequal levels in administrative hierarchy—Calcutta Metropolitan District an area of 490 square miles which includes 3 municipal corporations, 31 municipal towns, 32 non-municipal towns, one notified area authority and 450 rural mouzas is one typical example. Added to this, the responsibility of city development is shared by a number of agencies like the City Development Authority, Water Supply and Sewerage Board, Electricity Board, Slum Clearance Board, Town Planning Department, and City Transport Authority. Thus the overlapping responsibilities are several. This only leads to conflicts between the development decisions of the sectoral authorities and urban regional development authorities. Yet another area of conflict is between the urban development authorities with their superior status and technical skills and the municipal authorities with their popular base and potential for resource mobilization at one level, and the municipal authorities and the adjoining rural panchayats at another level.

In metropolitan cities and rapidly developing cities, a new zone, the city fringe is emerging, which is recognised neither by the city authority nor by the rural panchayat. This tends to become the problem zone, as it defies both the city authority and the rural panchayat. This is not only the zone of rapid population growth, mainly non-agricultural population employed in the city, but is also characterized by mixed land-use and occupational structures. It is in such zones fringing the cities that 'rurban' authorities should be created with the main objective of promoting orderly development, conserving the rural landscape structure (Naidu Ratna 1978). The rurban authority could be located in a small town or a large village, central to the rural neighbourhood with an appropriate level of urban services and amenities. Such an authority acts as a buffer between the metropolitan authority and the rural panchayats.

It needs to be stressed that any plan to decentralize authority has no meaning without decentralized decision making powers and administrative and financial devolution within an overall development framework.

Policy instruments

To operationalize the urban development policy goals/objecttives, there is the need for powerful planning instruments. But the instruments should be judiciously used to properly implement policies without defeating the very policy objectives. The devastating impact of the Urban Land Ceiling Act in 1976 on urban land though concerned with only a limited number of cities, is too well known to need repetition. The Act had stripped the urban dweller wholly of any capability to obtain land, and has priced him out of the land market. Private speculation has been replaced by public speculation. The Act is still casting its shadow (Chandrasekhara 1979).

While national and regional policies (e.g. counter magnets, new towns, medium and small towns, growth centres in resource rich and less developed regions) require a set of instruments e.g. investment incentives, tax subsidies, licensing, etc., the intra-city and city-regional developments require another set of instruments—zoning and land-use controls, restriction on high rise residential apartments etc. The problem is not the non-availability of these instruments but the lack of "power" in implementation. The question is, how to insulate these instruments and the planners who take rational decisions from the powerful vested interests and political pressures? Some administrators and planners of experience think that the citizen and community participation in urban development programmes could provide the necessary insulation and facilitate successful implementation, and also, modify the plans, where necessary. The 1976 Habitat conference on Human Settlements had issued a call for "full participation of all residents in the decision-making that determines policies for their settlements". The State Town and Country Planning Acts provide for inviting suggestions and comments from the public at various stages of the preparation of development plans. The varied ways in which developments are taking place in our cities and the city-regions, whether in the location of residential layouts, shopping complexes, or alignment of arterial roads tearing apart residential layouts, or location of traffic terminals, without any regard to locational rationale, only suggest that public consultation either failed in its function, or the programmes did not receive the due and appropriate publicity. But it must be noted here, to quote Sherry R. Arnstein, that "citizen participation is a categorical term for citizen power . . . participation without redistribution of power is an empty and frustrating process for the powerless. It allows the power holders to claim that all sides were considered but makes it possible for only some to benefit. It maintains the status quo". How to rationalize citizenship participation which is an elusive element, is still an unresolved question.

Urban planning in India, both at the inter-city and intra-city levels, more often follows urban development instead of directing development according to a predesigned plan. This only leads to regularising irregular urban sprawl. The basic city planning instrument, the city "master plan", the Procrustean bed' of land-uses, has become only too static, too defective and too outmoded, to be of much value in monitoring the changing structure and pattern of development in the city and the city region. What further compounds the problem is the time-lag between the formulation of the plan and its implementation. It is known that plan implementation is exposed to rough weather from (1) the different agencies involved in city development, pulling in different directions, (2) the rigidity of rules and regulations, (3) the inadequate machinery for implementation, and (4) above all, inadequate finances. All these conspire with the "master plan" and its defects. These harsh realities lead to non-implementation and are stressed again and again in the different town planning conferences and seminars, and periodical reviews of city master plans (Dhar 1978).

At the policy level, the national planners are shifting their emphasis on urban development, while the state planners faithfully follow the shifts, with the result that urban centres develop without direction. If the Indian urban system is lopsided, it is only because the urban system is still subservient to industrial development and the socio-economic class and regional imbalances. The major problem is the increasing imbalance between the urban and rural population growth and the rapid growth of cities beyond their economic capacity to sustain, given the existing local government system.

The present study has brought out that urbanization in India has at least three major facets, those based on metropolitinization/industrialization, commercialization and urbanization of the countryside. The urban base in the rural areas is sub-standard, and the intermediary link with the metropolitan apex, through market towns, is weak. Commercialization with its multipliers and industrialization with its multipliers are two separate processes, each influencing an urban centre in a totally different manner. If the sharp inter-state and inter-regional variations in urbanization are given their due weight, there is a strong case for state/regional urbanization policy which need not necessarily conform to national urbanization policy. Instead of every state, every sub-region and micro-region, mechanically following the same pattern of urban development—counter-magnets, satellite towns, ring towns, ring railway and ring roads, alternative urban development models related to the region's resource development patterns and potentials should be worked out, indicating the costs and benefits of each model. At the intra-city level, alternative land-use allocation models should be worked out before taking the final decision.

While Maharashtra should discourage metropolitanization,

Orissa should encourage metropolitanization. In Andhra State, there is a case for sub-regional urban development models (Telangana, Coastal Andhra and Rayalaseema), each with at least one regional metropolis, and with Hyderabad developing both as a part of the national urban system and also as a part of the sub-regional urban system (Telangana). In contrast to this, all the states and all the sub-regions should urbanize the countryside with a focus on the development of urban infra-structure, both economic and social, not only in the small towns but also in the large central villages. In this context, the urban and the rural sectors are two sides of the same coin, and hence require complementary development programmes.

BIBLIOGRAPHY

Ajo, R. (1965): On the structure of population density in London Field, *Acta Geographica*, 18.

Alam, S.M. and W. Khan (1972): *Metropolitan Hyderabad and its Region : A Strategy for Development*, Asia Publishing House, New Delhi.

Alam, S.M.; B.P.R., Vital; and N.K. Sen (1974): *Planning Atlas of Andhra Pradesh*, Government of India and Andhra Pradesh, Hyderabad.

Alonso, W.C. (1964): *Location Theory in Regional Development and Planning, A Reader*, Ed. J. Friedmann and W. Alonso, MIT Press.

Andrews, R.B. (1942): Elements in urban fringe pattern, *The Journal of Land and Public Utility Economics*, 18, pp. 167-183.

Appalaraju, Jaya and M. Safer (1976): Growth centre strategies in less developed countries, *Development Planning and Spatial Structure*, Ed. A. Gilbert, John Wiley and Sons.

Arnstein, S.R. (1969): A ladder of citizen participation, *Journal of American Institute of Planners*, 35, p. 216.

Avachat, Anil (1978): Beedi Workers in Nippani, *Economic and Political Weekly*, 13 (22), 29 July.

Bahl, H.D. (1979): Heat Island studies at Delhi, *Mausam*, 30, (1), pp. 119-122.

Barry, R.G. and R.J. Chorlay: *Atmosphere, Weather and Climate*.

Bawa, V.K. and V.L.S. Prakasa Rao (1981): Planning the metropolis: Trends in southern cities, *The Hindu*, 24-11-81, Madras.

Beavon, K.S.O. (1977): *Central Place Theory: A Reinterpretation*, Longman.

Belicher, M. (1892): *Statistiche Beschreibung Der Stadt.*, Frankfurt Am Main Und Threr Bevolekerung, Frankfurt Am Main.

Berry, B.J.L. (1971): The passing of central place theory, Research Institute—Lectures on Geography, *Special Report*, ETL-SR-71-1, pp. 113-118 (Mimeo).

Berry, B.J.L. (1972): Hierarchical Diffusion, the basis of development, filtering and spread in a system of cities, *Growth Centre in Regional Economic Development*, Ed. N.M. Hansen. The Free Press.

Berry, B.J.L. (1973): *The Human Consequences of Urbanisation*, The MacMillan Press Ltd.

Berry, B.J.L. (1977): Transformation of the Nation's Urban System: Small city growth as zero-sum growth in small cities in transition, *The Dynamics of Urban Growth and Decline*, Ed., H.J. Bryee, Ballinger, pp. 283-300.

Berry, B.J.L. and W.L. Garison, (1958): The functional bases of central place hierarchy, *Economic Geography*, 34, pp. 145-154.

Berry, B.J.L., J.W. Simmons, and R.J. Tennant (1963): Urban population densities, Structure and change, *Geographical Review*, 53.

Berry, B.J.L. and V.L.S. Prakasa Rao (1968): *Urban-Rural Duality in the Regional Structure of Andhra Pradesh*, Franz Steiner Verlog GMBH, Wiesbaden.

Bhaskar Rao, B. (1977): Integrated development of rurban regions, *Proceedings of the COSTED Seminar*, Madras, pp. 176-198.

Bhat, L.S. (1976): *Micro-Level Planning—A Case Study of Karnal Area, Haryana—India*, K.B. Publishers, New Delhi.

Bhooshan, B.S. *et al.* (1979): *The Role of Small and Intermediate Towns in the Rural Development : A Pilot Study in Mandya District*, IDS, Mysore University, Mysore.

Blakie, P.M. (1976): Communication scale and change—The case of India, *Development Planning and Spatial Structure*, Ed. A. Gilbert, John Wiley & Sons, London.

Bogue, D.J. (1949): *The Structure of Metropolitan Community:*

A Study in Dominance and Sub-dominance, Ann Arbor University of Michigen.

Bose, Asish (1970): *Urbanization in India*, Academic Books, New Delhi.

Boudeville, T.R. (1966): *Problems of Regional Economic Planning*, Edinburgh University Press.

Bradnock, R.W.. (1974): The Hinterlands of Bangalore and Madras, *The Indian Geographical Journal*, 49, 1.

Brahme, Sulbha (1977): The role of Bombay in the Economic Development of Maharashtra, *Indian Urbanization and Planning*, Ed. A.G. Noble and A.K. Dutt, Tata McGraw Hill, New Delhi.

Bredo, W. (1961): Industrial decentralization in India, *Indian Urban Future*, Ed. R. Turner, Berkely, pp. 240-260.

Breese, G. (1966): *Urbanization in Newly Developing Countries*, Modernisation of Traditional Societies, Prentice Hall of India Private Ltd., New Delhi.

Bremen, Jan (1978): Seasonal migration and co-operative capitalism—Sugar Factories of Bardoli, *Economic and Political Weekly*, 12, Nos. 31, 32 and 33.

Brush, J.E. (1968): Spatial pattern of population in Indian cities, *Geographical Review*, 58.

Casettie, E. (1967): Urban population density patterns: An alternative explanation, *Canadian Geographer*, 11.

Casettie, E. (1969): Alternative urban population density models: An analytical comparison of their validity range, *Studies in Regional Science*, Ed. A.J. Scot, Pion, London.

Census of India (1971): Primary Census Abstract, Series I, India: Part II, A (ii).

Chandrasekhara, C.S. (1979): State control over urban land and social objective, *Urban Research Bulletin, No. 1*, July, pp. 4-8.

Cheyne, J.I. and J.S. Lloyd (1975): Development of rural health services in third world, central authority or local autonomy, *Research Paper CESRP*, Centre for Environment Studies, London.

Christaller, W. (1966): *Central Places in Southern Germany*, (translated by C.W. Baskin), Prentice Hall, Englewood Cliffs, N.J.

Clark, C. (1951): Urban population densities, *Journal of the Royal Statistical Society*, Series A, 114.

Connel, J. *et al.*, (1976): *Migration from Rural Areas: The Evidence from Village Studies*, Oxford University Press, Madras.

Craig, J. (1972): *Population Potential and Population Density*, Office of the Population Census and Survey, U.S.A.

Desai, P.B. *et al.* (1969): *Regional Perspectives of Industrial and Urban-Growth—The Case of Kanpur*, MacMillan, Bombay.

Derwent, D.F. (1969): Growth poles and growth centres in regional planning—A Review, *Environment and Planning* 1, pp. 5-32.

Deshpande, C.D. (1976): Trends in cities and towns of western India (1961-71), *Urbanization in Developing Countries*, Ed. S.M. Alam and V.V. Pokshishevsky, Osmania University Press, Hyderabad, pp. 321-347.

Deshpande, C.D. *et al.* (1979): *South Kolaba—A Study in Settlement Hierarchy and Rural-Urban Inter-relations*, Bombay University (Mimeo).

Dhar, V.K. (1978): Study of city master plans—Uttar Pradesh, *Urban Research Bulletin*, National Institute of Urban Affairs. 1 No., 7-8, July, Aug., pp. 5-9.

Directorate of Town Planning, Hyderabad, (1972): *Report on the Delimitation of Hyderabad Metropolitan District*.

Duncan, O.D. (1957): The measurement of population distribution, *Population Studies*, 11, 1.

Dutta, A. (1976): Human settlements and Local Government in India 2000, Seminar on Human settlements, University of Rajasthan, Jaipur (Mimeo).

Ellefsen, R.A. (1962): City-hinterland relationships in India, *India's Urban Future*, Ed. Roy Turner, Oxford University Press, pp. 94-116.

Escap (1977): *Report of the Export Group Meeting on Migration and Human Settlements*, UN Series No. 38.

Fisher, H.B. and G. Rushton (1977): Integrated rural area planning in India—Experience of the pilot research project on growth centres, 1969-74, *Man, Culture and Settlement*, Ed. K.N. Singh and R.P.B. Singh, Kalyani Publishers, New Delhi.

Fiery, W. (1946): "Ecological considerations in Planning for urban fringe, *American Sociological Review*, 11 (4), pp. 411-423.

Folke, Steen, (1968): Evaluation of plantations, migration and population growth in Nilgiris and Coorg, *Collected Papers Denmark*, Ed. N.K. Jacobsan and R.H. Jensen, 21st International Geographical Congress, New Delhi.

Friedmann, J. and J. Miller (1965): The urban field, *Journal of the American Institute of Planners*, 31, pp. 312-319.

Friedmann, J. (1966): *Regional Development Policy: A Case Study of Venezuela*, MIT Press.

Friedmann, J. (1966): Two concepts of urbanization: A comment, *Urban Affairs Quarterly*, pp. 78-84.

Friedmann, J. and W. Robert, (1976): The urban transition: comparative study of newly industrialising societies, *Progress in Geography*, 8, Ed. Edward Arnold, pp. 4-93.

Gaile, G.L. (1980): The spread and backwash concept, *Regional Studies*, 14. 1, pp. 15-25.

Gist N.P. (1957) : The ecology of Bangalore : An east-west comparison, *Social Forces*, 35.

Greenwood, M.J. (1971): An analysis of the determinants of internal labour mobility in India, *Annals of Regional Science*, 5, pp. 137-151.

Hagget, P. and Gunawarden (1964): Determination of population thresholds for settlement functions by Reed-Muench methods, *Professional Geographer*, 16, pp. 6-9.

Hansen, N.M. (1967): Development pole theory in regional context, *Kyklos* 20, pp. 709-27.

Hansen, N.M. (1978): *Human Settlement Systems*, Ballinger.

Hansen, N.M. (1978): Border regions: A critique of spatial theory and a European case study, *Human Settlement Systems*, Ed. N.M. Hansen, Ballinger, pp. 247-261.

Hanspal, Ranjana (1977) : Urban structure of Bangalore city: A spatial analysis, unpublished Ph.D. Thesis, Institute for social and economic change, Bangalore.

Hasan, M.F. (1970): *Bangalore Through the Centuries*.

Hermensen, T. (1972): Development poles and related theories: A synoptic view, *Growth Centres in Regional Economic Development*, Ed. N.M. Hensen, The Free Press.

Holland, Stuart, (1977): *Capital Versus Regions,* The MacMillan.

Hyma, B. (1971): The rural-urban fringe of a growing Metropolis; Madras, University of Pittsburg Ph.D. Thesis (Unpublished).

Isard, W. (1972): *Location of Space Economy,* The MIT Press.

Jafferson (1939): The Laws of the primate city, *Geographical Review*, 29, pp. 226-232.

Jagadish Singh (1979): *Central Places and Spatial Organization in Backward Economy—Gorakhpur Region*, Study in integrated regional development. UBBP Publishers, Gorakhpur.

Jensen, R. (1966): *High Density Living*, Leonard Hill, London.

Johri, N.B. (1980): Emerging industrial profile vis-a-vis development plan of greater Bombay, *Urban India* 1, October-December, No. 2, pp. 22-26.

Johnson, E.A.J. (1970): *The Organization of Space in Developing Countries,* Harvard University Press.

Jones, E. (1970): *Towns and Cities*, Oxford University Press, London.

Kantseboskaya, I.V. (1976): Some definitions of urbanization in geographic literature and relevant ideas, *Urbanization in Developing Countries*, Ed. S.M. Alam and V.V. Pashishevsky, Osmania University Press, Hyderabad, pp. 1-23.

Kar, N.R. (1962): Growth distribution and dynamics of the population load in Calcutta (Mimeo).

Khan, W. (1973): A note on growth centering policy for Telangana, Planning Department, Government of Andhra Pradesh, Hyderabad (Mimeo).

Kirk, W. (1975): The rural-urban interface as an index of social change, Indo-British Geography Seminar, Delhi University, Delhi (Mimeo).

Lakdawala, D.T. *et al.* (1974): *Regional Variation in Industrial Development*, Monograph 2, Sardar Patel Institute of Economic and Social Research, Ahmedabad.

Linsky, A.S. (1965): Some generalisation concerning primate cities, *Annals of Association of American Geographers*, 55, pp. 506-513.

Lösch, A. (1954): *The Economics of Location*, Trans. W.H. Kloglan, Yale University Press.

Mackay, B. (1962): *The New Exploration: A Philosophy of Regional Planning*, University of Illinois Press, Urbana.

Manmohan Singh, H.K. (1979): Population pressure and labour availability in agriculture and selected activities, *Economic and Political Weekly*, 14, 11 March.

Mathur *et. al.* (1968): *Cost of Urban Infrastructure for Industry as Related to City Size in Developing Countries*, Stanford Research Institute, Menlopark, California.

McGee (1971): *The Urbanization Process in the Third World*, Bell and Sons, London.

McNulty, M.L. and G. Rushton (1980): A comparative analysis of the locational efficiency of rural service delivery systems, A Research Design (Mimeo).

Mills, E.S. (1980): Three essays on urbanization in India, Princeton University (Mimeo).

Misra, R.P. (1972): Growth poles and growth centres in the context of India's urban and regional development problems, *Growth Pole and Growth Centres in Regional Planning*, Ed. A.R. Kuklinski, Mouton.

Misra, V.N. *et al.* (1975): Economic base and multiplier analysis: A study of Indian Towns and Cities, *Indian Journal of Industrial Relations*, 2, No. 2, October, pp. 177-191.

Mitra, A. (1965): *Levels of Regional Development*, Census of India, 1, Part I, A (i) and (ii), New Delhi.

Mitra, A. (1978): *India's Population*, 1 and 2, Abhinav Publications, Delhi.

MMDA (1978): Resource mobilization and investment planning for Madras Metropolitan Area (Mimeo), Operation Research Group, Baroda.

Mosley, M.J. (1974): *Growth Centres in Spatial Planning*, Pergaman Press.

Munnich, C.E. (1974): Central place theory and regional planning: West German experience, *Transport and Urban Environment*, Ed. J.G. Rothenberg and I.G. Heggie, The MacMillan.

Naganna, C. (1975): The structure of the terrain around Bangalore (Mimeo).

Naidu, Ratna (1979): Organizational structure of Hyderabad

urban development authority: Problems and Possibilities, *Nagarlok*, 11, No. 2, April-June, pp. 134-152.

Nangia, S. (1976): *Delhi Metropolitan Regions*, K.B. Publications, New Delhi.

National Council of Applied Economic Research (1980): Household income and its disposition, Bengal Press, New Delhi.

Neef, E. (1950): Das Probleum der Zentralen Orte, *Petermanns Geographicsche*, Mitteilungen, 94, p. 12.

Newling, B.E. (1967): Urban Population; The mathematics of structure and processes, paper presented at the St. Louis Meeting of the Association of American Geographers.

Newling, B.E. (1968): The spatial variation of urban population densities (Mimeo), paper contributed to the 21st IGU Congress, New Delhi.

Office of the Registrar General of India (1980): *Sample Registration Bulletin*, 14, 2, December.

Olds, E.B. (1949): On the use of spatial divisions for statistical purposes, *Journal of American Statistical Association*, 44, 248.

Padmanabhamurty, B. (1979): Isotherms and Isohumes in Pune on clear winter nights—A meso-meteorological study, *Mausam*, 30. 1, pp. 134-138.

Padmanabhamurty, B. and M.S. Hirt : The Toronto heat island and pollution distribution, *Atmospheric Environment Service*, Toronto, Canada.

Pal, M.N. (1975): Regional disparities in the level of development in India, *Indian Journal of Regional Science*, 7, 1.

Papaioannou, (1969): Comment on the 'Corridor' Concept, *Ekistics*, 28, 168, November, pp. 354-355.

Parvathi, C. (1977): Market, centres and spatial development in Coimbatore—Nilgiris region, Ph.D. Thesis, Mysore University, Unpublished.

Pathak, C.R. (1975): Spatial variation in urban industrial growth in India, *Indian Journal of Regional Science*, 7, 1, pp. 1-10.

Perroux, F. (1964): Economic space: Theory and applications, *Regional Development and Planning A Reader*, Ed. J. Friedmann and W. Alonso, The MIT Press.

Planning Commission (1970): Fourth Five Year Plan, Government of India.

Planning Commission (1980): Sixth Five Year Plan 1980-85: A Framework, Government of India.

Pothanna, V. (1979): Urban growth rates in Andhra Pradesh: An economic analysis, Ph.D. Thesis, Andhra University, Waltair, Unpublished.

Prakasarao, V.L.S. (1963): *Regional Planning*, Indian Statistical Institute, Calcutta.

Prakasarao, V.L.S. (1964): *Towns of Mysore State*, Indian Statistical Institute, Calcutta.

Prakasarao, V.L.S. (1971): *Some Aspects of Urbanization*, Prasaranga, Mysore University, Mysore.

Prakasarao, V.L.S. (1976): *Development Strategy for an Agriculture Region*, University of Mysore, Mysore.

Prakasarao, V.L.S. and A.T.A. Learmonth (1961): Industrialization and Urbanization in Mysore State, *Applied Economic Papers* 102, pp. 41-52.

Prakasarao, V.L.S. and R. Ramachandran (1971): Mobility and choice of central places, *Analytical Geography*, 1, Delhi University, Delhi.

Prakasarao, V.L.S. and R. Ramachandran (1973): Socio-economic study of Vijayawada City, Department of Geography, Delhi University, Delhi, (Mimeo).

Prakasarao, V.L.S., V.K. Tewari and H. Ramachandran (1978): Urban systems and regional economy, *Indo-French Seminar on Probleums of Urban Growth*, New Delhi (Mimeo).

Prakasarao, V.L.S. and V.K. Tewari (1979): *The Structure of an Indian Metropolis: A Study of Bangalore*, Allied Publishers, New Delhi.

Prakasarao, V.L.S. and V.K. Tewari (1980): An exercise in re-grouping administrative units: A study of Karnataka, (Mimeo).

Prakasarao, V.L.S., B. Bhaskara Rao, and N. Naganna (1980): Migration and resettlement: Rural-urban policies, 4, Social Welfare and Development Centre for Asia and the Pacific, Manila.

Prakasarao, V.L.S. and V.K. Tewari (1978): *Urbanization in India: Spatial Dimension*, Institute of Social and Economic Change, Bangalore.

Pred, A. (1965): Industrialization, initial advantages and American metropolitan growth, *The Geographical*, 55, 2.

Pred, A. (1976): The Inter-urban transmission of growth in advance economics, Empirical Findings Versus Regional Planning Assumptions, *Regional Studies*, 10, pp. 151-171.

Premi, M.K. (1978): Migration to cities, Its socio-economic correlates, Jawaharlal Nehru University, New Delhi (Mimeo).

Premi, M.K., (1981): Role of migration in the urbanization process in Third World Countries: A case study of India, *Social Action*, Vol. 31, July-September 1981, pp. 291-310.

Preston, R.E. (1971): The structure of central place systems, *Economic Geography*, 47, pp. 136-155.

Ramachandran, Neera (1979): Commodity flows and regional organization of the Indian economy, Unpublished Ph.D. Thesis. CSRD, JNU, New Delhi.

Ramachandran, R. (1976): Identification of growth centres and growth points in south-east resource region, *National Geographical Journal of India*, 22, Part I & II.

Ramegowda, K.S. (1972): *Urban and Regional Planning*, Prasaranga, Mysore University, Mysore.

Rao, H.C. (1930), *Mysore, Gazetteer*, Vol. 5, Government Press, Bangalore.

Rao, M.S.A. (1978): Tobacco development and labour migration planning for labour welfare and development, *Economic and Political Weekly*, 13, 29 July-22.

Raza, Moonis *et al*. (1979): Spatial organization and urbanization in India: A case study of underdevelopment, *Rural Area Development Perspectives and Approaches*, Ed. R.P. Misra and K.V. Sundaram, Sterling, pp. 333-377.

Reed, L.J. and Muench, (1938): A simple method for estimating fifty per cent end points, *American Journal of Hygiene*, 27, pp. 493-497.

Reid J. and Learmonth, A.T.A. (1966) : Applications of statistical sampling to geographical studies with special reference to cartographic presentation of sampling error. Department of Geography, Australian National University, School of general studies, Occasional Papers, No. 5 Canberra, July, pp. 22-25.

Richardson, H.W. (1973): *The Economics of Urban Size*, Saxon House, Lexington Books.

Richardson, H.W. (1973): Growth pole spillover: The dynamics of backwash and spread, *Regional Studies*, 10, pp. 1-9.

Rogers, Andrei (1978): Urbanization, Resources and Development, *An Alternative for Growth*, Ed. H. McHains and L.W. Willex, Ballinger, pp. 149-217.

Roy, P. and B.R. Patil (1977): *Manual for Block Level Planning*, MacMillan.

Rushton, G. (1911): Postulates of central place theory and the properties of central place systems, *Geographical Analysis*, 3, pp. 140-156.

Satyanarayana, B. and V.P. Subrahmanyam (1979): Meteorological factors in relation to air pollution—A Case Study, *Vayumandal*, 5, 2 to 3, pp. 56-57.

Sen, L.K., *et al*. (1971): *Planning Rural Growth Centres for Integrated Area Development*, National Institute of Community Development, Hyderabad.

Seers, Dudley, (1978): The meaning of development, United Nations Asian Pacific Development Institute (Mimeo).

Shanbhag, Vinod (1977); Evaluation of the impact of central investment subsidy scheme in Surendranagar district centre for environmental planning and technology, School of Planning, Ahmedabad, (Mimeo).

Sharma, A.K.V., *et al*. (1977): Estimation of population threshold, *Behavioural Sciences and Community Development*, 11, 1.

Sherrat, G.G. (1960): A model for general urban growth, management sciences, *Models and Techniques*, Ed. O.W. Churchman and M. Verhulst, Pergamn Press, New York.

Singh, R.L. (1964): *Bangalore: An Urban Survey*, National Geographic Society, Varanasi.

Sita, K. (1972): Some aspects of urbanization in south Konkan, *Bombay Geographical Magazine*, 21, 1 December, pp. 31-48.

Sita, K. and V.S. Padke (1980): Declining towns of India—1971, Transactions—*Institute of Indian Geographers*, 2, 2 July.

Smailes, A.E. (1969): The Indian city: A descriptive model, *Geographische Zeit Schrift*, 57. 3.

Smailes, A.E. (1971): *Urban Systems*, Presidential address, Institute of British Geographers, University of Sussex.

Srivastava, Bina (1976): The rural-urban fringe of Delhi: Structural and functional patterns, Ph.D. Thesis, Delhi University, Delhi, Unpublished.

Stewart, J.Q. and W. Warntz (1958): Physics of population distribution, *Journal of Regional Science*, 1.

Subrahmanyam, V.P. and V.M. Sastry (1976): Temperature inversions and Stable layers in the atmosphere over Visakhapatnam, *Vayumandal*, 6, 2-3.

Subrahmanyam, V.P.; V.M. Sastry; and Sachidevi, S. (1978): A comparative study of temperature and vapour pressure distributions in urban and non-urban locations, *Geographical Review of India*, 40, 1.

Sundaram, K.V. *et al.* (1974): *A Case Study of Meerut*, U.N. Centre for Regional Development, Nagoya.

Tanner, J.C. (1961): Factors affecting the amount of travel, *Road Research Technical Paper No. 1*, Department of Scientific and Industrial Research, London.

Tennant, R.J. (1961): Population density patterns in eight Asian cities, Paper read at West Lakes Division Meeting of the Association of American Geographers.

Tewari, V.K. (1976): Inter-State disparities in the level of industrialization and per capita total consumer expenditure in India, *Golden Jubilee Volume, The Indian Geographical Society*, Madras.

Tewari, V.K. (1978): A Model of Bangalore Metropolis, Human Geography and Ecology Unit, Institute of Social and Economic Change, Bangalore (Mimeo).

Ullman, E. (1970): A theory of location of cities, *Analytical Human Geography*, Ed. Peter Ambrose, Longman, pp. 135-137.

Venugopal, B. (1970): Urbanization in Telangana, Ph.D. Thesis, Osmania University, Hyderabad, Unpublished.

Vittal Murthy, K.P.R.; V.M. Sastry; and V.P. Subrahmanyam (1977): Seasonal and annual variation of ground concentration of air pollutants for Visakhapatnam, *Indian Journal of Ecology*, 41, pp. 1-22.

Warntz, W. (1967): Macroscopic analysis and some patterns of the geographical distribution of population in the United States 1790-1980, *Quantitative Geography* Part 1. Ed., W.L. Garrison and D.F. Marble, North-Western University Studies in Geography, Illinois.

Whebell, C.F.J. (1969): Corridors: A theory of urban systems, *Ekistics*, 28, 168, November, pp. 348-353.

Wherein, G.S. (1942): The rural-urban fringe, *Economic Geography*, 18, (3), pp. 212 228.

Wolf, L.G. (1967): Metropolitan tidel wave in Ohio, 1900-2000, *Economic Geography*, 45, 2.

Williams, A. and R. Anderson (1975): *Efficiency of the Social Services*, Basil Blackwell, Oxford.

Wise, M.J. (1966): *Advancement of Science*, London, pp. 571-588.

INDEX

NAME INDEX